Stafford Henry Northcote

Twenty Years of Financial Policy

Stafford Henry Northcote

Twenty Years of Financial Policy

ISBN/EAN: 9783337812928

Printed in Europe, USA, Canada, Australia, Japan

Cover: Foto ©Suzi / pixelio.de

More available books at **www.hansebooks.com**

TWENTY YEARS OF FINANCIAL

POLICY.

TWENTY YEARS OF

FINANCIAL POLICY.

A SUMMARY OF THE CHIEF FINANCIAL MEASURES

PASSED BETWEEN 1842 AND 1861, WITH

A TABLE OF BUDGETS.

BY

SIR STAFFORD H. NORTHCOTE, BART.

M.P. FOR STAMFORD.

LONDON:

SAUNDERS, OTLEY, AND CO.

BROOK STREET, HANOVER SQUARE.

1862.

TO

THE REVEREND EDWARD COLERIDGE,

FELLOW OF ETON COLLEGE,

THIS VOLUME IS INSCRIBED BY HIS AFFECTIONATE

FRIEND AND PUPIL,

STAFFORD H. NORTHCOTE.

July, 1862.

PREFACE.

THE germ of this volume will be found in the Table of Budgets contained in the Appendix. I have myself often felt the want of a convenient summary of the financial measures of recent years, and I hope that what I have here drawn up for my own use may also be found useful by others.

The explanatory notes which I had intended to add to the Table have grown into a volume; and the Table, which should have been the text, has shrunk into an Appendix.

It was my wish to add a chapter upon the system of Public Accounts, and another upon the

viii *Preface.*

financial progress of some other countries besides our own during the period of which I have here treated; but I have not yet found time to write them; though I do not abandon the idea, as I think a short popular account of our Financial System would be useful to many persons who have not the opportunity of studying it in detail; and I am sure that a comparative account of the progress of other countries would throw much light upon that which we have made ourselves.

I have to thank my friend Mr. Anderson, of the Treasury, for his kindness in revising the Table of Budgets, and several other portions of the work.

STAFFORD H. NORTHCOTE.

July, 1862.

SUMMARY OF CONTENTS.

CHAPTER I.

(1842—1844).

	Pages
NTRODUCTORY Remarks	1—5
Budget of 1842-3	5
Financial Position of the country	5—7
Prevalence of distress	7
Position of the Ministry	7—9
The Penny Postage	9
Why the Whigs were the Free Traders	10—12
Sir R. Peel's Budget Speech, March 11, 1842	12—21
Review of Fiscal Policy since 1816	21—26
Principles of Sir R. Peel's Financial Policy	26—32
Views of the Conservatives in 1842	32
Opposition of the Liberals to the Income Tax	33—37
Arguments of Sir R. Peel and his colleagues	37—41
Disappointment of Sir R. Peel's calculations	41—47
Soundness of his general policy	47
Budget of 1843-4, May 8, 1843	48—50
Budget of 1844-5	50—53
Conversion of the Three-and-a-half per cents	53—58
Term of Income Tax expires	58

x *Summary of Contents.*

CHAPTER II.

(1845—1847).

	Pages
Budget of 1845-6	59
Renewal of Income Tax proposed	61—64
The Surplus and its application	64—67
Comparison of the Budgets of 1842 and 1845	67—72
Lord J. Russell's criticism	72—75
Mr. Roebuck and Mr. C. Buller on the Income Tax	76
Success of the Budget of 1845	77
Repeal of the Corn-laws	79
Free Trade Measures of 1846	79—80
Budget of 1846-7, May 29, 1846	81
Sir R. Peel quits office	82
Sugar duty Bill	82
Financial prosperity coincident with national distress in 1846	83—86
Causes of the condition of the country	86—93
Budget of 1847-8, Feb. 22, 1847	93
Loan of 8,000,000*l.*	94
Dissolution of Parliament	97

CHAPTER III.

(1847—1852).

Meeting of New Parliament	98
Relaxation of Bank Charter Act	98
Fear of Invasion	99
West Indian Committee	100
Budget of 1848-9, Feb. 18, 1848	100—105
Unpopularity of the Budget	105

Summary of Contents. xi

	Pages
Proposed increase of Income Tax abandoned	106
Controversies respecting the Income Tax	107—109
Debates on the Sugar duties, and Financial Statements of June 30 and Aug. 25	109—115
Other questions discussed in this Session	116
Financial Reform movement	116—118
Mr. Cobden's Motion for reduction of Expenditure	118
Budget of 1849-50, June 22, 1849	121—123
Budget of 1850-1, March 15, 1850	124
Repayment of advances	127—130
Opposition to the proposed Stamp duties	130—133
Defeats of the Government on financial questions	133
Question of the renewal of the Income Tax, 1851	134—137
Budget of 1851-2, Feb. 17, 1851	137—142
Resignation and recall of the Ministry	143
Financial circumstances of the crisis	143—149
Different views respecting the Income Tax	149—151
Position of the Conservatives	151
Budget again brought forward, April 4	152
Alteration in the House Tax	153
Other changes in the Budget	155
Mr. Herries' Motion for reducing the Income Tax	156
Mr. Disraeli's Motion—Claims of Agriculturists	158
Mr. Gladstone criticises the Budget	160
Mr. Hume's Amendment, limiting duration of Income Tax to one year	161
Select Committee on the Income Tax	163
Other defeats of the Government	165

xii *Summary of Contents.*

	Page
Mr. Disraeli and Mr. Gladstone criticise the financial arrangements	166—170
Change of Government	170
Budget of 1852-3, April 30	171—173
Dissolution of Parliament	173
Budget of December, 1852	174—180
Budget rejected. Resignation of Lord Derby's Government	180

CHAPTER IV.

(1853).

Financial importance of the year 1853	182
Budget of 1853-4, April 18, 1853	183
Mr. Gladstone's arguments respecting the Income Tax	185—192
His Plan for its gradual extinction	193
Succession duty and other taxes	194—195
Remissions of taxation	197
General character of the Budget	199
Sir E. B. Lytton's amendment on the Income Tax	201
Mr. Palmer's Amendment	202
The Succession duty	203—210
Mr. Pitt's Plan of Legacy and Succession duties	210
The increase of the Irish Spirit duties	212—214
Failure of Plan for revising trade licences	215
Repeal of Advertisement duty	217
Abolition of minor Customs' duties	217
Soap duty repealed	218
Revision of Assessed Taxes	218
Conversion of 3 per cent. Stocks	220—226

Summary of Contents. xiii

	Pages
Expectation of a Fall in the rate of interest	226
Reduction of interest on Exchequer-bills	231
Remarks on these operations	233

CHAPTER V.

(1854—1856).

Introduction of system of paying gross revenue into the Exchequer	237
Financial character of 1854	239
The Budget of 1854-5	243
Mr. Gladstone's View as to Loans in time of war	246
Second Budget, May 8	250
Issue of Exchequer-bonds	251
Controversy respecting Mr. Gladstone's financial arrangements	255—257
The question between Loans and Taxes	258—264
Change of Government	264
Budget of 1855-6	265
Loan of 16,000,000*l.*	265
Opposition to the proposed Sinking-fund	274
Further issue of Exchequer-bills	275
Sardinian and Turkish Loans	276
Further Supplementary Estimates and a fresh Loan of 5,000,000*l.*	278
Budget of 1856-7	279
Sir G. Lewis' Remarks on the War	281
Observations on the effect produced by the war on the National Expenditure	283
Third Loan, 5,000,000*l.*	288
Sir G. Lewis' Remarks upon the State of the Debt, and on the Pressure of Taxation in this and other countries	289—290

xiv *Summary of Contents.*

	Pages
Mr. Disraeli's and Mr. Gladstone's Remarks upon the Necessity of Economy	291—292
Prorogation of Parliament	293

CHAPTER VI.

(1857—1861).

Financial character of 1857	294
Cost of the war	295
State of trade	296
Moral effect of the war	297
Agitation against the " war ninepence "	298
State of Foreign Affairs	299
Opening of the Session. Debate on the Address	300
Budget of 1857-8, Feb. 13, 1857	306
Sir G. Lewis' Views as to the Remission of Taxes	308
His Proposal for the coming year	310
Income Tax reduced to 7*d.*	311
Tea and Sugar duties fixed for three years	311
Mr. Disraeli's Resolution	313
Sir G. Lewis' Answer	316
Mr. Gladstone's Speech	318
Remarks on the Budget of 1857	318
Expense of Persian and Chinese wars	321
Speeches of Lord J. Russell, Mr. Cardwell, and Mr. Milner Gibson	321—323
Resolution defeated	323
Defeat of the Government on Mr. Cobden's Motion respecting China	324
Financial Measures in anticipation of a Dissolution	324
Estimates brought forward in New Parliament	326

Summary of Contents. xv

	Pages
Supplementary Estimates, July 17	327
Tea and Sugar duties fixed for three years, Aug. 12	328
Circumstances of the Autumn of 1857	329
Commercial Pressure	329
Bank Restriction Act suspended	331
Meeting of Parliament; Committee on the Bank Acts	333
Defeat of the Government on the Conspiracy Bill, Feb. 19, 1858	333
Change of Government	334
Estimates for 1858-9 brought forward	334
Budget, April 19	335
Budget of 1858-9	337
Repeal of War Sinking-fund	340
Postponement of Exchequer-bonds	340
Equalisation of Spirit duties	340
Discussion on the Budget, and on the Exchequer-bonds' Bill	342—343
Financial Results of 1858-9	347
Necessity for increased Estimates in 1859	349
Budget of 1859-60	350
Budget of 1860-1	351
Mr. Ducane's Resolution	355
Opposition to the Repeal of the Paper duty	355
Supplementary Estimates and second Financial Statement	356
Financial Results of 1860-1	357
Budget of 1861-2	358
Mr. Horsfall's Amendment on the Tea duty	360
Review of Financial Policy from 1842-1861	361

APPENDIX A.

Table of Budgets from 1842—1861 . . 375

APPENDIX B.

I. General Taxation not falling directly on
   Property 396
II. General Taxation falling directly on Pro-
    perty 397
III. Local Taxation 398

TWENTY YEARS OF FINANCIAL POLICY, 1842—1861.

Chapter I.

THE last twenty years have witnessed a great change in the financial system of England; and concurrently with that change we have seen a marked development of the wealth and prosperity of the country. It is as yet too early to pronounce an historical judgment upon these events; for we cannot entirely divest ourselves of the feelings of actors, or of interested spectators; nor indeed can we yet look upon them as matters belonging to the past, since the change alluded to is still in progress, and it may be some time before we can regard it as complete.

The very circumstances, however, which prevent the writing of a regular history of this

Chap. I.

Introductory remarks.

CHAP. I.
Introductory remarks.

financial revolution, appear to render a short and informal account of it desirable. A new generation of public men, and of men who, though not engaged in political life, are interested in the study of public affairs, are growing up, and find themselves in the midst of a work of which it is difficult to understand the nature without studying it from the beginning. But nothing is more troublesome than the study of a history which has not been written. It is very much easier to read up the reigns of the Stuarts, or of the Roman Emperors, than that of Queen Victoria; and, though a writer, who attempts to deal with the events of his own time, is sure to commit a great many faults, it is not unreasonable on his part to hope that, in condensing and bringing together information, which is scattered over a large number of blue books, and a great many volumes of Hansard, he is rendering a service to some of his contemporaries, if only by inducing them to go over the same ground in order to correct his blunders.

The period reviewed is that commencing with Sir Robert Peel's imposition of the Income Tax in 1842, and extending to the Repeal of the Paper Duties in 1861. The fortunes of the Income Tax, its origin, the change which has

Financial Policy.

taken place in its character, and the work which has been done by its aid, give a kind of dramatic unity to this period, which would alone be sufficient to make the study of it interesting; but, in addition to this, we have in the course of these twenty years seen our financial system exhibited in all its bearings; and examples have been given of almost every kind of financial problem. We have seen how large surplusses have been applied, and how large deficits have been met; we have had peace taxation and war taxation; loans of various kinds, contracted upon different principles; successful and unsuccessful operations upon the interest of the debt; we have repealed an enormous mass of taxation with one hand, and have laid on a still larger amount with the other; we have revised our Commercial Policy, and to some extent our Monetary Policy also. These proceedings render the history of the time worthy of the attentive examination of us all; and an indication of its main outlines, such as is here attempted, can hardly fail to render that examination less laborious and more compendious.

If individual opinions are too freely expressed in any part of the book, I beg pardon both of those whom they may displease and of the general reader. It has not been my intention to enter into controversy; but there is something so repulsive to human nature in the simple reproduction of defunct budgets, that I could not have got through my task without stepping a little aside, from time to time, to touch upon questions of principle, or even of party, arising out of the narrative.

There is one more observation of a general character which I must make at the outset. I have attempted in the following pages to examine an important period of our history from a very limited point of view. I have treated of the policy of the last twenty years under its financial aspect alone. This would be a serious error in a work which laid claim to the title of a history. Perhaps it may be thought a mistake even in so much more confined a treatise as the present. Financial policy can never be regarded as entirely distinct from commercial and social policy; and if this be true as a general proposition, it is peculiarly true when applied to the case before us. The financial measures of 1842, 1845, 1853, 1860, and indeed of the whole period under review, were largely influenced, and sometimes governed, by considerations of commercial policy; and even these were, to a great extent,

Financial Policy.

subordinate to others of a still higher character. Mr. Gladstone, in his budget-speech of 1861, pointed out in eloquent language that the policy of the last twenty years should be judged by its political, social, and moral, as well as by its economical, results. I fully subscribe to this doctrine; but I have not attempted so high a flight of criticism as would enable me to take a comprehensive view of the whole of this great field of inquiry. I am content to act the part of the critic upon Garrick's acting, and to look only at the financial stop-watch; but in doing so I think it well to guard against misconstruction, by saying, once for all, that I am quite aware how inadequate a test the stop-watch alone would be of the merits of the great performance to which I propose to apply it.

CHAP. I.
Introductory remarks.

I will now begin at once with the account of Sir Robert Peel's financial statement of March 11, 1842.

Budget of 1842-3.

Probably no budget was ever awaited with more interest, anxiety, or curiosity, than that of 1842. Serious financial difficulties had been accumulating for several years. Five times in succession the revenue had fallen short of the expenditure by amounts averaging about a million and a-half per annum. In 1837-8 the

Financial position of the country.

deficiency had been 1,428,000*l.*; in 1838-9 it had been 430,000*l.*; in 1839-40, 1,457,000*l.*; in 1840-1, 1,851,000*l.*; and for 1841-2, the year just drawing to a close, it had been estimated at 2,421,000*l.* In each of the four years, 1837-1840, the estimates of the Chancellor of the Exchequer had been falsified by the result, to an amount in the whole of no less than 3,569,000*l.*; and in three out of the four the failure had been due to a deficiency in the anticipated income, rather than to the occurrence of any unexpected expenditure. In the year 1840-1, the estimate of income had been 48,591,000*l.*, and the amount realized had been only 47,433,000*l.*; showing an error of more than a million sterling in the estimate, and indicating a state of things which might well be thought alarming; since the failure had occurred in that portion of our revenue upon which we mainly depended, and which then constituted about four-fifths of the whole, namely, the revenue from the customs and the excise; it followed upon a well-meant and, in its way, a bold attempt to obtain a balance of income and expenditure by an addition to taxation; and it appeared to imply an exhaustion of the resources of the people, more serious than any deficit in the Exchequer, and

Financial Policy. 7

which was unhappily but too much in accordance with other disheartening and distressing signs of the times.

CHAP. I.
1842.

There was at this period a great deal of suffering among the lower orders, and especially among those engaged in manufactures; there was a scarcity of employment, and provisions were at a high price. As a consequence, there was much political discontent. Chartism was exciting serious uneasiness; the new Poor Law, against which the Chartist movement was mainly directed, was pressing hardly upon the people; who had not yet become fully accustomed to it; and who were suffering from it all the more severely on account of the badness of the recent harvests, the slackness of employment, and the growth of the population, which had not yet learnt to relieve itself by emigration.

Prevalence of distress.

To these causes of uneasiness were added others connected with the position of the great political parties in the State. The Whigs had held office, with a short interruption, for ten years; they had gradually lost the popularity which they had enjoyed at the beginning of their administration; and had for some time been maintaining themselves with difficulty, in an equally divided House of Commons, by the sup-

Position of the Ministry.

port of the extreme Liberals, and of the Irish party, then led by Mr. O'Connell. They were popularly accused of sacrificing both their own convictions and the interests of the State to the necessity of conciliating these important allies; and the measures which they brought forward were on this account regarded with suspicion and dislike, and were sure of being severely criticised. This was especially the case with regard to their financial projects; financially they were in bad odour with almost everybody. Since the accession of Lord Melbourne to power, in 1835, they had found it necessary to increase our naval and military expenditure by several millions sterling; we had been brought to the brink of a war with France; to an actual war with China; to a serious and, as it proved, a disastrous struggle in India; besides having to deal with an insurrection in Canada, and a Chartist rising at home. All this had told upon the estimates; and we had paid 15,536,000*l.* for army, navy, and ordnance in 1841, instead of 11,730,000*l.*, the amount in 1835. This increase of expenditure was unpopular among the extreme Liberals; but they had been to some extent conciliated by the unwillingness which the Government had shown to add proportionately to the taxation;

Financial Policy. 9

and especially by the concession made in 1839 of the Penny Postage,—a measure of undoubted social and general advantage, but extremely inconvenient in a financial sense; and the adoption of which, at that particular time, was thought to be due to the political necessities rather than to the convictions of the Ministry.

This surrender of an important branch of our revenue had been opposed by Sir Robert Peel and the Conservatives generally; and they regarded it both as financially wrong, and as an indication of a want of moral firmness on the part of the Government. Hopes had been held out by the advocates of the measure, that the rapid increase which would take place in the correspondence, and the economy which might be effected in the management of the Post Office under the new scheme, would soon replace the revenue which was to be given up; but a very short experience of the working of the system proved that this recovery of the revenue, though it might ultimately be realized, could not take place for many years. The lessons drawn from this experiment, therefore, were,—First, that the Government could not be trusted to resist a popular demand for a remission of taxation; and, secondly, that the sanguine promises of the

Chap. I.
1842.

Penny Postage measure.

CHAP. I.
1842.

advocates of remission, to the effect that the revenue they proposed to sacrifice would be speedily made up, were not to be relied on. These considerations had a powerful bearing upon the much greater struggle of which the year 1841 witnessed the commencement, and of which we feel the consequences to the present day.

Why the Whigs were Free Traders rather than the Conservatives.

Judging from the antecedents of the two parties, I see no particular reason why the Whigs should have been the Free-traders, and the Conservatives the Protectionists, of 1841. If the questions raised had been simple questions of political economy, it is probable that the doctrines of Pitt and of Huskisson would from the first have found their supporters among the political descendants of those statesmen. But the discussion was complicated by the fact that the Anti-Cornlaw Leaguers belonged to the Radical party; and that their language and proceedings alarmed the Conservatives; while the Whigs were supposed to be naturally anxious to conciliate so important a section of their political supporters, and were suspected of having political ends in view when they gave their assent to economical reforms. No doubt the partial adoption of a Free-trade policy by Lord Melbourne's Cabinet, in 1841, was in a great measure due to

Financial Policy.

the progress of conviction, to the arguments which such men as Mr. Poulett Thomson, Mr. Deacon Hume, and others, had for some years been addressing to the Ministry, and to the remarkable evidence collected by the Import Duties Committee of 1840. But however genuine their convictions may have been, they did not get much credit for sincerity. It was thought that they took up Free-trade as a last and desperate card, and played it for the sake of strengthening their alliance with the Radicals, and of getting up a cry in the country, which might be of service to them at a general election. The fact that the budget of 1841 was so greatly at variance with the principle of the budget of 1840, added much to the grounds for suspecting that the Government were either swayed by some unavowed considerations, or else were in a difficulty as to their course, and were floundering in hopes of finding firm ground, without well knowing in which direction to look for it. In 1840 Mr. Baring had attempted to restore an equilibrium in the finances by a general increase of duties. In 1841 the same Chancellor of the Exchequer proposed to effect the same object by the directly opposite course of reducing certain duties, with a view to obtain a greater revenue from them. In doing so he was, in truth, only acting upon a financial principle already well known, and generally, though not universally, acknowledged to be sound; but the apparent inconsistency in his conduct gave an air of uncertainty to his proceedings; and the recollection of the results of the Postage Reform, coupled with the general suspicion attaching to all policy likely to conciliate Radical support to the Ministry, deprived his measure of any fair chance of success. Accordingly, the budget of 1841 had proved the occasion for the ejection of the Melbourne Ministry from office; and the reins of power had been transferred to Sir Robert Peel and a Conservative Cabinet, commanding a majority of more than ninety in the New Parliament.

Sir Robert Peel had spent the autumn and winter in maturing his plan of finance, and on the 11th of March, 1842, he laid it before the House of Commons in a speech of very great ability.

After stating his grounds for thinking that the deficiency for the year then expiring would be about 2,350,000*l.*, he proceeded to lay down his estimate of Income and Expenditure for the year 1842-3, as follows:—

Financial Policy.   13

Income.

	£
Customs	22,500,000
Excise	13,450,000
Stamps	7,100,000
Taxes	4,400,000
Post Office	500,000
Crown Lands	150,000
Miscellaneous	250,000
Total Income	£48,350,000

Expenditure.

	£
Debt (funded and unfunded)	29,427,000
Charges on Consolidated Fund	2,368,000
Army	6,617,000
Navy	6,739,000
Ordnance	2,084,000
Miscellaneous	2,800,000
Canada, Clothing of Volunteers	108,000
Expedition to China	675,000
Total Expenditure	£50,819,000

The net result of this estimate was, of course, an anticipated deficiency of 2,469,000*l.* This, however, did not, in Sir Robert Peel's opinion, represent the full extent of the liabilities of the country. He pointed out that, although he had reason to think that the sum of 500,000*l.*, which he had taken in the military estimates on account of the hostilities in China, would probably be sufficient provision to make within the year, yet a further expenditure of 700,000*l*. or 800,000*l*. would in all likelihood be ultimately incurred, and must be met at some future time. He glanced at the possible demands from Australia and other of our colonies, and at the serious cost which the recent events in Affghanistan were likely to entail upon us. Finally, for the purpose of bringing before the House a full and complete view of the financial position of the country, he referred to the growing deficit in the finances of India. " I am quite aware," he said, " that there may appear to be no direct and immediate connection between the finances of India and those of this country; but that would be a superficial view of our relations with India, which should omit the consideration of this subject. Depend upon it, if the credit of India should become disordered, if some great exertion should become necessary, then the credit of England must be brought forward to its support, and the collateral and indirect effect of disorders in Indian finances would be felt extensively in this country."

Having thus shown both the actual deficiency to be met, and the circumstances under which it was to be met, and having pointed out that, unless an exertion were now made, the aggregate deficiency of the six years, 1837-1843, would amount to 10,072,000*l*., Sir Robert Peel proceeded to state his views as to the various modes in which the necessary amount of revenue might be provided. His statement is a good instance of that exhaustive form of argument in which he excelled, and which he sometimes pushed so far as to provoke a smile. On the present occasion he used it like a master.

First, he swept away all idea of meeting the difficulty with financial nostrums, disguised loans, application of savings' banks' monies, issue of exchequer bills, or any other expedient for easing off the crisis. Then, having expressed his conviction that matters could not be brought round by a reduction of expenditure, and having thus arrived at the conclusion that there must be an addition to our taxation, he opened the question, what the nature of that addition should be. Not increased charges on articles of consumption, he said; for, besides that he felt great reluctance to add to the burdens of the labouring classes, he was convinced, by the results of Mr. Baring's experiment, that we had " arrived at the limits of taxation on articles of consumption." Mr. Baring had expected, by adding 5 per cent. to the customs and excise duties, to gain 1,895,000*l*. and he had only gained 206,000*l*. To repeat Mr. Baring's attempt, therefore, would be to repeat Mr. Baring's failure.

But if this could not be recommended, what then? Should he revive some of the abandoned taxes? Should he increase the rate of postage? No; he was unwilling to disturb the working of an experiment fraught with so many advantages to the labouring classes. Nor would he re-impose the duties on salt, on leather, or on beer; nor lay taxes on railways or on gas. To all such modes of raising the revenue he objected, partly on the ground of unwillingness to interfere with the comforts of the labourer, partly on that of respect for the interests of manufacturing industry.

One more method remained to be examined, before he came to his own conclusion. Should he follow the example of his immediate predecessors, and attempt to increase revenue by diminishing taxation? Upon this question he argued at some length, expressing his concurrence in the opinion, that reductions of duty on articles of consumption have a tendency to replace the revenue surrendered in order to make

Financial Policy.

them, and that increased revenue may ultimately be realized from diminished taxation; but adding, that a long period must elapse before that end could be attained, and that a plan for reducing taxation with a view to ultimate improvement would not provide the means of meeting the existing deficiency. This view he confirmed and illustrated by referring to the reductions which had been made in the duties on wine, tobacco, coffee, hemp, rum, and sugar; in only two of which cases, (those of coffee and rum), had the revenue recovered to the extent of the reduction of duty; and even in the case of coffee, which was by far the most favourable, it had taken three years to do so. If, therefore, we were to have recourse to the reduction of taxation as the only means of supplying the deficiency, it would be necessary to resort for a time at least to the objectionable system of loans and other devices, to which he for one could not consent to be a party.

Having thus exhausted all other alternatives, Sir Robert Peel addressed "an earnest appeal to the possessors of property, for the purpose of repairing this mighty evil." He said, "I propose, for a time at least—(and I never had occasion to make a proposition with a more thorough con-

C

viction of its being one which the public interest of the country required)—I propose that, for a time to be limited, the income of this country should be called on to contribute a certain sum for the purpose of remedying this mighty and growing evil. I propose that the income of this country should bear a charge not exceeding 7*d.* in the pound, which will not amount to 3*l.* per cent., but, speaking accurately, 2*l.* 18*s.* 4*d.* per cent., for the purpose of not only supplying the deficiency in the revenue, but of enabling me with confidence and satisfaction to propose great commercial reforms, which will afford a hope of reviving commerce, and such an improvement in the manufacturing interests as will react on every other interest in the country; and, by diminishing the prices of the articles of consumption, and the cost of living, will, in a pecuniary point of view, compensate you for your present sacrifices; whilst you will be at the same time relieved from the contemplation of a great public evil."

This tax, he proceeded to explain, was not to extend to Ireland. Persons having incomes not exceeding 150*l.* a-year were to be exempt from it. Tenant-farmers, and occupiers of land, were to be assessed upon one-half of the rental. The

Financial Policy.

produce of the tax might, he thought, be taken at 3,771,000*l.* The period for which he hoped that Parliament would, if necessary, sanction its duration was five years; but, in order to afford an earlier opportunity for reconsidering the subject, he proposed to lay it on in the first instance for three years only.

In order that Ireland, which was not to contribute to the Income Tax, might nevertheless bear her share in the additional burdens thus thrown upon Great Britain, Sir Robert Peel proposed to raise the duty on Irish spirits from 2*s*. 8*d*. per gallon to 3*s*. 8*d*., the amount charged on Scotch spirits;* and to equalise most of the stamp duties of England and Ireland, by raising those affecting property in the latter country to the English level. By the former of these operations he expected to gain 250,000*l*., and by the latter 160,000*l*., so that Ireland would contribute in the whole 410,000*l*. additional revenue.

One more new duty he had to propose; namely, the extension of the export duty of 4*s*. per ton on coals carried in foreign ships, to coals carried in British ships. From this source he calculated on obtaining 200,000*l*., making the

---

* The duty on English spirits was 7*s*. 10*d*.

whole amount of revenue to be derived from additional taxation 4,380,000*l.** Deducting from this sum the estimated deficiency on actual votes, 2,570,000*l.*, he arrived at a probable surplus revenue of 1,800,000*l.*, subject, of course, to some possible diminution on account of further claims connected with the Chinese war, and the hostilities in Affghanistan. That surplus he proposed to apply to a great reform and reduction of the commercial tariff of the country.

It is not proposed to enter here into a discussion of Sir Robert Peel's commercial reforms. It may be sufficient to say that he proposed to expend about 1,200,000*l.* of his surplus upon the reduction of the duties on foreign and colonial timber, on coffee, and upon about 750 various articles in the tariff, repealing at the same time the export duties on British manufactures, and reducing the duty on stage coaches. He reserved a balance of 520,000*l.* for the pur-

---

	£
* Income Tax	3,770,000
Irish Spirit Duties	250,000
Irish Stamp Duties	160,000
Export Duty on Coals	200,000
	£4,380,000

pose of meeting either any additional charges arising out of the Chinese or the Indian war, or any additional reductions of duty, which we might be called upon to make in the event of the conclusion of any of the commercial treaties then in course of negotiation.

CHAP. I.
1842.

Sir Robert Peel concluded this great speech by an appeal to his hearers to follow the example set by their fathers, who, in the hour of their greatest distress, "with a mutiny at the Nore, a rebellion in Ireland, and disaster abroad, yet submitted with buoyant vigour and universal applause (with the funds as low as 52) to a property tax of 10 per cent." Speaking after twenty-five years of peace, at a time of increasing prosperity, wealth, and comfort among the upper classes, but of increasing financial embarrassment in the country, he expressed his confidence, that the appeal he had made would be successful, and that the representatives of the people would not "throw away the means of maintaining the public credit by reducing in the most legitimate manner the burden of the public debt."

The great fiscal engine thus brought into play by Sir Robert Peel had been laid aside, but not forgotten, since the conclusion of the war; having been rejected by the House of Commons,

Fiscal Policy since 1816.

in March, 1816, by a majority (against ministers) of thirty-seven. Since that time considerable alterations, chiefly in the direction of remission, had been made in our system of taxation. Duties to the estimated amount of about 27,000,000*l.* had been taken off, and duties to the estimated amount of between 7,000,000*l.* and 8,000,000*l.* had been laid on. Much had been done, especially by Mr. Huskisson, to relieve trade and industry; and, while taxation had been lightened, the revenue from the customs and excise had not diminished to any considerable extent. Mr. Labouchere was able to point out in 1840* that, while customs' and excise duties to the amount of 5,982,000*l.* had been taken off since 1830, the revenue from those two sources had only diminished by 1,091,000*l.*

The various remissions which had been made, however, had been made as it were piecemeal; though there had not been wanting financiers and statesmen, who had, at different times since the conclusion of the war, urged the importance of a general revision of the whole system of taxation upon a settled plan, with a view to the relief of industry, and to a more judicious ad-

* May 15.

Financial Policy. 23

justment of the burdens of the people. Such a revision was particularly demanded about the year 1830, towards the close of the series of Tory Administrations which was finally cut off by the accession of Lord Grey to power, and by the passing of the Reform Act. Sir Henry Parnell, Mr. Poulett Thomson, and Mr. Huskisson, were among the leading advocates of Financial Reform. Sir Henry Parnell had hoped to bring the whole question of the incidence of taxation before the celebrated Finance Committee, appointed at his instance in 1828; but the labours of that committee were cut short, and Sir H. Parnell was obliged to content himself with publishing his views in his elaborate and useful tract upon the subject. Mr. Poulett Thomson brought the question of taxation before the House of Commons, and moved for a Committee upon it, on the 25th of March, 1830. The Committee was not granted, but the debate, especially the mover's speech, is interesting and instructive. Mr. Huskisson, who supported Mr. P. Thomson on this occasion, had a few days before (on the 18th March) explained his own views in a speech upon the state of the nation. All these three gentlemen, though differing upon certain points, agreed in recommending large remissions of taxation upon various raw materials of industry and articles of consumption; and all agreed also in expressing themselves as favourable to the imposition of a Property or Income Tax.

There is, however, a difference between the tone in which Sir H. Parnell and Mr. Thomson respectively speak of the propriety of imposing such a tax. Mr. P. Thomson, while proposing large and important remissions of taxation, and dealing with a revenue of some 16,000,000*l*., is cautious and even timid in suggesting the idea of a Property Tax; and, though avowing his own disposition to adopt it, takes care to disclaim it as an essential part of his plan; he even goes so far as to recommend recourse to a loan to cover the bold experiments upon the revenue, which he hopes will lead to its ultimate recovery and improvement. But Sir Henry Parnell, in a more statesmanlike spirit, lays down as essential the doctrine, that a financier ought not to run risks. Accordingly, although he expresses his conviction that the reduction of duties on many articles, which he names, will lead to little or no ultimate loss of revenue, and although he embodies in his plan some proposals for considerable reductions in the public expenditure, he states

Financial Policy.

that, in his opinion, it would not be right to depend on these reductions alone for the means of making good the revenue. "The proper principle," he says, "on which the proposed reduction of taxation and expenditure should be conducted, is, that the securing of a sufficiency of revenue should never be a matter of doubt; and therefore it is particularly desirable that, when a measure is taken for reducing taxes, there should at the same time not only be some measure to produce a reduction of expense, but also a new tax, which shall be of such a nature as to make quite certain of receiving from it full as much revenue as will be wanting for all the public services. In selecting a new tax," he adds, " there seems to be but one opinion with respect to what tax that ought to be. Persons who hold the most opposite doctrines on the subject of our financial, commercial, and agricultural difficulties, in suggesting remedies, have made an Income Tax a part of them."*

It may be observed, by the way, that, although the last-quoted paragraph is literally accurate, inasmuch as there were many persons of very different sentiments on other points who con-

---

* Parnell's Financial Reform, p. 252.

curred in recommending an Income Tax, it is not to be inferred from this that all the financial reformers of the day were prepared for such a measure. The extreme timidity of Mr. P. Thomson's reference to it in the speech already mentioned, and the distinct protest entered against it by Lord Palmerston, on the same occasion, though his Lordship supported Mr. Thomson's motion, sufficiently indicate the reception which a proposal to revive that tax would probably have met with. It is still more significant that Lord Althorp, though personally in favour of an Income Tax, did not venture to propose it while he himself was Chancellor of the Exchequer.

Sir R. Peel's Policy identical with Sir H. Parnell's. The policy insisted on by Sir Henry Parnell, in 1830, was the policy actually adopted by Sir Robert Peel in 1842, which contrasts with that contemplated by his immediate predecessors in this, among other respects, that he covered his operations upon the tariff by a new tax which ensured his receiving a full amount of revenue, whether the remodelling of the tariff proved financially successful or not, while the Whig budget of 1841 rested entirely on the merits of its scheme of readjustment and remission of duties, and must, if that readjustment had failed to in-

Financial Policy.

crease the revenue of customs, have led to an augmentation of debt. It can hardly be doubted that Sir Robert Peel's was the sounder and safer principle. At the same time it is not to be forgotten that, in calling in the aid of the Income Tax for a temporary object, the nation exposed itself to the fate of the horse in the fable, which gained its victory indeed over the stag, but at the expense of permanent subjection to its rider:—

CHAP. I.
1842.

" Non equitem dorso, frenum non depulit ore."

It would be a curious, and not an unprofitable, subject of speculation, whether the Tariff Reforms of 1842, or anything approaching them, could have been successfully carried through without the aid of the Income Tax; but it must be obvious to every reader of Sir Robert Peel's great budget-speech that these Reforms were but an object of secondary importance in his estimation, compared with the maintenance of the public credit, and the restoration of a surplus revenue. Any one who refers to the language used by Sir Robert Peel, not only upon that occasion, but for several years before, will see that the maintenance of a proper equilibrium in our finances was the object uppermost in his

Sir R. Peel's first object was to restore the finances.

mind, and that it was one which he kept steadily in view; while he gave but a cold and negative approval to the projects of those who desired to effect, what they thought, great improvements in the whole system of our taxation. His opinions upon commercial finance had indeed been gradually maturing for a considerable time, and frequent foreshadowings of particular changes adopted in 1842 and 1845 are to be found scattered in his speeches between 1830 and 1840; but his general views on the subject of great financial changes are pretty nearly as he stated them in 1833. " He thought the noble lord (Lord Althorp) had acted wisely in maintaining the system of taxation as it stood at present. All attempts to effect an extensive commutation of taxes causing, as it necessarily must in the present artificial state of society, the unsettlement of capital, must be productive of great injury. Another system of taxation might be proved by reason *à priori* to be better than the present; but the present being established, and the habits and occupations of the people having accommodated themselves to it, it might, though abstractedly less perfect, be on the whole preferable to any substitute." It may be worth remark that Sir Robert Peel had always looked coldly on an Income or Property Tax as a substitute for other taxation. In 1830, referring to Mr. Huskisson's great speech on the distress of the country, he said,—" His right honourable friend seemed to recommend a more extensive commutation [of taxes] than had yet been thought of, and the levy of taxes, too, on something else, in lieu of what for the relief of industry might be repealed. The House could not fail to observe that his right honourable friend most skilfully avoided the enunciation of what that something else was to be; but his drift was not to be concealed. The House might naturally suppose that amongst the various subjects connected with the finances of the country, which had occupied the attention of Government, the question of a Property Tax had not escaped them; it was one of those which they had most seriously mooted. * * * They had most attentively considered the bearing of such a tax as affecting the commercial, the professional, and the landed incomes of the country; and also the question, if such a tax were resolved upon, of confining it to landed incomes, and excluding the other two classes. After those mature deliberations, then, the conclusion at which they arrived was, that they should best discharge the duty they owed to the country by repealing this year 3,400,000*l.* of taxes. * * * The course which they had adopted pretty plainly proved that they had not resolved upon submitting to Parliament any proposition for a Property Tax."

So again, when in opposition in 1833, he commended Lord Althorp for not proposing an Income Tax with a view to the reduction of other taxation; and declared that in his opinion nothing but a case of extreme necessity could justify Parliament in imposing an Income Tax in time of peace. In 1835, when in office, he opposed the motion of Lord Chandos for a repeal of the Malt-tax, and warned the agriculturists to beware how they exchanged " the light pressure of a malt duty for the scourge of a Property Tax." In 1839, when opposing the proposal of the Government to reduce the postage duty, and to pledge the House to make up any consequent deficiency in the revenue, he expressed his conviction that by such a pledge the House would virtually commit itself to a Property Tax; and he added that possibly such a tax might be the one to which in such a case it would be the wisest to resort. " But would the House do so," he said, " merely to raise one or two millions of money?" In 1839 his mind

Financial Policy. 31

was clearly not made up in favour of a Property Tax. Nor was it so in 1840, when he approved Mr. Baring's attempt to meet the deficiency by an addition to our indirect taxation rather than by a direct impost.

But while he felt so little inclined to try experiments upon our fiscal system, and entertained so little love for an Income Tax, his convictions as to the necessity of maintaining our revenue and supporting public credit were decided and strong. Nothing can be warmer than his denunciations, in 1832, of the principle of reducing taxation for the relief of the people without regard to the obligations, for the fulfilment of which the taxes were a security. "The strongest apprehension that he had entertained from the infusion of democratic power into the House of Commons by the measure of reform was, that the House would hereafter find it very difficult to resist proposals for immediate relief at the expense of good faith and of the true permanent interests of the country." It was on this occasion that he denounced, with all the force of his eloquence, the doctrine propounded by Mr. Poulett Thomson, that the deficiency in the revenue was to be regarded not as money lost, but as money left to fructify in the pockets of the

CHAP. I.
1842.

people; and he expressed his own conviction that it was essentially necessary that a surplus revenue to a certain amount should be maintained for the support of the public credit. In entire conformity with this language is that which he used in 1839, upon the question of the reduction of the duties of postage; in 1840, upon Sir John Yarde Buller's motion against the Melbourne Ministry; and in 1841, in the debate on the budget, and again in support of his own vote of want of confidence in the Administration. A review of these and other speeches seems clearly to establish that Sir Robert Peel, in proposing the revival of the Income Tax, was actuated much more by his desire to restore public credit and the balance between Revenue and Expenditure, than by a deliberate intention of altering the incidence of taxation.

Views of the Conservatives generally.

However this may have been as regards his own secret motives, there can be no doubt that it was upon the financial ground that the great bulk of his followers gave their support to his proposals. Many of them had little faith in the elasticity of a reduced tariff; very many disliked the reduction in the tariff exceedingly, and were so far from seeing in it a compensation for the

Financial Policy.

burden of the Income Tax, that they looked upon it as an aggravation of the evil. But all felt that the financial position of the country was a serious one; all believed that their leader was the only man to grapple with its difficulties; and they set aside for a time their feelings of dissatisfaction and alarm at some parts of his policy, in order that they might carry him triumphantly through the opposition, with which the adherents of the late Ministry assailed his plan.

For the proposed Income Tax received no quarter from the Liberal party in either House of Parliament. It is true that on the night of the Financial Statement itself there was little appearance of opposition; but within three days afterwards Lord Brougham laid upon the table of the House of Lords a series of resolutions condemning some of the leading provisions of the tax, and declaring the importance of making every effort to provide for its early cessation; and when, on the day after the discussion in the House of Lords Sir Robert Peel moved in the House of Commons the resolution in favour of the Income Tax, a debate was begun, which continued for eight nights; and the resolution was not adopted until the 13th of April. Nor did the opposition stop there. Lord

CHAP. I.
1842.

Opposition the Income Tax in botl Houses of Parliament.

John Russell had declared his intention of opposing "the resolutions, and the report of the resolutions, and the first reading, the second reading, and the third reading of the bill;" and he kept his word. Every stage of the bill was keenly contested, the members of the previous cabinet taking the lead against it; there were as many as sixteen divisions taken upon it in the House of Commons, without reckoning those upon mere questions of adjournment, or those connected with the reception of petitions against it. At length the third reading of the bill was carried, on the 31ft of May, by a majority of 106; and the bill was sent up to the House of Lords, where it was warmly debated, and where several protests were entered against it after it had passed.

Arguments of the Opposition. The arguments of the Opposition were directed partly against the structure of the tax, and partly against the whole financial scheme of the Government. Mr. Baring, in particular, as ex-Chancellor of the Exchequer, defended the proposals of the late Cabinet, and impugned some of the reasoning on which Sir Robert Peel's proposals were founded. Sir Robert Peel had argued that the results of the budget of 1840 had shown, that increased revenue was not to be obtained by increasing indirect taxation; and that

Financial Policy. 35

the proposals of 1841, for meeting the deficiency by a diminution of taxation, were too uncertain to be relied on; whence he drew the conclusion that, since the deficiency could not be met either by increasing or by diminishing the general taxation, recourse must be had to a new impost. Mr. Baring, in reply, observed—First, that the experiment of 1840 had by no means turned out so badly as Sir Robert Peel represented; and secondly, that his description of the proposals of 1841 was an unfair and incorrect one. Sir Robert Peel had stated that the addition of five per cent. to the customs' and excise duties had produced an increase of only one-half per cent. in the customs' and excise revenue; but Mr. Baring showed that, in making this calculation, Sir Robert Peel had included the duty received from corn, which had not been altered, and upon which a very great amount of the loss had accrued; and he argued that, if the amount of revenue derived from corn were excluded from the accounts of both the years (1838-9 and 1840-1) between which Sir Robert Peel had drawn a comparison, the increase of the revenue from the other customs' and excise duties would be found to be,—not 206,000*l.*, as Sir Robert Peel had stated it, but—1,007,000*l.* He contended, therefore, that the resources of indirect taxation were not exhausted, as it was said they were; and that there was no real necessity for "a recurrence to that odious impost," the Income Tax. With regard to the proposals of 1841, he considered it unfair to represent them as an attempt to increase revenue by simply diminishing the rates of certain duties; the mode in which they were intended to increase the revenue was, by reducing the amount of protection afforded to the home and colonial producers, and by introducing into the market a quantity of foreign produce at a rate of duty, which would be more productive to the Exchequer than the duty on the colonial article, while the consumer would gain by the reduction in price. Thus, in the case of sugar, he had expected to gain 700,000*l.* by reducing the duty on foreign sugar from 63*s.* to 36*s.* per cwt., not so much because he hoped that the reduction would stimulate consumption sufficiently to produce this increase of revenue, as because he calculated that a quantity of foreign sugar, which was excluded by the high duty of 63*s.*, would come in at 36*s.*, and would displace a corresponding quantity of colonial sugar, which only paid 24*s.* The same would have been the case had the

Financial Policy. 37

timber duties been altered from 55*s.* a load on foreign, and 10*s.* on colonial, to 50*s.* on foreign, and 30*s.* on colonial timber. It was, therefore, not fair in Sir Robert Peel to argue against the plan of 1841 from the experience of the reductions on wine, tobacco, and other articles, as he had done; and Mr. Baring maintained that, both as regarded the experiment of increasing indirect taxation in 1840, and the proposals for altering its incidence and for diminishing protection in 1841, the foundation of alleged necessity for the Income Tax would prove to be an unsound one, and that the tax was really not required to maintain the revenue. Mr. Baring further argued, and in this he was supported by many of his party, that Sir Robert Peel's whole scheme of commercial reform was objectionable, as being founded on the doctrines of Protection. The details also of the Income Tax were much objected to; and most of the arguments which have since been urged against its inequalities and its alleged unfairness were brought forward in the course of the protracted debates to which its imposition gave rise.

Sir Robert Peel, however, adhered to his assertions that the result of the increase of indirect taxation in 1840 showed that such taxation had

CHAP. I.
1842.

Arguments of Sir R. Peel and his colleagues,

almost reached its limits; and that the budget of 1841, besides being open to other objections, would not have produced a revenue sufficient to meet the expenditure; and it was on this ground mainly that his party appear to have supported the proposed Income Tax. The following extract from the speech of Mr. Goulburn, the Chancellor of the Exchequer, shows the view taken of the matter by one of his principal colleagues:—

"He (Mr. Goulburn) and his colleagues had laboured most anxiously to avoid having recourse to the measure now proposed by Her Majesty's Government, knowing the opinion which would be entertained against it by some portions of the people, and the burdens which it must throw upon many; but he did most sincerely believe that under the present circumstances of the country, encumbered with a debt that must be discharged, bound to maintain a receipt equal to the expenditure, equal to the preservation of our empire abroad, and our character throughout the world, it was only by the imposition of a tax affecting the property of the country, that it was possible successfully to cope with difficulties so gigantic."*

---

* Debate of March 18, 1842.

Financial Policy.

The language of another leading Minister, Lord Ripon, is equally remarkable. Lord Brougham had proposed a string of resolutions in the House of Lords, to the adoption of which Lord Ripon objected as unnecessary and inconvenient. Speaking of one of these, he said,— "Entirely concurring, as he did, in the noble and learned lord's declaration that the proposed tax was a resource to which Parliament ought not to have recourse except under the pressure of dire necessity, still, unless the noble and learned lord thought he had reason to believe * * * that there existed a design on the part of the Government to entrap Parliament into the passing of this Act on the plea of absolute necessity, and for a limited period only, * * * unless the noble and learned lord thought them mean and shabby enough so to trick Parliament in order to get the measure passed, and then afterwards to continue it as a permanent tax, * * * he did not see why, as a preliminary step, their Lordships should be called upon to declare by resolution their opposition to it."*

Such, then, were the arguments by which Sir Robert Peel and his colleagues supported

---

* Debate H. L., March 17, 1842.

their financial policy. Their first object was, to put a stop to the series of deficits by a bold measure of direct taxation; their second was, to readjust the system of indirect taxation, so as to relieve the springs of industry from the undue pressure which was weighing upon them, preserving at the same time the principles of protection to native and to colonial industry, upon which they had taken office. They rejected the principles upon which their predecessors had proposed to deal with the great articles of corn and sugar, on the ground that the British corn-grower was entitled to a better kind, and larger amount, of protection than a fixed duty of 8s. a quarter on wheat would afford, and that the colonial sugar-planter ought not to be exposed to competition with the slaveholders of Cuba and Brazil. They rejected the principle on which it had been proposed to alter the timber duties, because, although Mr. Baring's plan would have produced a larger revenue from that source than their own, it would have imposed an additional burden upon the industry of this country by raising the price of a most important raw material. Finally, they rejected the whole principle of the budget of 1841, because it failed to secure the revenue against the possibility of a

Financial Policy.

further heavy deficit, and a further addition to the public debt. This was the position which Sir Robert Peel took up, and which he eloquently and successfully defended throughout the session.

CHAP. I.
1842.

It is not a little curious, after studying the debates of 1842, to turn to those of 1843, and to inquire into the immediate results of the great measures we have been describing. They were somewhat startling. Sir Robert Peel had reckoned on a surplus of 520,000*l.* ; but, although the Income Tax had proved more productive than he had anticipated, instead of realizing a surplus, he had to announce a deficiency of 2,200,000*l.*

1843. Disappointment of Sir R. Peel's calculations;

The first and most obvious cause of this disappointment was an oversight with regard to the time of collecting the Income Tax. Sir Robert Peel had taken credit for a whole year's tax ; but, as the collection was arranged to take place half-yearly, the time for calling up the second half did not arrive till the financial year had expired ; so that one-half only, and not, as had been expected, the whole, of the tax became available for the service of the year. Against this, however, had to be set the fact that the tax had proved a much more productive one than had been foreseen ; and that, instead of

causes of it.

3,770,000*l.*, it was worth about 5,100,000*l.* per annum. Of this amount 2,500,000 had been realized within the year; so that the difference between the estimate and the result, as regarded this tax, was only 1,270,000*l.* against the latter.

But Sir Robert Peel's hopes had been seriously disappointed as regarded other branches of the revenue. The Customs had fallen short of his estimate by 750,000*l.*; the Excise by 1,200,000*l.*; the Stamps by 200,000*l.*; and the Taxes by 135,000*l.* In short, the income of the year, leaving out the produce of the Income Tax, had been estimated at 47,640,000*l.*, and had reached only 45,600,000*l.* To the loss of 2,000,000*l.* thus sustained must be added the loss by miscalculation on the Income Tax, 1,270,000*l.*, making the total deficiency of income realized, as compared with income anticipated, 3,270,000*l.* But, on the other hand, a sum of 725,000*l.* had been received for the ransom of Canton, which had not been included in the preceding year's estimate; and the expenditure of the country had been also reduced by 222,000*l.* below what it had been taken at; and, by deducting these sums from the deficiency of 3,270,000*l.*, Mr. Goulburn reduced it to a deficiency of 2,422,000*l.*, from which again he

Financial Policy. 43

took off 202,000*l.*, as the amount of loss by forged Exchequer-bills, which he said ought not to be reckoned as part of the year's expenditure, and arrived at a net balance of 2,200,000*l.*, as representing what he considered to be the real deficit.*

CHAP. I.
1843.

Few budgets have presented so remarkable a picture of miscalculation as was here shown; and it is no slight evidence of the confidence which Sir Robert Peel had inspired, that his reputation as a financier did not suffer from the exhibition of his mistake. The peculiarity of the case lay, not so much in the amount of the discrepancy between the estimate and the result, as in the details of that discrepancy. With regard to the produce of the Income Tax, for instance, it is curious that Sir Robert Peel should not have foreseen that a moiety of it could not be collected within the financial year. That he should have been unable to form a correct estimate of the produce of the tax was not surprising; and he had himself pointed out the

Remarks on this miscalculation.

---

* These figures are taken from Mr. Goulburn's budget-speech, May 8, 1843; they do not exactly agree with the figures given in the table of Budgets (Appendix A), which are taken from the Quarterly Balance Sheets presented to Parliament.

difficulty of doing so; but that he should not have perceived what the effect of his own arrangements for its collection would be, is certainly startling. As regarded the deficiency in the other branches of the revenue, although the same remarks do not altogether apply, there were circumstances which could not fail to excite unfavourable criticisms on the sagacity of the minister. The Customs' revenue had fallen short of his expectations by 750,000*l.*; and this, notwithstanding a very large amount of revenue (1,378,000*l.*) received from corn, a source of income upon which it was generally thought imprudent for a minister to rely, on account of the great uncertainty attending it. Upon this it was obvious for Mr. Baring to retort upon Sir Robert Peel the argument which the latter had used in the preceding year against Mr. Baring's own budget of 1840. Mr. Baring's addition of 5 per cent. to the Customs'and Excise duties had been pronounced a failure, because in the result it had produced an increase of only 206,000*l.*, instead of 1,895,000*l.* to the revenue. By parity of reasoning, Sir Robert Peel's reform of the Tariff might be termed a financial failure, because in the result it had produced a loss of nearly 2,000,000*l.*, instead of 1,000,000*l.* as

Financial Policy. 45

had been anticipated. The argument, as Mr. Baring said, was not a very strong one, but it was as good in the one case as in the other; and Sir Robert Peel had certainly made a good deal of it the year before. The truth seems to be, that a single year's experience does not afford sufficient ground for such sweeping arguments.

But there were other points calling for notice. Amongst the articles upon which the greatest amount of loss had been sustained, wine stood the first. The deficiency in the wine duties reached the sum of 500,000*l.* Yet there had been no alteration in the rate of duty, nor did there appear to be any tendency to a diminution in the consumption of wine in the country. The loss was wholly attributable to the uncertainty into which the wine trade had been thrown by the long protracted and at length fruitless negotiations for a Commercial Treaty with Portugal; or, in other words, to the adoption by the Government of a line of policy with regard to Reciprocity Treaties, which had been the subject of very serious criticism in the preceding session. The loss on the timber duties, again, had exceeded the expected amount, being 676,000*l.*, instead of, as had been expected, 600,000*l.*; and this, too, appeared to have been partly due to the paralysis of trade caused by the suspended alteration in the duty,— another instance, as might be said, of a failure on the part of the Minister to foresee the consequences of his own measures. Then the great deficiency in the Excise was in part attributed by Mr. Goulburn to the falling off in the malt duty for 1842-3, on account of the badness of the harvest of 1841 ; but, while it was perfectly true that, according to the system of malt credit then in force, the malt revenue for one year depended mainly upon the harvest of the year before, it was also to be remembered that this very circumstance naturally gave a Minister, when framing his estimates, the advantage of knowing pretty accurately what the former harvest had been ; and that in point of fact Sir Robert Peel had taken the badness of the harvest of 1841 into account, and had made, as he said, a very moderate estimate of the malt revenue on that ground. Moderate as it was, however, it exceeded the actual result by no less than 880,000*l.*

Moreover, of the three measures which Sir Robert Peel had adopted for increasing the revenue, two had proved failures. The export duty on coal, from which he had expected to receive 140,000*l.* additional duty, had pro-

Financial Policy. 47

duced not quite 80,000*l.* within the year,* and of this it was said that some 9000*l.* was the produce of the old duty, and not of his addition to it. His other and more signal failure was in the results of the addition to the Irish spirit duties, from which he had reckoned on getting 250,000*l.*, but got only 56,000*l.*; and this at the cost of a fearful addition to illicit distillation in Ireland.

CHAP. I.
1843.

Such were the failures of the budget of 1842; yet, in spite of those failures, its policy was upon the whole beginning to be recognized as sound; and discerning eyes could see that as a whole it was likely to prove not a failure but a success. The very disappointments, which had been experienced in the financial results of the increase of some, and the reduction of many duties, brought more clearly into sight the value of the Income Tax as a financial engine. A stronger conviction than ever began to be entertained, that no shifting or readjusting of our indirect taxation would have brought us through our difficulties; and the bold effort which the Go-

Soundness of his general policy.

---

* It had only been in operation for three-fourths of the year, but Sir Robert Peel had framed his calculations on an expectation of receiving 140,000*l.* or rather 200,000*l.* within the year.

CHAP. I.
1843.

vernment were making to maintain the public credit, and to meet the public exigencies, by recourse to even an unpopular tax rather than to loans or similar expedients, afforded ground for confidence in the soundness of our position. Symptoms of reviving trade, and of the approaching termination of that long period of manufacturing distress, which had told so seriously upon the revenue, as well as upon the other interests of the country, and to which the great decrease in the Excise in the past year was mainly attributable, were now becoming general; the returns of every department of the revenue for the last quarter of the financial year had been far more satisfactory than those for the first three quarters; the tone of the trade circulars was encouraging; the prices of provisions were low; the mills of Yorkshire and Lancashire were working full time again; and, what was perhaps the most cheering consideration of all, though the Ministry could take no credit for it to themselves, the prospects of the harvest were, for the first time in several years, extremely good.

Budget of 1843-4. May 8.

These, and similar considerations, enabled Mr. Goulburn to take a firm and cheerful tone in introducing the budget of 1843-4. After

Financial Policy. 49

explaining the manner in which the deficiency had arisen, he invited the House of Commons to allow the Government to meet it out of the revenue of the coming year, rather than by any special provision in the way of loan or of fresh taxation.* He proposed, however, to take a Vote of Credit for 2,000,000*l.*, to be repaid hereafter out of the Chinese indemnity, in order to enable him to meet two charges which would come in course of payment in the ensuing year, viz.— 1,250,000*l.* compensation to the holders of opium destroyed by the Chinese, and 800,000*l.* due to the Indian Government for expenses incurred during the China war. At the same time he reckoned on receiving and carrying to the revenue of the year a sum of about 870,000*l.* from the Chinese indemnity. This arrangement exposed him to some criticism. It was said in effect that, instead of raising 800,000*l.* by a Vote of Credit, to pay what was due to the East India Company,*

CHAP. I.
1843.

---

* The course pursued was, to take a credit on the Consolidated Fund for more than it could produce, and to meet the demand at the end of each successive quarter by a large issue of Deficiency-bills; and to such an extent was this done, that on the 5th of January, 1843, the Deficiency-bills amounted to 8,567,729*l.*; and in the course of the ensuing April the amount borrowed was 7,549,440*l.*—(SIR C. WOOD'S *Speech*, August 25, 1848.)

E

CHAP. I.
1843.

he ought to have paid it out of the 870,000*l.* he was about to receive from China; and that the Vote of Credit was, under the circumstances, only a roundabout way of borrowing a sum of money to make up a surplus for the year. The mode in which the Chinese indemnity was employed upon this occasion will come under consideration when I come to treat of Votes of Credit, and of War receipts and expenditure, of which, unfortunately, more than one instance occurs in the period now under review.

Confining myself for the present to the working of the new scheme of taxation, and to the result of Sir Robert Peel's effort to restore the balance between revenue and expenditure, I have now to pass on to the budget of 1844, when the experiment had had a fair time for trial, and when its real results had begun to show themselves pretty clearly.

Budget of 1844-5.

In 1843, Mr. Goulburn had formed an estimate showing a probable surplus of 763,000*l.* He had taken the revenue at 50,150,000*l.* and the expenditure at 49,387,645*l.* But when, on the 29th of April, 1844, he came to state the actual results of the year, it appeared that the revenue had reached 52,835,125*l.*, the expenditure had only been 48,669,000*l.*, and the sur-

Financial Policy.

plus therefore was no less than 4,165,000*l*. Setting aside 2,749,000*l*. to pay off the deficit of the preceding year, he still found himself in possession of a surplus of 1,400,000*l*.; that is to say, the financial plan of 1842 had in the first two years of its operation placed that amount of surplus in the hands of the Government, and had thus enabled the Chancellor of the Exchequer to strengthen the balances in the Exchequer, and had relieved him of the necessity, under which his predecessors had lain, of relying for support upon the coffers of the Bank of England.

This was a satisfactory state of things; and as the greatly improved condition of trade was leading to an increased revenue, while the conversion of the $3\frac{1}{2}$ per Cents into $3\frac{1}{4}$ Stock* was leading to a diminished expenditure, the prospects of 1844-5 were naturally bright. Mr. Goulburn estimated the income for that year at 51,790,000*l*., and the expenditure at 48,643,170*l*., showing an apparent surplus of 3,146,130*l*.; but, inasmuch as a part of this arose from an alteration in the time of paying the dividends on the Three-and-a-half per Cents in consequence of the conversion, he reckoned the real surplus at no more than 2,376,930*l*.

Chap. I.
1844.

---

* See *infra*, p. 53.

The effect of changing the time of paying the interest of the debt was, to throw over one quarter's payment into the next year. This was a real gain to the year 1844-5, not leading to any corresponding loss in the following year, though in the following year the gain, of course, could not be repeated. It was analogous to the case of an anticipation of revenue by the shortening of a credit. The difference which it made to 1844-5 was 1,400,000*l*. But Mr. Goulburn would not consent to reckon this windfall as part of his surplus; and took credit only for the permanent gain of 313,000*l*., obtained, not by the change in the time of paying the interest, but by the change in the rate of interest itself. At the same time he treated as expenditure for the year the sum paid to the dissentients who had claimed to be paid off on the reduction.

Out of the surplus thus estimated, Mr. Goulburn proposed to apply about 400,000*l*. only to the remission of taxation,—selecting for that purpose the duties on certain kinds of glass, on vinegar, on marine insurances, on currants, on foreign coffee, and on wool; some of which he abandoned altogether, while others he reduced in a greater or less degree. It was at this time

Financial Policy. 53

also that he announced the intention of the Government to make an alteration in the sugar duties, with a view to admit foreign sugar, the produce of free labour, at a moderate rate, while slave-labour sugar should continue to be excluded by duties virtually prohibitory. This alteration was made in the course of the session, and the distinction between free and slave labour was maintained in our Statute-book for a short time; but it was abandoned by the successors of Sir Robert Peel, immediately upon their coming into office.

The importance of the year 1844 in a financial sense is derived, not from these alterations of duty, but, in the first place, from the proof afforded by the large surplus revenue that the experiment of 1842 had succeeded; in the second place, from the conversion of the Three-and-a-half per Cents; and in the third place, from the measure for the regulation of the currency known as the Bank Charter Act.

The conversion of the Three-and-a-half per Cents into Three-and-a-quarter, and ultimately into Three per cent., Stock, was a measure of very great consequence. The reduction was effected upon a sum of nearly 250,000,000*l*., an amount much larger than had ever been simi-

Chap. I.
1844.

Conversion of the Three-and-a-half per Cents.

larly operated on before; it produced an immediate saving of 625,000*l.* a-year, and an ultimate saving of 1,250,000*l.* a-year; it involved no addition whatever to the capital of the debt; and it was carried into effect not only without a dissentient voice in Parliament, but with an exceedingly small number of dissentients among the stockholders whose interests were affected by it; the total amount required to meet their claims being but 250,000*l.*, a sum which it was found perfectly convenient to take for the purpose out of the surplus revenue of the year.

Mr. Goulburn brought forward his plan for this conversion on the 8th of March, 1844. It was not the first occasion upon which he had had to perform such a task; for it had fallen to his lot, in 1830, to propose and carry a reduction of interest upon a large part of the very stock with which he was now again to deal; and it was natural that he should feel gratification at being a second time able to propose so material a relief to the country. He was able, too, to claim for the Government of which he was a member a considerable share of credit for the policy which had contributed to bring about the satisfactory state of the money-market which rendered his operation possible. How far the

Financial Policy. 55

revival of trade and of the industry of the country was to be attributed to their measures was, of course, a matter open to question ; but it was evident that their firm determination to avoid a recurrence to any system of loans for the purpose of meeting the deficiencies of the revenue, and to supply those deficiencies by fresh taxation, and their success in strengthening the balances in the Exchequer, and dispensing with the necessity of leaning on the Bank for support, had directly tended to raise the price of the funds. At the accession of the Government to power Consols had stood at 89 ; they now stood at 99. The balances in the Exchequer, which at the commencement of the year had been as low as 1,400,000*l.*, had risen to 4,700,000*l.* There were no Deficiency-bills unpaid, nor had it been necessary to have recourse to the Bank for advances in anticipation of supplies during the whole year. The amount of Exchequer-bills in circulation was between 18,000,000*l.* and 19,000,000*l.* only, an amount then considered low in comparison with previous years ; the interest upon them was but 2*l.* 4*s.* per cent., and they commanded a premium of 3*l.* 13*s.* per cent. in the market. There could be no doubt that the firmness of the Government and of Parliament in submitting to the Income Tax, rather than stave off the evil of a growing deficiency by resorting to a loan, had contributed materially to this satisfactory state of things; and the country was now to reap the just reward of its exertions for the maintenance of the public credit, in the reduction of the rate of interest to the public creditor.

Various plans, said Mr. Goulburn, had at different times been adopted for the reduction of the interest on portions of our debt. Sometimes an addition had been made to the nominal capital of the debt, in order to induce the creditor to accept a reduced amount of annuity; sometimes the interest had been augmented for a limited period, in order that it might be reduced afterwards. In the present instance it was possible to reduce the 3½ per Cents either to a 3 per cent. or to a 2 per cent. Stock, by adding a sufficient amount to the nominal capital of the debt. By the former operation a gain of between 800,000*l.* and 900,000*l.* a-year might immediately be obtained to the taxpayer at the expense of an addition of 10,000,000*l.* or 12,000,000*l.* to the capital of the debt. By the latter the gain would be 1,200,000*l.* a-year, but the addition to the capital of the debt would be no less than 50,000,000*l.* Mr. Goulburn rejected both these plans; and, preferring the ultimate to the immediate gain, proposed a reduction of the interest on this portion of the debt to 3¼ per cent. for ten years, and to 3 per cent. for at least twenty years more; adding nothing to the capital of the debt, and securing a saving of 625,000*l.* a-year till 1854, and of 1,250,000*l.* a-year afterwards until 1874, when the debt will be convertible or redeemable at the option of Parliament should circumstances permit.

It may be as well to mention, in connection with this subject, that Mr. Goulburn took advantage of the flourishing state of the revenue, not only to pay off all the dissentients to this arrangement, thereby reducing the principal of the debt by 250,000*l.*, but also to extinguish an annuity payable to the South Sea Company out of the revenue of Customs under an arrangement made in 1815. The uses, therefore, to which he put the large surplus of revenue in 1843-4 were, for the most part, of a kindred nature. With the exception of the small amount of 400,000*l.* applied to the remission of taxation, the whole was spent in improving the credit and diminishing the permanent burdens of the country, by strengthening the balances in the

CHAP. I.
1844.

Bank Charter Act.

Term of Income Tax expires.

Exchequer, and by redeeming or reducing the interest of the debt.

The other great measure of 1844, the Bank Charter Act, demands separate consideration.

We now come to the year 1845, when the first term of the Income Tax expired. This may, however, be considered a fit place to close the present chapter, which has been devoted to showing what were the circumstances under which that tax was originally imposed; what were the disappointments which its framers at first met with; and what the success with which they were ultimately rewarded. We have now to inquire into the effect which this great success had upon their subsequent policy.

Chapter II.

HEN Parliament met in the beginning of 1845, it was announced in the Speech from the Throne that a renewal of the Income Tax was in contemplation; and within ten days after the opening of the session, Sir Robert Peel rose to explain the policy of the Government. He said that the hopes expressed by Mr. Goulburn the year before had been more than fulfilled; and that, as far as it was then possible to judge, the surplus of revenue for the year ending on the 5th of April, 1845, would not be less than 5,000,000*l.* About 500,000*l.* of this surplus would be due to casual receipts, such as the Chinese indemnity, which could not be reckoned on as permanent items of revenue; and the amount of the Income Tax (5,190,000*l.*) was by itself more than the whole amount of the

CHAP. II.
1845.
Financial statement for 1845-6.

surplus. Looking forward, however, to another year, and estimating the ordinary revenue for 1845-6, according to the data afforded by the experience of the year past, Sir Robert Peel was of opinion that it would amount, without the Income Tax, to 47,900,000*l.*, to which would have to be added 2,600,000*l.* on account of the proportion of Income Tax remaining uncollected from the previous year, and 600,000*l.* on account of the expected receipts from China. The revenue for 1845-6, therefore, even supposing the Income Tax not to be renewed, would amount to 51,100,000*l.*, or considerably more than was necessary for the expenditure. The expenditure of the year in which he was speaking had amounted, or was likely to amount, to 48,243,000*l.*; but he pointed out reasons for proposing an increase of this sum in the following year, and especially for adding 1,000,000*l.* to our Navy Estimates for the purpose of increasing our fleet, which would bring the expenditure up to 49,690,000*l.* in the whole. This would still be considerably within the estimated revenue of 51,100,000*l.* for that single year; but it was not to be forgotten that, if the Income Tax were not renewed, the receipt of 2,600,000*l.* would

Financial Policy.

not recur; and the question therefore arose,— "Will you run the risk of entailing a deficiency in future years by making no provision for the time to come; and, seeing that in 1846 the Revenue will be sufficient to meet increased expenditure, will you postpone the consideration of what will be fitting to do until that year shall have expired?" To this question the reply of the Government was, that such a course would not be a prudent one; and that, looking forward to the future necessities of the public service, they felt it their duty to propose a renewal of the Income Tax for a further term of three years.

CHAP. II.

1845.

Government propose a renewal of Income Tax.

Had Sir Robert Peel closed his statement at this point he would simply have been seeing in 1845 what he foresaw in 1842. When in 1842 he laid on the Income Tax, and reduced the Tariff, he expressed a hope that the ordinary revenue of the country, apart from the Income Tax, would right itself in five years; and though he laid on the Income Tax for three years only, five years was the term which he thought a fair one for his experiment. The three years had expired; and the ordinary revenue had nearly, though not quite, reached the amount at which he had estimated it in 1842 before making his tariff reductions. In 1842 he had estimated it at 48,350,000*l.*; in 1845 he was able to estimate it at 47,900,000*l.*, notwithstanding the important remissions of duties which he had made. The experiment had succeeded so far; but, as the revenue had originally been too small to cover the expenditure, it was necessary that it should do something more than right itself, and that it should rise to a higher point than that at which it had stood in 1842. That it was still rising, and would rise further, was evident. In 1842-3 the ordinary sources of revenue, excluding the Income Tax and the China payments, had produced 45,770,000*l.*; in 1843-4 they had produced 46,670,000*l.*; in 1844-5 they had produced 48,500,000*l.*; and it was estimated that in 1845-6 they would produce 47,900,000*l.* It was reasonably to be expected that in two or three years more they would produce 50,000,000*l.*, a sum sufficient to cover the whole expenditure of the country at the rate then contemplated.

But while it would have been imprudent to have parted with the Income Tax until this level had been attained, it was evident that to keep the Income Tax at its existing rate for two or three years longer would have brought into the

Exchequer so large an amount of surplus revenue, that an irresistible pressure would have been brought to bear upon the Government for a remission of taxation. It is true that 6,000,000*l.* or 8,000,000*l.* of such surplus would not have been much more than enough to counterbalance the deficits of former years, and that such an amount might very fairly have been applied to the reduction of the debt; or, if this were not thought possible, an arrangement might have been made for the gradual extinction of the Income Tax by the reduction of its rate, as was afterwards proposed by Mr. Gladstone in 1853. In short, if Sir Robert Peel's own views had not undergone a change or a development since 1842, a plan might easily have been devised for giving complete effect to his original proposal, and dispensing altogether with the Income Tax at the end of five years from its imposition.

The experience, however, of the last three years had led both the nation and the Ministry to look with a different eye upon our system of indirect taxation. The seeming paradox, that a larger revenue might be obtained from smaller duties, had turned out to be the simple expression of an economical law, which appeared capable of more extensive application than it had yet

Objects of this renewal.

received. Duties had been largely reduced and even in some cases repealed; yet the revenue was as large as before, and was evidently growing. Perhaps this fact did not conclusively prove that the increase of revenue was caused by the remission of the duties; but it undoubtedly afforded a fair presumption that there was some connection between them. At all events, Sir Robert Peel, the shrewdest modern observer of passing events and of the temper of the times, thought the occasion one for a repetition on a larger scale of the experiment of 1842; and, frankly acknowledging that there was no absolute financial necessity for his course, and that the supplies of the year might have been provided without resorting to additional taxation, announced his proposal of continuing the Income Tax for a further period of three years,— "not for the purpose of providing the supplies for the year, but distinctly for the purpose of enabling us to make this great experiment of reducing other taxes."

The surplus which the renewal of the Income Tax was to place at the disposal of the Minister would be, for the year 1845-6, 3,409,000*l*. Of this sum he proposed to surrender no less than 3,338,000*l*. in remissions and reductions of taxation. In thus stating the available surplus, however, Sir Robert Peel excluded from his estimate of income 600,000*l.* which was to be received from China, looking upon it as a merely temporary addition to our revenue. If this sum were taken into the account, his plan would leave a surplus, after all reductions, of 672,000*l.*

Having thus a sum of more than three millions to deal with, it became, as he said, a matter of importance for him to consider well the mode in which it should be applied. We were, in the first place, to consider the claims that might be urged in favour of a reduction of heavy taxes on articles of general consumption. We were also bound to consider what taxes pressed most on the raw materials of manufacture; what taxes were disproportionately expensive to collect; and what taxes there were, the removal of which would give more scope to commercial enterprise, and occasion an increased demand for labour. The changes which he proposed were framed with a view to all these objects. In the first place, 1,300,000*l.* was to be given up by an important reduction in the sugar duties, which were brought down from 25*s.* 3*d.* to 14*s.* per cwt. in the case of colonial muscovado sugar, and from 35*s.* 9*d.* to 23*s.* 4*d.* in the case of foreign free-labour sugar. Various other rates were imposed upon sugar of other qualities. Slave-grown sugar was still excluded by a prohibitory duty. All remaining export duties were removed, including that on coal, which had been the occasion of much controversy for the last two or three years. The loss on these was taken at 118,000*l*. About 430 articles, producing small amounts of revenue, were swept altogether from the tariff; many of these were articles used in manufactures, such as silk, hemp, flax, and furniture woods. The loss on the whole of these articles was about 320,000*l*. A more important sacrifice of revenue was made by the removal of the duty on cotton-wool, amounting to 680,000*l*. Under the head of Excise, Sir Robert Peel abolished the auction duty, and the duty on glass. The former involved a sacrifice of 250,000*l*., and the latter of 640,000*l*. In stating the grounds for the abolition of the auction duty, against which, he admitted, no complaint had been raised, Sir Robert Peel observed that it was a duty which pressed upon the transfer of property in one particular mode, while all other modes of transfer were altogether free from duty; that it had been found necessary to pass no less than thirty-two different Acts in order to exempt particular classes of property from its operation; and that it was so extensively evaded, that, out of 45,000,000*l.* worth of property exposed for sale by auction in the year 1840, no more than 8,000,000*l.* paid the duty. His argument for the repeal of the duty on glass turned chiefly on the great amount of the tax in proportion to the price of the article; the impediments offered by excise restrictions to the extension of a manufacture, for carrying on which we had many natural advantages; and the importance of the uses to which glass might be applied, if those restrictions and the heavy tax of 200 or 300 per cent. on the value of the article were removed. The estimated loss in the first year from all these reductions together was, as has been said, 3,338,000*l.*

Such was the second great operation of Sir Robert Peel upon our system of taxation—an operation, in one sense, much more extensive than that of 1842, since the amount of remission was nearly three times as great, and the principle of absolutely repealing instead of merely reducing duties was now introduced; but when it is remembered that the budget of 1842 was brought forward at a time of national distress, with a deficit of 2,500,000*l.* to be met, and an

Chap. II.
1845.

Budgets of 1842 and 1845 compared.

absolute uncertainty whether the Income Tax would be accepted by the country, what would be its produce if accepted, and what effect its imposition would have upon the other branches of our revenue; while the situation of the country in 1844 was in every one of these respects exactly the opposite of what it had been in 1842; we cannot hesitate to give the palm to the earlier and bolder measure.

In proposing his second scheme, Sir Robert Peel held nearly the same language with regard to the duration of the Income Tax as in proposing his first. He did, indeed, express an opinion that the taxes which he intended to reduce pressed more heavily upon the community than did the Income Tax; and he invited the House of Commons to retain the Income Tax in order to enable him to get rid of those more onerous burdens; but he did not recommend it as a permanent substitute for them; he asked for it only as a temporary resource, to be used while the ordinary revenue was recovering itself. He thought, as in 1842, that the experiment would probably require five years for a full trial; but, as in 1842, he proposed to give it only three years, and hoped that that period might prove sufficient. "I have been asked," he said, a few days after the introduction of the budget, "what assurance I could give that this tax should expire at the end of three years? * * * I feel bound to say that for so extensive an experiment three years is rather a short period. * * * If I could have been perfectly sure of success, I would have proposed it for five years; at the same time I do think there are good grounds for hoping that at the end of three years we may be at liberty to discontinue it. I see the population of the country increasing; the capital of the country rapidly accumulating; and I think, if we facilitate the application of that capital to new branches of industry and manufactures, that the effect will be greatly to increase the demand for labour; and, with the demand for labour, to increase the consumption of articles subject to taxation. * * * I see many causes combining to increase the prosperity of the country. The establishment of railways, rendering travelling more easy, and traffic less expensive, a surplus capital, instead of seeking for investments on foreign security, and an increasing population, are circumstances calculated, I think, to justify the hope, that at the end of no very remote period there will be an increase in the consumption of articles subject to duty, and

with it an increase* of production. * * *
I cannot so far foresee events and occurrences as to be able to guarantee that this tax may not be necessary at the end of that period. Nay, at the expiration of the present time the House may be of opinion, although no Government may ask them for renewal, that there ought to be a continuance of the tax, * * * but I have every reason to think that there will be a fair opportunity for the House to consider, at the end of that period, whether this tax ought to cease."†

In comparing the language of Sir Robert Peel on this point in 1845 with that which he and his colleagues had used in 1842, it is impossible not to feel that there is a difference of tone, indicating a perhaps unconscious change of sentiment. Not that in 1845, any more than in 1842, Sir Robert Peel intended to impose the Income Tax as a permanent tax, or contemplated its becoming such in time of peace; but he had become a little blinder to its faults, a little kinder to its merits, and, above all, a little

---

* There is some flaw in the report here ; Sir Robert means that the increased consumption of duty-paying articles would lead to an increase in the revenue.
† Sir Robert Peel's Speech, Feb. 17, 1845.

Financial Policy.

more alive to the magnitude of the work that might be done by its aid. He was becoming conscious that the principles he had laid down would carry him still further in the work of commercial reform; and he probably foresaw, what, whether he foresaw it or not, was, as we can now see, very certain, that more reductions and remissions of duty would have to be made before his work was complete; and that to render these possible, further recourse must be had to the Income Tax.

In comparing the financial policy of 1845 with that of 1842, we may, as has already been said, give the palm for boldness of conception, so far as the Minister was concerned, to the measures of the earlier year; but if we are to look to the comparative importance of the measures adopted, and to the indications they afford of the temper and views of Parliament, we must acknowledge that the step taken in 1845 was far in advance of that which preceded it. In 1842 the House of Commons, under pressure of a great financial difficulty, adopted the Income Tax as the only means of saving the national credit. In 1845 that difficulty was at an end; the equilibrium had been restored between revenue and expenditure; a surplus was secure

CHAP. II.
1845.

for the coming year; and, as Sir Robert Peel himself pointed out,* an increase of a penny in the postage of letters, or an addition of a small percentage to our import duties, would have been amply sufficient to meet the probable wants of future years. Moreover, in 1842 the Income Tax was untried, and the exact measure of its burden was unknown; but in 1845 every one knew precisely what that burden was, and what was the price they were paying for commercial reforms when they agreed to purchase them with a three years' Income Tax. It was therefore a deliberate and a voluntary step which Parliament took, when, on the invitation of the Minister, it decided to renew the Income Tax, and to renew it without alteration, in order to diminish and to readjust the burden of other taxation.

Lord John Russell's criticism of the budget.

The step was not taken in the dark. On the first day of the discussion † which followed the opening of the budget, Lord John Russell, as leader of the Opposition, delivered an elaborate speech upon the whole ministerial plan. He stated his conviction that the Income Tax, imposed under such circumstances, and accom-

---

* Sir Robert Peel's Speech, March 10, 1845.
† Feb. 17, 1845.

panied by such extensive reductions in our other taxation, must be looked on as virtually permanent. For his own part, he said that he regarded it as a tax which, though it might be necessary in times of great emergency, was subject to some of the greatest objections which could be urged against any tax. He described it as a tax in which " inequality, vexation, and fraud were inherent." After dwelling at some length on these defects, he observed that Sir Robert Peel did not deny their existence, but argued that they were inseparable from the nature of an Income Tax; and, though not himself prepared to endorse that argument, he admitted that Sir Robert Peel's authority on such a point was of great weight. He concluded, therefore, that such a tax ought not to be imposed in time of peace under circumstances that would probably render its further continuance a matter of necessity, " without a declaration on the part of the Government that such is the intention; and without answering this question :—Whether they consider the Income Tax to be one of the best sources of permanent revenue? If they are of that opinion," added his lordship, " let the House fairly deliberate upon that point; and let it ascertain, likewise, either through the intervention of a Select Committee, or by means of a Committee of the whole House, whether some of the great injustice and inequality of the tax may not be diminished." Lord John Russell criticised with some severity the commercial policy of the Government. Admitting that many of Sir Robert Peel's proposals were good, while he thought others doubtful, he urged that their adoption would not restore the revenue which the repeal of duties was about to destroy, and that there was but one true road to financial prosperity,—the abandonment of protective duties, more especially upon the great articles of sugar, timber, and (apparently he meant to add) corn, and the consequent extension of our foreign trade, stimulating the demand for our labour, and augmenting the consumption of those articles which we restricted by our system of "imaginary favour and protection." "Then indeed," he said, " you might look forward, at the end of three or five years, to the abolition of your Income and Property Tax; but if the question be between a perpetual Income Tax and the continuance of monopoly and restriction, I declare for the Income Tax and a diminution and final abolition of all monopoly. Entertaining these opinions, I certainly cannot give any

Financial Policy.

hearty assent to the proposition in the hands of the chairman. At the same time I see that it is impossible for me to refuse my assent to the renewal of the Income Tax for three years; but I give it, not from the wish of making the tax permanent. I regret that the right honourable gentleman has taken a course which may make it necessary to continue this burden from time to time; but my hope is that the pressure of this inquisitorial impost will at length open the eyes of the people to the disadvantages they suffer as consumers from existing restrictions and monopolies, and induce them to seek to set trade free, not only in order to procure greater benefits and enjoyments, but to put an end to a tax which I think in time of peace ought not to be imposed."

Whatever may be thought of the logic of these arguments, the conclusion at which Lord John Russell arrived at least showed that he had advanced considerably from the position he had taken up in 1842, when he pledged himself to oppose the resolutions and the report of the resolutions, and the first reading, the second reading, and the third reading of the bill. Some years later, when himself holding office, he justified both his opposition to the Income Tax in the earlier year, and his assent to it in the later; and there is no doubt that the authors of the budget of 1841 might with perfect consistency have objected to the impost as, in their view, unnecessary in the year 1842, when the most urgent business was to supply a deficiency, which they thought could be supplied, without any new tax at all, by the simple relaxation of some part of our protective system ; and yet might have approved of it in 1845, when it was reimposed for the purpose, not of stopping a deficiency, but of forwarding a work of reform in the whole system of our taxation upon principles more or less in harmony with those which they had themselves professed. At all events their support was given ; and, notwithstanding the expressions used by the leader of the Opposition respecting the unfairness and inequality of the tax, it was given to the tax as it stood ; although several independent members, such as Mr. Roebuck and Mr. Charles Buller, endeavoured to get alterations made in its structure. The arguments which had been put forward in 1842, with regard to the alleged unfairness of taxing all incomes alike, were urged again, and with somewhat more earnestness ; but Sir Robert Peel and Mr. Goulburn met them by saying, first, that the attempt to draw distinctions between different classes of incomes could only end in inextricable confusion ; and, secondly, that, inasmuch as the tax was proposed with the view of relieving the public from other taxes, and as that relief would be experienced by the owners of temporary incomes to at least as great an extent as by the owners of permanent incomes, it was but fair that those who had their full share of the benefit should bear their share of the burden. It is not immaterial to notice this circumstance ; because it has an important bearing on some of the subsequent controversies, which arose with regard to the assessment of the Income Tax. Whatever the abstract merits or demerits of that assessment may be, it is at least certain that the Parliament of 1845 deliberately adopted it; and that at a time when the tax was not proposed as a measure of urgency, as in 1798, or even in 1842 ; but when it was calmly weighed in the balance against cheap sugar, cheap glass, cheap cotton, and the rest, and found to be a price worth paying for these countervailing benefits.

The financial result of the budget of 1845 was extremely satisfactory. Instead of 672,000*l.*, the surplus amounted to 2,380,600*l.* Sir

CHAP. II.
1845.

Financial results of the budget of 1845.

Robert Peel had remitted Customs' and Excise duties to the amount of 3,300,000*l.*, but the revenue from those two sources only fell off by 2,436,000*l.*, so that he obtained from them nearly 900,000*l.* more than he had anticipated; while the revenue from Stamp duties and from the Post Office exceeded his estimate by 650,000*l.*; an increase " indicating perhaps more than any other the great extent of commercial transactions in the course of the year, and the multiplication of all those dealings throughout the country which are the great contributors" to those branches of the revenue. The produce of the Excise was undoubtedly the most striking feature of the year. The reductions effected in that branch of taxation had been absolute remissions of duty;—640,000*l.* had been given up on glass, and about 300,000*l.* on auctions; so that nearly a million of revenue had been absolutely abandoned; yet the Excise produced only 200,000*l.* less than it had produced in the previous year; and this will be considered the more worthy of remark, when we bear in mind that the year in which this happened was the year of the great potato blight, which destroyed an important portion of the people's food, not only in this country but in great part of Europe, and which

Financial Policy. 79

produced so sensible an effect upon our condition and prospects as to lead, first, to the breaking up of Sir Robert Peel's powerful Government; and then, on its reconstruction, to the repeal of the Corn-laws, and the consequent disruption of the Conservative party.

CHAP. II.
1846.

It is not necessary to enter here upon a discussion of the great events which have just been referred to. The repeal of the Corn-laws was not proposed on financial grounds; and though the political importance of the measure was immense, its direct financial importance was not very great. It may therefore be sufficient to remark that the Government, having come to the decision to strike this blow at the protective system, appear to have thought it desirable to carry the application of the principle of Free-trade further than they had contemplated in 1845; and that accordingly, at the opening of the session of 1846, Sir Robert Peel proposed, not only a great alteration and ultimate extinction of the duties on corn, but likewise some further material alterations in the rest of our customs' tariff; and duties, to the amount of more than 1,000,000*l.*, were again remitted in the course of this year.

Repeal of the Corn-laws.

Other measures of 1846.

The principal changes made were as follow.— The duties on tallow and on timber were reduced, in order to enable the manufacturer to obtain these important raw materials on better terms. The protective duties on the coarser kinds of cotton, woollen, and linen manufactures were abandoned, and those on the finer kinds reduced from 20 to 10 per cent.; on silk goods the protection was fixed at 15 per cent.; on most other manufactured articles the rate was fixed as nearly as possible at 10 per cent. Considerable reductions were made in the duties on soap, candles, boots and shoes, and foreign spirits; and a further reduction upon free-labour sugar was announced; but, in consequence of the change of Government in the course of the session, this was not carried into effect. The duties on seeds were greatly reduced; so also were those on butter, cheese, and hops; the duties on all kinds of meats were repealed; and so were those on live animals. Finally, the duties on corn were reduced to a low slidingscale, which was to continue in operation for three years, and to be followed on the 1st of February, 1849, by a nominal duty of one shilling a quarter upon grain of all kinds.

These various measures having been adopted by the House of Commons, and the Corn-bill having passed a second reading in the House of

Lords, Mr. Goulburn, on the 29th of May, brought forward the budget. The necessity for so doing was little more than formal; as the finance of the year had been practically settled by the progress already made. Mr. Goulburn's speech, however, possesses great interest; as it contains a clear and able summary of the results which, in the judgment of the Ministry, had been produced by their financial policy since their taking office nearly five years before. Such a statement, made within a few weeks of their approaching fall, cannot but be read with interest and attention. He called upon the House to observe that between January 1842 and January 1846 the balances in the Exchequer had been increased by 5,000,000*l*., the capital of the debt reduced by 7,000,000*l*., the average amount of Deficiency-bills by 4,000,000*l*., the annual charge for the debt by 1,500,000*l*., with the prospect of a further reduction of 600,000*l*. in a few years' time; and that this result had been brought about, not only without adding to the burdens of the people, but concurrently with a great diminution of them; for that, while new taxes to the amount of 5,624,000*l*. a-year had been imposed, taxes to the amount of 8,206,000*l*. had been remitted. He argued that this satisfactory state of things could not be attributed simply to the good harvests with which the country had for some years been blessed, because there had been equally abundant periods between 1820 and 1823, and again between 1833 and 1836, and yet the financial results in those years had not been comparable to those of the years 1842-1846. The conclusion, he thought, was obvious; the prosperity was in a large measure owing to the system of commercial and financial policy which had been adopted, and which had aided instead of counteracting the effects of the blessings of Providence.

Sir R. Peel quits office.

This was Mr. Goulburn's last budget-speech. The Government, of which he was a member, was defeated within a month afterwards on the Irish Life Protection Bill, and quitted office thereupon. The financial measures of the year were complete, except the annual Sugar Duties' Bill, which had still to be passed, and which it fell to the lot of Lord John Russell's adminis-

Sugar-duty Bill.

tration to settle. The distinction between slave-grown and free-grown foreign sugar was abandoned; and all foreign sugar admitted at the same rates of duty. The result of this measure was, to add about 300,000*l*. to the revenue of the year. Mr. Goulburn had estimated for a

Financial Policy. 83

revenue of 51,650,000*l*. The addition thus derived from foreign sugar would have made up that amount to nearly 52,000,000*l*. The actual produce was no less than 54,473,000*l*., and this in a year of the greatest distress which this country had for a long time experienced, for it was the year which witnessed the beginning of the Irish famine. A more remarkable result can hardly be imagined.

CHAP. II.
―――
1846.

It is difficult to understand how, in a system like our own, great financial prosperity can co-exist with national distress; and it may safely be affirmed that such a conjunction for any length of time is impossible. Yet the speech of Sir Charles Wood, in opening the budget of 1847-8,* presents a contrast of this description, which it is well worth the while of every statesman to examine. On the one hand, we find him stating that a calamity of the heaviest nature had fallen upon the country, and especially upon its weakest member; that thousands of persons in Ireland were actually famishing, and were only to be kept alive by large grants from the Government; that even in England the prices of provisions in consequence of the deficient har-

Financial prosperity of 1846 coincident with national distress.

―――
* Feb. 22, 1847.

vest were extremely high; that the scarcity was not confined to the United Kingdom, but extended to several neighbouring nations, thus at once depriving us of several sources of supply and raising up competitors for the food of more distant markets; and finally, that, concurrently with the high price of provisions, we had to contend against an unusually high price of cotton, the great staple of our industry, in consequence of which the demand for labour was slackening in the manufacturing districts, many mills were wholly or partially stopped, and many workmen thrown out of employment. On the other hand, he informs the House that the condition of the revenue was never more satisfactory; that the estimates of his predecessor had fallen far short of the result; that, for the first time within the memory of any financier in the House, it had been found unnecessary to have recourse to Deficiency-bills, the quarterly balance in the Exchequer having been sufficient to defray the payment of the dividends; that the increase in the revenue had taken place more or less in every one of its branches, but more particularly in the Excise; and that even in Ireland the produce of the Excise had increased, and not to an inconsiderable amount, in the course of the past year. Sir Charles Wood, therefore, thought himself justified in estimating the Income for the coming year at more than 1,000,000*l*. above the estimate which Mr. Goulburn had made the year before;* and this estimate, it may be observed in passing, fell very little short of the truth.

Before attempting to explain this apparently inconsistent state of things, it may be well to look on a little and see what was the end. Sir Charles Wood was speaking in February. In April there was a commercial panic, and many failures took place. In October and November there was another panic and more failures: within a few months no less than 220 mercantile houses of the higher class fell,—besides many of inferior importance,—the liabilities of 85 out of these 220 firms are estimated to have amounted to 12,000,000*l*., and the total loss occasioned by the whole of the failures is said to have been 30,000,000*l*.;† the bullion in the Bank sank

---

* Mr. Goulburn's estimate for 1846-7 was 51,650,000*l*., from which must be deducted 700,000*l*. for Chinese payments, leaving an estimate of ordinary revenue 50,950,000*l*. Sir Charles Wood's estimate for 1847-8, was 52,515,000*l*., of which 450,000*l*. was to come from China, leaving the ordinary revenue 52,065,000*l*.

† Mr. Herries' Speech in House of Commons, Feb. 17, 1848.

CHAP. II.
1847.

to less than 8,000,000*l.*, or about one-half the amount at which it had stood in the previous year; the rate of discount rose to a nominal 8 per cent., but in reality discount was not to be obtained by any but a few fortunate individuals; meetings were held all over the country to consider what could be done; Government was appealed to; the Bank act was suspended; and when the new Parliament met, in the month of December, it was expected that it would be called on to grant an indemnity for this necessary stretch of the prerogative.

Causes of the condition of the country.

Probably there were more causes than one for this course of events; but it can hardly be doubted that one of those causes was simply this: the nation had been spending its capital, and the process had produced the same effects as it usually does—temporary prosperity and subsequent difficulty and depression. Its working is very ably and clearly pointed out in a series of articles by the late Mr. Wilson, first published in the *Economist* of the day, and afterwards collected and reprinted, with the title "Capital, Currency, and Banking." According to Mr. Wilson's view, much both of the real and of the apparent prosperity of the years 1842-7, and a great part of the calamities of the

Financial Policy. 87

last of them, were due to the same cause—the sudden and rapid developement of the railway system, and the large expenditure upon railways. It appears that, between the commencement of the century and the close of the year 1843, the number of railways constructed was 148; and the amount which the Railway Companies were empowered to raise, as capital or by way of loan, was 80,309,417*l*. Of this amount about 60,000,000*l*., or at the rate of 5,000,000*l*. per annum, had been raised in the last twelve years of the period; but in the year 1844 schemes involving an expenditure of nearly 15,000,000*l*. received the sanction of Parliament. In 1845 a further expenditure of nearly 60,000,000*l*., and in 1846 a still further expenditure of 110,000,000*l*., was authorized; making in three years an expenditure of 185,000,000*l*., to be met by a country, which had previously been spending only 5,000,000*l*. a-year on these undertakings. Now, although the circumstances of the Money-market ultimately rendered the execution of some of the proposed schemes impossible—at least within the time originally contemplated—still the mere commencement of so large an outlay upon new works, requiring a great number of labourers to execute them, had

CHAP. II.
1847.

of necessity a considerable effect upon the demand for the necessaries of life, and upon the consumption of taxable articles. A large body of "navvies" was at once created, who were well paid, worked hard, and fed highly. Hence there was a great consumption of corn, meat, beer, spirits, tobacco, coffee, tea, sugar, and other articles, all of which paid duty and contributed to keep up the revenue. The revenue from stamps, also, was much increased by the number of transactions to which the speculative tendencies of the day gave rise. Similar effects always follow from any large expenditure involving the employment of much additional labour. Even the unproductive expenditure of a war has a tendency to produce them; as is shown by the experience of our own great war, and as may now be observed in the case of the civil war in America. But the prosperity occasioned by the construction of our railways differed widely from the apparent and temporary prosperity which often accompanies a war. They were works calculated, not only to set a large amount of money in circulation, but to produce an ample profit upon the outlay which they involved, and enormously to increase the national wealth by liberating a great quantity

Financial Policy. 89

of fixed capital, and by making the returns of trading profits more rapid than before. The time requisite for sending goods from one part of the country to another was so greatly shortened, that in many cases that could be done in a day which it had hitherto taken a week to do. In such cases the quantities of goods which must necessarily be always upon the road between the two places, in order to keep up a regular supply, were at once diminished to one-seventh of the previous amount. This was tantamount to a real addition to the stock of goods in the country; and the merchant was a gainer to the full extent of the profit which he had previously lost upon six-sevenths of his goods *in transitu*. Again, very large savings were effected by the reduction of the cost of transport. One instance is referred to of an inland city, where the cost of coal was reduced ten shillings a ton by the opening of a railway—a benefit which is said to have been equivalent to a gift of the whole house-rent of the city to the inhabitants. Many other advantages from the opening of railways might easily be pointed out; but it is unnecessary to take up time in proving what every one will admit. There can be no doubt that the large outlay upon these works in the years 1845 and

CHAP. II.
1847.

1846—or, indeed, it may be said in the years from 1840 to 1846—had both directly and indirectly a very important effect upon the condition of the country. The effect was partly immediate and partly postponed. In so far as it was immediate, that is to say, as regarded the great demand for labour and consequently for articles of consumption, and as regarded the disengaging a quantity of capital by diminishing the quantities of goods *in transitu*, it was temporary and has passed away; but the postponed effects, the quickening and cheapening of communication, and the consequent stimulus to trade, were permanent, and we feel them now, and shall always feel them.

Still, great as these benefits have been, the fact remains, that in the years 1845 and 1846 the country undertook to spend upon the construction of railways a larger amount of capital than it could conveniently spare. Too much was undertaken at once, and the consequence was the crash of 1847. Various circumstances combined to increase the difficulties under which we laboured in that year. The harvest of 1846 had failed, and the harvest of 1847 also failed. The great distress in Ireland, consequent upon the destruction of the potato crop, caused a heavy

Financial Policy.

demand to be made upon the national Exchequer, as well as upon private charity. At the same time the manufacturers were suffering under a serious failure in the supply of cotton, the price of which had risen nearly 50 per cent.; and, while extensive purchases of food, and a heavy outlay on cotton, were thus rendered necessary, the industry of the people was largely directed to making railways instead of to the production of exportable commodities, so that a drain of gold naturally began.

The effect which the outlay on railways produced upon the stock of gold in the country appears to have been as follows. In the first place, the demand for capital to construct them led to the calling in of money advanced upon foreign loans, much of which was paid into the banks in the shape of railway deposits, and contributed to swell the reserve in the Bank of England. Then again, the opening of some of the earliest and most important lines, those between London and the chief manufacturing towns, disengaged considerable quantities of goods *in transitu*, and thus enabled the country to go on for a time with smaller imports than would otherwise have been necessary. At the same time, the cost of production being cheapened by the new facilities thus given to our producers, we were enabled to manufacture cheaply, and to export largely; and, the excellent harvests of 1843 and 1844 having rendered any very great importation of corn unnecessary, more bullion came into the country to pay for our manufactures than left it to purchase our supplies. The bullion in the bank, therefore, which had fallen as low as 2,500,000*l*. in 1839, and did not exceed 4,500,000*l*. at the close of 1841, rose to no less than 16,000,000*l*. in 1844, and maintained the same high level for two or three years. Of course this large amount of money enabled the bank to discount bills freely, and to sustain the activity of our trade. By degrees, however, the railway deposits began to be drawn out in order to pay the labourers; the labourers expended their wages upon commodities brought from abroad; and the failure of the harvefts of 1846 and 1847 rendered it necessary that these commodities should be largely paid for in gold. The deposits withdrawn from the bank did not come back to it, but went out of the country to pay for corn, and other articles of consumption. Meanwhile the railway shareholders were bound to pay up fresh calls; but their means of doing so were no longer what they had been. The money out on foreign loans had to a great extent been called in. Credit was no longer as easy as before, for the means of the bank were reduced. It was necessary to starve the other business of the country in order to find the capital required for these new undertakings; and so, one cause acting and reacting upon another, came pressure, and panic, and heavy loss.

The extent of the mischief was not foreseen at the time of the opening of the budget of 1847-8. Parliament had, however, been called together at an unusually early period (January 19th), in order to take prompt measures for the relief of Ireland. The Corn-laws and Navigation-laws had been suspended. Lord John Russell had given an account of the outlay already made by the Government, in pursuance of the authority given by the Acts of the last session relating to Ireland; and had explained, and made some progress towards carrying, other measures which would entail upon the country a still larger expense. Sir Charles Wood, therefore, had, in bringing forward his budget, to make provision for this expenditure. He stated the amount already spent at about 2,000,000*l*.; and he estimated that 8,000,000*l*. more would be expended before the conclusion of the next harvest. The 2,000,000*l*. had been provided out of the balances in the Exchequer. The 8,000,000*l*. he proposed to borrow. He remarked that in doing so he did not add that whole sum to the amount of the permanent debt, because one-half of the advances for public works was repayable in ten years by the Irish landlords. The interest on the loan would, he expected, be about 280,000*l*., as he calculated on borrowing at or under 3½ per cent. He found himself, too, under the necessity of raising the interest on Exchequer-bills from 1½*d*. to 2*d*. per day, and thus making a further addition of 142,000*l*. to the amount of interest payable by the Treasury. The net result of his calculations was a revenue of 52,515,000*l*. (including a payment of 450,000*l*. from China), an expenditure of 52,183,000*l*. (including a vote of 185,000*l*. for the excess on the Navy estimates of the year before), and a surplus of 332,000*l*.

Loan of 8,000,000*l*.

The loan of 8,000,000*l*. was shortly afterwards obtained at the rate of 3*l*. 7*s*. 6*d*. per cent. It was negotiated in Consols at the price of 89*l*. 10*s*. for every 100*l*. stock. The stipulations made were, that 12 per cent. should be paid up at once, and the remainder spread over seven months, the last payment (16 per cent.) to be made in October. No discount was allowed for prompt payment, as the Government did not require the whole sum at once; but subscribers were allowed to pay their instalments in advance, and to receive stock for them immediately; and all persons paying their instalments before the 10th of July were to be entitled to the half-yearly dividend in October. Mr. Hume and Mr. Williams objected to this mode of borrowing, because more was added to the capital of the debt than was raised for the public service; but Sir Charles Wood replied that the course taken was the same as that which had usually been followed, and that it appeared to the Government to be the most advantageous they could adopt.

This addition of 8,000,000*l.* to our national debt in a single year, and that, too, a year of profound peace, and (but for a single calamity) of general prosperity, is a striking illustration of the immense importance of a good harvest. Only nine months had elapsed since Mr. Goulburn had made his last budget-speech, had reviewed the situation of the country in the terms which have been already alluded to, and had pointed with satisfaction to the diminution of

7,000,000*l.* which had been effected in the capital of the debt in the course of four years; and now in a single year the work of those four years was undone. In that speech Mr. Goulburn had referred to the succession of good harvests with which the country had been blessed, and to the influence of which many persons, as he said, seemed disposed to attribute the prosperous condition of our trade and our finances; and he had argued that the prosperity of 1846 was greater than could be accounted for in such a manner. Yet now, though the system of commercial and financial policy, to which he believed our situation to be chiefly due, was in full operation, the beneficial results of that policy were at once outweighed by the mysterious dispensation of Providence, and the failure of a single crop. Such a lesson at such a time was well calculated to humble us, by showing us how entirely the weal and woe of the country are in the hands of a Higher Power than our own; and that, as the " race is not always to the swift, nor the battle to the strong," so neither does success always attend the counsels of the wise. It is but fair towards Mr. Goulburn to add that he only claimed for his policy the merit of having " aided instead of counteracting the blessings of Provi-

Financial Policy. 97

dence;" and that it cannot be doubted that the effects of that policy did to some extent mitigate, though they were powerless to avert, the calamities of 1847-8.

CHAP. II.
1847.

The Parliament of 1841 was now coming to its end. Elected to maintain the system of commercial restrictions for the protection of native and colonial industry, it had in six years almost destroyed it. It had overthrown the Ministry which it had in the first instance brought into power, and had replaced that which it had begun by setting aside. It had called forth the Income Tax to accomplish a particular task, and, having thus displayed the power of this mighty fiscal engine, it was about to bequeath to its successor the fruits of its experience and the benefit of its example. It had, as it were, passed direct and indirect taxation through a crucible, had tested their merits, their capabilities, and their weaknesses. It was dissolved in the autumn of 1857. The Income Tax, renewed for three years in 1845, was legally to expire in April 1848, and the new Parliament would therefore be technically at liberty to renew it or not as it should think fit. Its freedom of choice, however, as will presently be seen, was far more nominal than real.

Dissolution of Parliament.

H

Chapter III.

Chap. III.
1847.
Meeting of new Parliament.

Relaxation of Bank Charter Act.

HE new Parliament was called together in the autumn of 1847. It was, as has already been said, a time of great commercial pressure and panic. So severe had been the strain upon the Money-market that the Government had taken upon themselves the responsibility of authorizing the Governor and Deputy-Governor of the Bank to transgress the limits laid down by the Bank Charter Act of 1844, and to issue notes in excess of the stock of bullion and the 14,000,000*l.* of securities which that Act admits as the basis of the paper currency. The authority had not been acted on; the knowledge that money might thus be obtained having proved sufficient to allay the panic. The distress had, however, been very great; and one of the first acts of the new House of Commons was

Financial Policy.

to appoint a Select Committee to inquire into its nature and causes.

Another kind of uneasiness had, at the same time, taken hold of the public mind. There was a great dread of a French invasion; and much alarm was expressed at the state of our coast defences. It is unnecessary to touch on the causes of this fear, to which allusion has only been made on account of its effect upon the estimates. It is sufficient to observe that the Government themselves appear either to have shared in the alarm, or, at all events, to have thought that it was desirable to take advantage of it in order to carry further the measures, which their predecessors had begun to take, for strengthening our naval and military position. Nor was this alarm the only cause for an increase in our military expenditure; for we were unfortunately engaged in a Kafir war, which had broken out at the Cape in the course of the year 1845, and had continued throughout 1846 and 1847. The accounts of the expenditure connected with this war had but recently been received; but a considerable vote to meet them was now becoming necessary.

Another topic of interest connected with the finance of the year was the distressed condition

Chap. III.
1847.

Fear of invasion.

West Indian distress.

CHAP. III.
———
1848.
Lord G.
Bentinck's
Committee.

of the sugar and coffee planters in our colonies. Lord George Bentinck, impressed with the belief that the distress was, to a great extent, caused or aggravated by recent legislation, applied for, and at the beginning of 1848 obtained, a Select Committee, upon the conduct of which he bestowed immense labour, and is thought to have thereby shortened his life.

Budget, Feb. 18, 1848.

These various subjects having been introduced to the notice of the House at its meeting in December, 1847, or on its reassembling after the Christmas recess, and great anxiety prevailing with regard to the financial condition of the country and the plans of the Government, Lord John Russell, as First Lord of the Treasury, himself brought forward the budget on the 18th of February. Premising that the period of the last eighteen months had been one of almost unparalleled vicissitudes; that, in twelve months, the price of wheat had gone from 49*s*. up to 102*s*., and down again to 49*s*. 6*d*., the rate of discount from 3 per cent. up to 8 per cent., and down again to 4 per cent., and the stock of bullion from 15,000,000*l*. down to 7,800,000*l*., and up again to 13,800,000*l*., he pointed out that such changes, and the commercial and manufacturing embarrassment and stagnation, of which

Financial Policy.

they were at once the cause and the consequence, could not have failed to produce a serious effect upon the revenue. He then proceeded to comment upon the balance-sheet of Income and Expenditure for the year ending the 5th of January, 1848, and to state his expectations as to the probable result of the complete financial year ending April 5th. The ordinary income would, he thought, fall short of the amount at which it had been estimated the year before by about 700,000*l*. Besides this, the sum of 450,000*l*., which was due from China, and had been reckoned on last year, had been stopped at the Cape and paid into the commissariat chest there, in order to meet the expenses of the war in that colony. The whole revenue, therefore, would fall short of the estimate by 1,150,000*l*. The expenditure, too, would exceed by about 132,000*l*. the amount calculated upon when the budget of 1847 was introduced; so that, instead of there being, as was anticipated, a surplus of 332,000*l*., there would be a deficiency of about 950,000*l*. on the 5th of April. So much for the finance of 1847-8, of which, however, the actual results were not quite so bad as Lord John Russell at this time anticipated; the ordinary revenue having fallen only 438,000*l*. below the estimate.

The loss was mainly upon the Excise; under which head no less a diminution than 1,400,000*l.* took place in the receipts from malt and spirits alone; though the improvement in other branches of the Excise revenue was sufficient to bring up the whole produce to within 425,000*l.* of the estimate.

As regarded the prospects of 1848-9, the case was still worse. Lord John Russell could only reckon on a revenue, exclusive of Income Tax, to the amount of 46,050,000*l.*; and, supposing that tax to be renewed at the existing rate of 7*d.* in the pound, it would only raise the total income to 51,250,000*l.* But the expenditure upon the scale of 1847-8 would amount to 52,315,000*l.*; and there was required, in addition, a vote of 245,500*l.*, to defray the Navy Excess for 1846-7, and a vote of credit of 1,100,000*l.* on account of the Kafir War. Nor was this all; for the Government thought it right, looking to the state of our defences, and to the naval expenditure of other countries, to make some considerable additions to our estimates, the effect of which would be to render necessary an expenditure in the whole of 54,596,541*l.*, leaving a deficit of 3,346,541*l.* to be in some way provided for.

It is impossible not to pause here and look back. Six years had passed since Sir Robert Peel had been reckoning on an income (without Income Tax) of 48,350,000*l.*, an expenditure of 50,819,000*l.*, and a deficit of 2,469,000*l.* It was to meet this deficit, and at the same time to develope the resources of the country, that he had then imposed the Income Tax for the limited period of three years. At the end of that period he had been again able to reckon on an income (without Income Tax) of 48,500,000*l.*, and upon an expenditure of 49,690,000*l.* The ordinary income would thus have fallen short of the expenditure, in 1845, by 1,200,000*l.*, instead of by 2,469,000*l.*, as in 1842. He had then renewed the Income Tax for another three years, and now, in 1848, the income (without that tax) could only be taken at 46,050,000*l.*, while the expenditure had reached the amount of 54,596,000*l.*, showing a deficiency in the ordinary income, as compared with the expenditure, of more than 8,500,000*l.* Our ordinary revenue had been reduced since 1842 by upwards of 2,000,000*l.*; our expenditure had been increased by upwards of 3,750,000*l.*, and a deficiency of 2,500,000*l.* had been converted into one of 8,500,000*l.* The Income Tax, therefore,

CHAP. III.
1848.

instead of being a temporary staff, which might be thrown aside when it had served its turn, had become a permanent and necessary support, upon which it was evident that we should have still to lean, and to lean more strongly than ever. Whether the consciousness that such a support was available had tended to encourage our financiers to indulge in a more extensive abandonment of other sources of taxation, and a greater liberality of expenditure, than was upon the whole desirable, is a question which every one must consider and answer for himself, and which lies at the root of most of the financial questions of the present day.

Arrangements for 1848-9. Increase of Income Tax.

To return to Lord John Russell's statement. Having to provide for a deficiency of 3,346,000*l*., and being reluctant to disturb the trade of the country by the uncertain experiment of an addition to indirect taxation, especially for the purpose of meeting difficulties of a temporary character, he proposed, as the best mode of raising the necessary amount of revenue, a renewal of the Income Tax for five years, and an increase of its rate for the first two of them from 7*d.* to 1*s.* in the pound. By this step he expected to raise 3,500,000*l.* more in the coming year, of which he proposed to give up 40,000*l.* by

Financial Policy. 105

the abandonment of the duty on copper ore, and to leave a surplus on the year of 113,000*l*.

CHAP. III.
1848.

This scheme was received by the House of Commons and by the public with great disapprobation. The renewal and increase of the Income Tax, for the purpose (partly) of adding to the expenditure for military and naval purposes, was peculiarly disagreeable to Mr. Hume and his friends; and, in the week following the opening of the budget, that gentleman, not satisfied with the announcement that the Government proposed to submit the whole of our expenditure to the scrutiny of two Select Committees, moved a resolution to the following effect:*—" That it is expedient that the expenditure of the country should be reduced, not only to render the increase of taxation in this session unnecessary, but that the expenditure should be further reduced, as speedily as possible, to admit of a ·reduction of the present large amount of taxation." This resolution was lost by a majority of 98 ; but, though the House of Commons and the country appeared generally willing to support the Government in strengthening the national defences, the feeling against

Unpopularity of the Budget.

---

* Feb. 25, 1848.

the proposed increase of the Income Tax was too strong to be disregarded; and on the 28th of February the Chancellor of the Exchequer (Sir C. Wood), after elaborately re-stating, and in some particulars correcting, the budget brought forward by Lord J. Russell on the 18th, announced that the Government, in deference to the feelings of the House and the country, would not press those resolutions which implied an addition to the Income Tax, but would simply ask for its renewal at the old rate for a period of three years. He proposed no substitute for the source of revenue which he thus abandoned; but stated that the balances in the Exchequer would be sufficient to meet the charge for the Kafir War and the Navy Excess of the preceding year, amounting together to 1,345,000*l*.; and that, after placing these items to the account of 1847-8, there would be a deficiency for 1848-9 of from 1,500,000*l*. to 2,000,000*l*. This deficiency, too, he hoped to meet out of the Exchequer balance, observing that one of the advantages of maintaining high balances in ordinary times was, that " by this means we might be enabled to bridge over a time of temporary pressure." He avowed his regret at finding himself forced to take this course, as he thought that, "under the present circumstances of the country, there was great safety in a full Exchequer," and he was very sorry at the thought of having to fall back upon those balances which on a former occasion proved so useful, as the means of affording immediate relief to Ireland. "Still," he added, "I do not think it would be wise to attempt to force upon an unwilling House an addition to an unpopular tax."

CHAP. III.
1848.

The attempt to raise the rate of the Income Tax having thus failed, two other questions respecting the impost remained. The first was, whether it should be renewed for a term of years; the second, whether it should be renewed in its existing shape. Upon the first point the opposition was led by Mr. Hume, who desired to limit the duration of the tax to one year; upon the second by Mr. Horsman, who desired to introduce a distinction between incomes arising from professional and precarious sources and those derived from realized property. Mr. Horsman was defeated on the 3rd of March by a majority of 175;* and Mr. Hume on the 13th by a majority of 225;† and the proposal

Controversies respecting the Income Tax.

---

* 316 to 140. † 363 to 138.

of the Government was eventually adopted. A somewhat smaller majority was recorded against Sir B. Hall on the 17th of the same month, when he proposed to extend the tax to Ireland. The last mentioned proposal was resisted by the Government on the ground of the distressed condition of that country, and was negatived by a majority of 80.*

These results are not a little remarkable. That the popular feeling against the Income Tax was very strong, both in the House of Commons and out of it, is shown by the concession which the Government were forced, against their own judgment, to make in respect of the proposed addition to its rate. They were defeated upon this point, just in the same manner as Lord Palmerston's Government were afterwards defeated upon the question of the " War Ninepence" in 1857, by something like general consent. Yet, at the same time, the House by overwhelming majorities declined to attempt to alter the character of the tax, either by introducing distinctions between different kinds of income, or by converting it into an annual instead of a periodical impost. A triennial Income

---

* 318 to 238.

Financial Policy.

Tax of 7*d*. in the pound, upon every kind of income alike, seemed to have taken its place among the recognized institutions of the country, and to be equally impregnable by ministers and by amateurs. The voice of the new Parliament had confirmed in the most decided manner the financial policy of its predecessor, and had not only renewed the most important of its measures, but had renewed it in precisely the form in which it had at first been adopted.

The debates on the Income Tax were succeeded by debates upon the Sugar Duties, and upon the measures to be taken for the relief of West Indian distress. The proposals of the Government included a guaranteed loan of 500,000*l*. for the promotion of immigration, and a prolongation of the term of protection to colonial sugar. In the course of the discussion of these proposals the Chancellor of the Exchequer took occasion (on the 30th of June) to make a fresh financial statement, showing what reductions had been effected in the estimates, and what addition might be expected to the amount of revenue on which he had calculated in February. He explained also his intention to apply what are called the "appropriations in aid,"—that is to say, the sums arising from the sale of old stores and other transactions,—to the service of the year instead of holding them over till the next year. He expressed a hope, that the deficiency, instead of reaching 2,000,000*l.*, as he had at one time thought it might, would not exceed 500,000*l.*; but he promised a fuller statement before the close of the session. This promise he redeemed on the 25th of August, when he reviewed at length the finance of the year, and produced what was called his fourth budget. There have certainly been few years in which so many statements of the kind have been made by a Chancellor of the Exchequer; but it is to be remembered that Sir Charles Wood's position was a peculiar one. The House and the country had rejected his proposal for equalizing the revenue and the expenditure by an addition to the Income Tax, and had thus virtually struck off 3,500,000*l.* from the revenue he was about to provide for the service of the year. At the same time there appeared to be no disposition to make good the loss by recourse to other taxation; and the idea of reducing the expenditure of the country by so large an amount at so short a notice, was, of course, entirely vain. The Minister, therefore, had nothing open to him but to shift as well as he could through the session, deferring his final arrangements till the latest moment; and, being naturally subject to curious inquiries from time to time as to the prospects of the revenue, he could hardly avoid the necessity of making statements varying somewhat from one another according to the variation of circumstances from time to time throughout the year. Had the first proposals of the Government been adopted, he need have said nothing more about his budget until the next session, when he would probably have had to announce a surplus on the year approaching 2,000,000*l*., after defraying the charge of the Kafir War and of the Naval Excess. It was the action of Parliament and of the country which drove him to a different course, and due allowance should be made for this fact in any criticisms which we may be disposed to make upon the undeniable inconvenience of his repeated financial statements.

The last of these statements was made, as has been said, on the 25th of August. Taking for his basis Lord John Russell's estimate of expenditure, amounting to 54,596,452*l*., the Chancellor of the Exchequer proceeded to show what reductions had been effected in this estimate in consequence of the reports of the two

CHAP. III.
1848.

Sir C. Wood's Statement, August 25.

Select Committees which had been appointed in the beginning of the year. The Navy estimates had, he said, been reduced by 208,000*l.*; the Army estimates by 150,200*l.*; the Ordnance estimates by 123,000*l.*; and the Miscellaneous estimates by 235,500*l.* The plan of embodying the militia having been abandoned, a reduction of 150,000*l.* was also made under that head; and the whole of the reductions together amounted to the sum of 866,700*l.* But some additions had been necessary, and these had reduced the amount of the actual saving to 828,700*l.* On the other hand, the income was likely to be higher than had been expected by Lord John Russell: the arrangements for paying the "appropriations in aid" at once into the Exchequer would add 500,000*l.* to the year's revenue; an unusual amount of malting had been carried on, and the Excise revenue was a considerable gainer in consequence, so much so that, notwithstanding a decrease in the receipts from stamps, a sum of 340,000*l.* beyond the estimate of February might now be expected; and lastly, a sum of 80,000*l.*, the last instalment of the Chinese indemnity, had been received in the course of the year. The income, therefore, which had been estimated at 51,210,000*l.* might now be taken at 52,130,000*l.*, and would fall short of the ordinary expenditure by only 292,335*l.* To this moderate deficiency, however, was to be added the amount of the extraordinary expenditure, consisting of the vote for the Kafir War, (1,100,000*l.*), the Naval Excess, 245,411*l.*, a sum of 262,545*l.* for Irish distress, and 130,965*l.* for the destitute emigrants to Canada, making 1,738,921*l.* in all, and raising the deficiency for the year to 2,031,256*l.* This statement shows a very great improvement in the position of the country within six months, and to some extent justifies the reluctance of the House of Commons to submit to an increase of taxation. In February, after the abandonment of the additional Income Tax, Sir C. Wood estimated the deficiency upon the ordinary expenditure at from 1,500,000*l.* to 2,000,000*l.*; in August he estimated it at only 292,000*l.* The main causes of this difference were, first, the reductions made in the estimates in consequence of the labours of the two Select Committees; and, secondly, the application of the "appropriations in aid" to the service of the year. The first of these was a real saving; the second was a mere change in the system of accounts, accidentally beneficial to the finance of the year in which the change was made, exactly as the anticipation of an excise credit is beneficial to a single year, or as the alteration in the time of paying the interest on the new 3 per cent. stock was beneficial to the finance of 1844-5. Had Sir. C. Wood been able to take the tone of Mr. Goulburn, he would hardly have reckoned this half million as a part of the revenue of the year; but his was a case of necessity, in which the strict financial law could not well be held to apply. In one important respect we find him, in August, taking a more prudent course than he had been disposed to pursue in February. In February he had intended to make good the expense of the Kafir War, the Naval excess, and the large anticipated deficiency of two millions, out of the balances in the Exchequer. In August, however, he informed the House that, looking to the amount of the advances from the Exchequer for drainage and other purposes which had been sanctioned by Parliament, he thought such a reduction in the balances could not safely be made; and, rejecting Mr. Goulburn's expedient of 1843, of meeting the demands of the public service by a liberal issue of Deficiency Bills, as too dangerous in the existing circumstances of the country, he proposed, as the best course open to him, to take power to raise the necessary amount by the issue of Exchequer Bills or the sale of Stock. This proposal was, after some discussion, agreed to. Mr. Hume objected to a loan in time of peace, and upon no peculiar emergency; and contended that the deficiency ought to have been met by a reduction of expenditure; but admitted very frankly that all his motions in that sense had been rejected by large majorities. Besides the divisions upon the general resolutions already mentioned, there had been majorities against several of his proposals on particular points; for instance, a majority of 347 to 38 against reducing the number of men to be voted for the navy, 293 to 39 against a similar proposal with respect to the army, and 216 to 80 against withdrawing the expensive blockading squadron from the West Coast of Africa. Lord John Russell justified the policy of the Government, observing that the practice of taking advantage of every surplus in the revenue to reduce taxation exposed the country to the risk of occasional deficiencies whenever a check to the national prosperity occurred; and that, if the House of Commons would not consent to supply such deficiencies by temporary taxation, the Government had no alternative but to resort to a loan.

CHAP. III.
1849.
Currency question.

Window-tax.

Exchequer receipts.

Colonial question.

Financial Reform movement.

Among the other subjects of interest connected with finance, which came under discussion this year, may be mentioned the state of the Currency-laws, which Mr. Herries brought forward on the 17th of February and on the 22nd of August; Lord Duncan's unsuccessful attempt to carry a motion condemning the Window-tax, (Feb. 24;) Dr. Bowring's resolution in favour of paying the whole of the gross revenue into the Exchequer, carried by a majority of one against the Government, (May 30;) and Sir William Molesworth's elaborate examination of our colonial system, which, though going far beyond questions of a merely economical character, included a full discussion of those questions; and which, considering how greatly finance depends upon policy, may fairly be called a financial speech.

The year 1849 was, in some sense, a year of great expectations. The duties on corn, which Sir Robert Peel had imposed at a moderate rate for three years from the period of his great measure, expired, or, to speak more correctly, were reduced to an almost nominal amount, on the 1st of February. The most important of the protective duties upon our tariff had now been swept away or prospectively condemned. The

Financial Policy.

old Navigation-laws were evidently inconsistent with the spirit of our legislation, and, though there had not been time to pass the bill for their repeal, which had been introduced in 1848, the debates and divisions which had taken place upon the ministerial proposals showed plainly that Parliament had made up its mind to the step. The great battle of Free Trade, in short, had been wellnigh fought out; and it was becoming a question what should be the next movements of the leaders who had won it. It seemed as though the organization which had repealed the Corn-laws were capable of doing a great deal more; and it was hardly visionary to expect that those who had given the impulse which had carried the great commercial measures of the last seven years against such powerful opposition, might successfully take in hand a reform of our financial and of our administrative system. It appeared, too, that there was some cause for their bestirring themselves in this direction. Whatever else Free Trade had done, it had not led to a diminution of the national expenditure. Our wealth, indeed, was increasing; but our burdens were beginning to increase with equal or even greater rapidity; and, what was peculiarly trying to the feelings of those who had seen in univer-

CHAP. III.
1849.

sal Free Trade only another name for universal peace, the increase was observable not only in our civil expenditure, but still more strikingly in our military and naval armaments. The Army, Navy, and Ordnance estimates had reached, in 1848, the sum of 17,645,000*l*.,* while in 1842 they had only amounted to 15,440,000*l*.,† and in 1835, to no more than 11,657,000*l*. It could not be denied that this advance was deserving of attention; and, considering how much might have been done if the burden of taxation could have been lightened, and commercial and other reforms thereby rendered easier, it must be admitted that the question, whether our expenditure was not pitched upon too high a scale, was well worthy the study of those who had taken so large a share in influencing our recent legislation.

Accordingly, between the sessions of 1848 and 1849, some of the leaders of the Anti-Cornlaw League undertook to act in concert for the purpose of obtaining a great reduction of expenditure; and, on the reassembling of Parliament, Mr. Cobden gave notice of a motion,

---

* Or, including the charge for the Kafir War, 18,745,000*l*.
† Or, including the charge for the Chinese Expedition, 16,115,000*l*.

Financial Policy.

which he brought forward on the 26th of February, for pledging the House of Commons to undertake a reduction of the expenditure of the country by about 10,000,000*l.*, and to bring it down to the standard of 1835. This motion was rejected by a majority of 197;* nor can it be supposed that even its mover expected any other fate for so extremely rough and ready a proposal; but it gave him and his friends an opportunity of drawing attention, in a forcible manner, to the growth of the estimates; and it called forth from the Government an explanation of the steps they had already taken in the direction of economy in consequence of the recommendations of the Select Committees which had sat in the preceding session. The estimates of 1848 had, in the course of the last session, been reduced by 828,000*l.* below the amount at which they had stood when first introduced; and in 1849 a further reduction of 1,447,000*l.* had been made; so that in the two years the proposed outlay on the Army, Navy, and Ordnance had been cut down by no less than 2,275,000*l.*

With such demands upon the part of such influential politicians, and with such promises, or

---

* 275 to 78.

indeed performances, on the part of the Government, it was not unreasonable to think that a tide of retrenchment was setting in, and to foretell that a few years would witness great progress in the direction in which matters appeared now to be tending. Certainly it could not then have been anticipated that in another twelve years the Military and Naval estimates would have increased from 17,645,000*l.* to 27,285,000*l.*,* and the Civil expenditure† from 6,533,000*l.* to 9,660,000*l.* The addition to our expenditure between 1835 and 1848 had no doubt been very considerable, but it has been entirely eclipsed by that which has been made between 1849 and 1861; and should the same rate of advance be maintained for another period of equal duration,

---

* This comparison between the estimates of 1848 and those of 1861 is favourable to the latter, because the charge for the Packet Service was included in the Navy estimates for 1848, while it is excluded from those of 1861. It is to be observed, on the other hand, that in 1848 a vote was only taken for the anticipated net expenditure on the services, allowance being made for a set-off in respect of the proceeds of the sale of old stores, and other " appropriations in aid," whereas the votes are now taken for the gross expenditure, and the " appropriations in aid " are carried to the account of revenue.

† Including the charges on the Consolidated Fund.

Financial Policy.

the budget of 1873 will be a budget of very respectable dimensions.

In his speech upon Mr. Cobden's motion, Sir Charles Wood held out very cheerful expectations with regard to the financial results of the still current year. As these expectations, however, were to some extent disappointed, it will be better to turn at once to the budget itself, which was not brought forward until the 22nd of June.

Referring first to the balance of income and expenditure for 1848-9, Sir C. Wood stated that in framing his estimates in the last session he had excluded from his calculation the duties to be received upon corn ; and that, exclusively of these, he had calculated on a revenue of 52,130,000*l*., and had realized one of 52,067,000*l*., or about 62,000*l*. less than he had anticipated. The chief falling off was under the head of Stamps, which had produced only 6,565,000*l*. against 7,319,000*l*. in the previous year, and 7,369,000*l*. in the year before that,— a decline marking the collapse of the fictitious prosperity which had inflated the revenue of 1846 and 1847. The duties on corn, however, had produced 950,000*l*., making the total revenue 53,017,732*l*. On the other hand, the expenditure, which had been estimated at 52,422,335*l.* had reached 53,287,110*l.*, showing an excess over income of 269,378*l.* This increase in the expenditure above the amount of the estimate was due in part to an unexpected charge of nearly 390,000*l.* for the relief of Irish distress, and in part to the excess of Naval expenditure for 1847-8, amounting to 323,787*l.*,— a Naval excess being about this time a chronic malady, to which all budgets appear to have been subject.

For the coming year, 1849-50, Sir Charles reckoned on an income of 52,262,000*l.*, and on an expenditure properly belonging to the service of the year of 51,515,000*l.*, to which, however, it was necessary to add no less a sum than 642,632*l.* to defray the excess of expenditure upon Army, Navy, and Ordnance votes in previous years. This addition would bring the expenditure up to 52,157,696*l.*, and would leave a surplus revenue of but 104,304*l.* The amount would, of course, have been much more considerable had it not been for the excesses which have been mentioned, and with respect to a portion of which Sir Charles offered the following explanation. They were, he said, in some measure caused by the reductions in our Navy.

Financial Policy. 123

The great payments of seamen's wages take place when ships are paid off; and although, when the force of seamen is kept up to a certain standard, the average sums voted for pay will usually cover the expense, yet, if in any year a considerable reduction of numbers takes place, a larger number of men than usual have to be paid off, and an excess of expenditure is occasioned without any fault on the part of the Admiralty. Notwithstanding the smallness of the surplus on which he was thus able to calculate in the current year, Sir Charles felt confident that the revenue was in a highly satisfactory condition, and that, notwithstanding the fall which was taking place in the duties both on corn and sugar, it would in two years be largely in excess of the current expenditure. This statement on the part of the Chancellor of the Exchequer, in 1849, seems to afford a fresh justification to the House of Commons and the country for having refused, in 1848, to submit to an increase in the Income Tax. Had the 1*s.* tax been voted, the estimated surplus for 1849-50 would have been 3,660,000*l.* The existence of so large a surplus would have given rise to a cry for the remission of taxation; and it is not improbable that such remission might have been made in a form and

CHAP. III.
1850.

Budget of 1850,
March 15.

to an extent which would have fastened the 1s. Income Tax upon the country for several years to come.

The budget of 1850 was brought forward at a much earlier period in the session than that of 1849. It was opened on the 15th of March. The financial year not having quite expired, Sir Charles Wood was not in a condition to give the precise figures with regard to it; but he was able to tell the House that the revenue had considerably exceeded, and the expenditure had considerably fallen short of, his estimates for the preceding year, and that the surplus of income over expenditure, instead of being 104,000*l*. would be about 1,895,000*l*.*

For the year 1850-1 he reckoned on an income of 52,285,000*l*. and an expenditure of about 50,785,000*l*., leaving a surplus of 1,500,000*l*. at

---

* This sum is arrived at by excluding from the calculation the sum put to the account of the "Excesses" of previous years paid in 1848-9. The income actually received in 1849-50 exceeded the estimate by 654,919*l*. The expenditure fell short of the estimate by 1,779,279*l*. These two sums make 2,434,198*l*.; to which must be added the amount of anticipated surplus, 104,000*l*., making the surplus about 2,538,198*l*.; but the "Excesses" amounted to 642,632*l*., and thefe ought fairly to be deducted from the surplus, as they were paid out of the revenue of the preceding year. Sir C. Wood anticipated a surplus of " two millions and a quarter."

Financial Policy.

his disposal. The knowledge that there would be a surplus had, he said, brought forward a number of advocates for the remission, reduction, or readjustment of taxation. After recapitulating the chief proposals which had been made, Sir Charles proceeded to remark upon the additions which had been made to the National Debt within the last twenty years, and to show that, after deducting the money applied to its redemption out of the surplus, the net increase in the capital of the debt had not been less than 27,000,000*l.* This fact alone seemed to constitute a reason for applying a portion of any surplus which might at any time be realized to the reduction of debt; but there was a special reason for taking that course on the present occasion. In 1848 it had become necessary to raise a larger amount of revenue than the ordinary sources of taxation would supply; the Government had proposed to meet this necessity by a temporary increase of direct taxation; but their proposal had been rejected, and they had been compelled to meet the demands of the year by a loan. A surplus was now available, and Sir Charles Wood most reasonably expressed a hope that the House would not insist that the whole of that surplus should be at once applied to the reduction of taxation without regard to the operations of the year 1848. "What," he said, "should we think of the conduct of a private man, who, whenever he found his income fall short of his expenditure, borrowed, but who never thought of paying off his debt when by some fortunate turn of affairs his income happened to exceed his expenditure? I must say that, if we hope to maintain the character, as a nation, which we consider indispensable to an individual, we ought, at least in a time of profound peace, to keep down our debt, and not go on, year after year, expending our surplus."

While laying down this principle, however, Sir Charles said that he did not consider himself precluded from applying a portion of the present surplus to the remission of taxation ; and, therefore, although he could not attempt to deal with such large amounts as were involved in the proposals to reduce the Tea-duties, or to abolish the Window-tax, he proposed to give up about 300,000*l.* upon Stamps, and about 455,000*l.* by the abolition of the Excise on bricks. These remissions would leave him with a surplus of about 750,000*l.*, of which he stated that he proposed to devote 250,000*l.* to redeeming a charge of 10,600*l.* a-year, known by the name

Financial Policy. 127

of the "Equivalent Fund," which had been imposed upon the revenues of this country at the time of the Union with Scotland. The remaining 500,000*l.* he proposed to retain in the Exchequer. He further proposed to employ a portion of the balances in the Exchequer by advancing 3,000,000*l.* out of them for the drainage and other improvements of landed estates in England, Scotland, and Ireland. Although this course might prevent the immediate application of the surplus revenue to a reduction of debt, yet it was to be looked upon only as a postponement of that operation;—" for," said he, " we are preparing the means which may enable some future Chancellor of the Exchequer to make considerable reductions. I hold that the making of these advances by the public is not a system which ought to be permanently continued; and I think that we should put an end to it as soon as possible, and consequently the repayments may soon permanently, and year by year, exceed the advances. I trust, therefore, that whoever succeeds me as Chancellor of the Exchequer will be able to apply considerable sums from these repayments to the extinguishment of debt."

These last remarks of Sir Charles Wood are not

unimportant at the present time. His anticipations, that in due course the repayments would considerably exceed the advances, are now being verified; and should the excesses be steadily applied, as he thought they would be, to the reduction of the debt, a saving of some consequence might be effected. Between 1841 and 1857 the excess of advances over repayments was 11,951,565*l.*; between 1857 and 1861 the excess of repayments was 2,273,079*l*. This amount has been received into the Exchequer; but, instead of being applied to the redemption of debt, it has been used to meet excesses of expenditure. It is curious enough to observe that the amount by which the expenditure of the year 1860-1 exceeded the income was as nearly as possible the exact amount* of the excesses of repayments in the four preceding years; that excess was defrayed partly out of the balances in the Exchequer, and partly by the interception of the repayments on their way to the Exchequer. Circumstances may

---

* Mr. Gladstone stated the amount of deficiency properly belonging to the year 1860-1 at 2,271,000*l*.

The total amount of deficiency which had to be provided for was 2,558,000*l*., of which 1,450,000*l*. was taken from the balances in the Exchequer, and 627,000*l*. was supplied by the interception of repayments.

render such a course justifiable; but it ought not to be forgotten that when we apply an excess of repayments to the service of the year in which it occurs, we are not dealing with the income of the year, and perhaps not with income at all. Advances have in some cases been made out of money borrowed by the State for the purpose of making them; and if, when those advances come to be repaid, the amount is applied to the expenditure of the year, the effect is precisely the same as if the State had raised it by a direct loan. Nor can we distinguish in principle between such cases as these and that of 1850, when Sir Charles Wood, having a considerable sum in hand, which he intended ultimately to apply to the redemption of debt, lent it out meanwhile for important national objects, with a distinct prospect of its being applied at last in the way which he recommended as the most consistent with a due regard for the national credit. Nothing could have been further from his intention, when he urged the House of Commons, in 1850, to deny itself the gratification of repealing taxes, in order that it might devote a portion of the year's income to the reduction of debt, than to provide some future House of Commons with the means of appropriating that portion to the remission of

CHAP. III.
1850.

Opposition to the propofed Stamp-duties.

taxes, say in 1870. It is however clear that, whatever were his intentions, the course he took was one which exposes his successors to this temptation; and it is therefore important that the point should not be lost sight of.

The abolition of the Excise-duty on bricks was carried without difficulty; but the proposals of the Chancellor of the Exchequer with regard to the Stamp-duties led to much discussion, and to a defeat of the Ministry upon an important point. The class of duties with which he announced his intention of dealing was that affecting transactions connected with landed property. The agriculturists were at this time suffering great distress; the prices of corn, meat, and other articles of food were very low; and the pressure actually caused by this circumstance was considerably enhanced by the general feeling of alarm with which both landlords and tenants regarded the prospects of British agriculture under the system of Free Trade. The suffering was so serious as to have called for remark in the Queen's speech at the opening of the session; and, although the Government remained firm in their adherence to the principles of Commercial Policy which had recently been adopted, and resolutely set their faces against the idea of any return to the system of Protective duties, they acknowledged the importance of taking any steps which could reasonably be expected to give relief and encouragement to the owners and occupiers of land. Mr. Disraeli had proposed, early in the session, to give this relief by transferring some of the local burdens to the Consolidated Fund; but this proposal had been resisted by the Government, and negatived by a majority of 21.* Sir Charles Wood in bringing forward his budget announced that the remissions of taxation which he had to propose had been selected with a view to the interests of the agriculturists. Besides advancing them 3,000,000*l.* for drainage and other improvements, he remitted the duty on bricks, thereby reducing the cost of cottages and farm-buildings; and he gave up a certain amount of revenue from the Stamp-duties on the conveyance and transfer of land, and on bonds and mortgages, so as to facilitate the sale of land, and the process of borrowing upon landed security. He also reduced the Stamp-duty on leases. The principle, however, upon which he proceeded was not that of simply reducing the ex-

---

* 273 to 252.

isting rates of duty, but that of revising and recasting them altogether. He found the duties upon small transactions disproportionately heavy when compared with those on larger ones; and he proposed to replace them by a new scale, in which the duties should bear a fixed ratio to the sums on which they were levied. The duty on mortgages or bonds for amounts under 50*l.* had been 1*l.*, or two per cent. *ad valorem;* he proposed to reduce this to 5*s.*, or one-half per cent.; and, making this his starting-point, to adhere to the same percentage throughout the scale. But though one-half per cent. was much below the old rate of Stamp-duty on small transactions, it was much above that on large ones; and the landowners and other mortgagers soon perceived that, though the new scheme would undoubtedly benefit small proprietors, it would, with equal certainty, increase the burdens of the large ones; and that the boon to the former would be given not solely at the expense of the Treasury, but at that of mortgagers or borrowers of sums above a certain amount. Many complaints were made by Railway and other companies, in consequence of the prejudicial effect which this increase of the Stamp-duty would have upon their debentures; and Sir Charles Wood ulti-

Financial Policy.

mately agreed to reduce his percentage rate to one-fourth instead of one-half, and to begin with a stamp of 2*s.* 6*d.* upon sums under 50*l.* as a starting-point. But this concession did not satisfy his opponents; and an amendment, moved by Sir Henry Willoughby, to make the starting-point 1*s.* instead of 2*s.* 6*d.* was carried in the Committee on the Bill by a majority of 29.* After this defeat the Government appear to have hesitated for some time; but, after about a month's delay, Sir Charles Wood stated that they were prepared to proceed with the bill, substituting 1*s.* 3*d.* for 1*s.* as the rate of duty on bonds under 50*l.*, and adhering to the same rate, or 2*s.* 6*d.* per cent. throughout the scale.

The session of 1850 was remarkably prolific of motions for the repeal or reduction of taxes; and, besides the defeat upon the Stamp-duties, the Government encountered more than one adverse division upon questions of taxation. Lord Duncan, indeed, was beaten, though only by a majority of 3,† in his annual attack upon the Window-duty; and Mr. Milner Gibson, Mr. Ewart, Mr. Macgregor, Mr. Cayley, and Col. Sibthorp, failed in their respective attempts

---

* 164 to 135. † 80 to 77.

CHAP. III.
1850.

to condemn the Paper-duty, the Duty on Advertisements, the Stamps on Marine Insurances, &c., the Malt-tax, and the Tenant-farmers' Income Tax: but Lord Robert Grosvenor succeeded in introducing his bill for the repeal of the duty on Attorneys' and Proctors' certificates; and, notwithstanding the opposition of the Government at every stage, carried it, by majorities varying from 2 to 19, to a third reading, when it was ultimately thrown out by a majority of 29:[*] and Lord Naas also succeeded in introducing a bill, which, however, he was unable on account of the lateness of the session to carry through, for altering the system of charging the duty on bonded spirits in Ireland. This bill he introduced again in the following session, and defeated the Government upon it more than once, though he was not ultimately successful in passing it. The principle of his measure was, however, conceded by Mr. Gladstone in 1853.

1851.
Question of the renewal of the Income Tax.

The struggles of 1850, however, were as nothing compared with those which awaited Sir Charles Wood in 1851. In the former year he had only to keep his surplus, or as much of it as he could; in the latter he had to get as well as to

---

[*] 113 to 84.

keep it. The Income Tax was now, for the third time, expiring; and again, as in 1845 and 1848, the questions,—whether it should be renewed,—in what shape it should be renewed,—for what period it should be renewed,—and for what considerations it should be renewed,—were pressing for decision. These questions were sufficiently grave in themselves; but what now rendered them the more embarrassing was, that the Government was far weaker than it had been in 1848, and immeasurably weaker than Sir Robert Peel's Government had been in 1842 and 1845. The authority of Sir Robert Peel, and the urgency of the circumstances, had led the country to take the first and most difficult step of consenting to the imposition of the Income Tax in 1842. The same authority, fortified by three years of successful finance, had renewed the tax in 1845, for the sake of benefits which the community at large believed to be well worth the price they were called on to pay for them. Lord John Russell, in 1848, did not perhaps command the same confidence in his financial skill as did Sir Robert Peel; and he was certainly at the head of a less compact and powerful party than that which had carried his predecessor through the first three years of his administration; but he had in his favour the disturbed condition of Europe, which rendered every one here averse from a change of Government; the disorganized condition of the Opposition in the House of Commons; the moral support of Sir Robert Peel; and the powerful argument of necessity, arising from the distress of the country and the impossibility of making good the revenue in any other manner. Even with these advantages, however, he had then encountered a serious, and to some extent a successful, opposition to his proposals with regard to the renewal of the Income Tax; and now, in 1851, when he had again to propose the same measure, all these advantages were lost to him. A change of Government was no longer a cause for national alarm; the Conservative Opposition had for some time been gaining strength, while the Government had been losing it; their Radical supporters had been showing a disposition to desert them, and the personal friends of Sir Robert Peel were alienated from them by the difference of their views on the Papal aggression, and the Ecclesiastical Titles Bill; the distress in the agricultural districts still continued, and sharpened the animosity of their opponents without calling forth any countervailing energy on the part of their friends; Sir Robert Peel, CHAP. III. who had often assisted them both by his advice 1851. and his countenance, was no more ; and finally, while they had no great inducements to hold out, and no overwhelming necessity to plead, in favour of a renewal of the Income Tax, the course which they had pursued in 1848 and the succeeding years had not tended to inspire the House of Commons with anything like implicit confidence in their financial sagacity, or in the firmness of their resolution. It was not forgotten that in 1848 they had proclaimed the necessity for an increase in the rate of the Income Tax, and that, nevertheless, when the House had shown itself unwilling to sanction that increase, they had shrunk from putting the question to the touch, had withdrawn their proposal, and had, after all, contrived to go on perfectly well without the increase they had demanded, and not only to bring the income and expenditure of the three years which had since elapsed to an equilibrium, but even to reduce other taxation to a not inconsiderable amount.

Sir Charles Wood brought forward his budget The Budget, on the 17th of February; but, early as that day Feb. 17. was, an important debate and division had already taken place upon a question closely connected with the incidence of taxation. Her Majesty had, in her opening speech, lamented the difficulties still felt by the owners and occupiers of land; expressing at the same time her confident hope that the prosperous condition of other classes of her subjects would have a favourable effect in diminishing those difficulties, and promoting the interests of agriculture. Upon these passages in the Royal Speech Mr. Disraeli had founded a motion, calling upon the Ministry to introduce forthwith such measures as might be most effectual for the relief of the distress of the agriculturists; and this motion, after two nights' debate, was lost in a full House by a majority of only fourteen.*

This indication of the temper of so large a portion of the House of Commons did not help to make the Chancellor of the Exchequer's task easier; and he appears to have felt some nervousness in beginning his statement; although he was able to do so with the satisfactory announcement that, as far as could then be foreseen, the surplus on the current year would probably amount to more than 2,500,000*l.* The prospects for the year to come were, however,

---

* 281 to 267.

Financial Policy.

not quite so favourable; he could reckon only on an Income of 52,140,000*l*., including the produce of the Income Tax, if that tax should be renewed; and, as the expenditure would probably amount to 50,247,171*l*., the surplus on the year 1851-2 would be no more than 1,892,829*l*. This being so, it was evident that the revenue would not bear the loss of the Income Tax, and of those Irish Stamp-duties which had been imposed along with it,—a loss, that is to say, of 5,500,000*l*. a-year,—unless the House were prepared to impose new taxes to the amount of about three millions and a-half. It was, however, his opinion that neither would the country agree to such a step, nor was it desirable to propose it. So far was he from thinking it possible to re-impose taxes on articles of consumption, or on the materials of industry, for the purpose of taking off the Income Tax, that he considered there were still many taxes which ought to be reduced or repealed before there could be any question of touching the Tax on Income. He proceeded to analyse the taxation of the country, showing that in the year 1850 there had been raised from duties on—

	£
Articles in the nature of Food (including Tobacco)	31,820,798
Manufactured Articles	2,452,658
Raw Materials	764,000
Duties affecting Trades and Professions	4,464,906
Conveyances	648,487
Newspapers and Advertisements	511,418
Assessed Taxes (except Window-tax)	1,491,308
Total of general Taxes not falling directly on Property	42,153,575
Add Local Tolls, Dues, and Fees	3,300,000
Total	£45,453,575

Land-tax, Window-tax, Probate, Legacy, and Insurance-duties, &c., and Schedules A and C of Income Tax	12,451,776
Local Rates	13,000,000
Total	£25,451,776

The total amount of taxation imposed upon property, therefore, was about twenty-five and a-half millions, and the amount of other taxation about forty-five and a-half millions.* Some exceptions might perhaps be taken to the principle of this division, and particularly to the mode in which the Schedules of the Income

---

* The revenue from the Post Office is excluded from this calculation; the gross revenue being considered as payment for work done, and the net revenue of 830,000*l.* being nearly absorbed by the charge for the Packet Service.

Financial Policy. 141

Tax are apportioned, as though a great part of the produce of Schedule D were not, in fact, the produce of a tax on property invested in trade. If, however, we accept the division as a basis of comparison, it may not be uninteresting to compare, as nearly as possible, the incidence of taxation in 1840 and 1860 with the calculations of Sir C. Wood in 1850. The comparison is made in a note,* in order that the account of the budget of 1851 may not be interrupted.

The Chancellor of the Exchequer having drawn from this analysis the conclusion that relief from taxation ought to be given rather to consumers than to the owners of property, and having stated the intention of the Government to propose a renewal of the Income Tax, proceeded to explain his views as to the application of the surplus of 1,892,000*l*., which would thus be placed at his disposal. He proposed to abolish the Window-duties, producing 1,856,000*l*.; but to substitute for them a House-tax, calculated to produce 1,155,000*l*., making the loss to the revenue on this head 701,000*l*. The Coffee-duties he proposed to reduce from 6*d*. per lb. on foreign, and 4*d*. on colonial, to 3*d*.

---

* See Appendix B.

per lb. on all coffee; thus relieving the consumer to the extent of 176,000*l.* The duties on foreign timber he would reduce by one-half, and the duties on agricultural seeds in a much larger proportion. Adding to these reductions the fall which was to take place this year in the amount of the Sugar-duties, he showed a relief to the tax-payer of 1,522,000*l.*; but, allowing for an increase of consumption, he thought the loss to the revenue would only be 1,130,000*l.* On the other hand, he proposed to relieve local rate-payers, by taking upon the Consolidated Fund a portion of the charge for pauper lunatics, thereby adding 150,000*l.* to the expenditure; and, deducting these two sums of 1,130,000*l.* and 150,000*l.* from the anticipated surplus of 1,892,000*l.*, he found himself with a margin of 612,000*l.*; or rather, for the present year, of 962,000*l.*, because there were arrears of Window-duty to be collected, which would amount to 350,000*l.* This surplus he hoped to be allowed to retain, with a view to operate upon the National Debt. He concluded by asking for a renewal of the Income Tax for a further term of three years.

The budget, as has been said, was brought forward on the 17th of February. The dis-

Financial Policy. 143

cussion of its merits was fixed for the 21st; but, before the 21st arrived, the Government had been defeated upon Mr, Locke King's County Franchise Bill, and were considering whether they should not send in their resignations—a step which they actually took in the course of the following day. A ministerial crisis of some duration followed; but at length, Lord Stanley* having found it impossible to form a Government strong enough to command a majority in the House of Commons, and an attempt to reconstruct a Liberal Cabinet on a broader basis having also failed, Lord John Russell and his colleagues were requested by Her Majesty to resume their offices; and the business of the session proceeded.

<small>CHAP. III.
1851.</small>

<small>Resignation of the Ministry.</small>

<small>Their return to office.</small>

The crisis was ostensibly of a political rather than of a financial character; but it is evident that considerations of financial policy entered largely into it. Lord Stanley expressed his own conviction that the defeat of the Ministry upon Mr. Locke King's motion was not the sole ground of their resignation; and that the unfavourable reception which the budget had met with at the hands of the public was, at least, one of

<small>Financial circumſtances of the crisis.</small>

---

* Now Earl of Derby.

the causes by which their retirement had been brought about. However this may have been, it is certain that it was chiefly owing to the difference of opinion upon financial policy between himself and the friends of Sir Robert Peel that Lord Stanley failed to secure their co-operation in forming a Conservative Administration; and the explanation which he gave of his own opinions with respect to the principles which should regulate our dealings with the taxation of the country, is sufficiently interesting and important in its bearings upon our financial policy to demand reproduction here, even at some length. He said,—" I begin by saying that financially I hold it to be an object not only of vital importance, but one to which the faith of successive Ministries has been pledged, that the Income Tax should not be permitted to degenerate into a permanent tax. In 1842 Sir Robert Peel introduced that tax. He introduced it for a limited period, with the express declaration that it was to enable him to deal with other portions of the financial system of the country in a mode which he hoped would conduce to the benefit of commerce generally, and would raise the revenue to an equality with the expenditure; and he pledged himself that at the expiration of that period the Income Tax should cease. Without that pledge there is not a man living who believes that the House of Commons, in 1842, would have consented to the imposition for an hour of a tax which has always been held to be the resource in time of war, which has always been deprecated in time of peace, and which, take it as you will, levy it as you please, must be full of anomalies and inconvenience, pressing variously upon different classes of the community with a complicated injustice that no modification can altogether remove. Sir Robert Peel anticipated, when he proposed the tax, that it would be continued for five years; but, in the first instance, he asked Parliament to sanction it for three years, expressing his assurance that Parliament would not refuse to continue it for the remainder of the time during which he believed it would be necessary, should circumstances prove that the system was working well. The first renewal, therefore, in 1845 was only the fulfilment of the original scheme of Sir Robert Peel, and the extension of the remainder of the term which he had anticipated, and announced as in his opinion necessary, when he introduced the measure. The year 1848, when the renewal of the Income Tax was proposed, was a period of the deepest distress, following immediately upon the disastrous year 1847; and to maintain the credit of the country it was absolutely necessary to continue it. But we have now arrived at a very different state of things. We have, in the first instance, a surplus of 2,500,000*l.* to deal with; we have, it is said, a state of general prosperity in the country. I do not wish to deny the existence of that prosperity; though I fear I see indications in some quarters that it is not as permanent, or as fully established, as some of your lordships may imagine. But, when the country is in a state of general prosperity, when we have a surplus revenue of 2,500,000*l.*, and at the expiration of nine years from the time when the Income Tax was imposed, I hold that a further renewal of that tax, without any security taken either for its modification or abolition, would be virtually declaring that the Income Tax shall be saddled upon the country for ever. When I remember, too, that the Chancellor of the Exchequer declared in his budget that there were various other classes of the community as well entitled to relief as the class which paid the window-duties; and that he stated that when he had disposed of the paper-duties, the tea-duties, and the tobacco-duties, and had equalized the system of taxation generally, he would be prepared to deal with the Income Tax; I think it is not assuming too much to suppose that, if Parliament had again allowed the renewal of the Income Tax, without any steps being taken for its limitation, they would virtually have imposed that tax upon the country permanently." Referring then to a proposal which had been made to him to resist the renewal of the Income Tax at all, Lord Stanley said,—" I could not support a measure which would leave a deficiency of at least 2,500,000*l.* in the revenue. I was, however, of opinion that a course should be taken, declaratory of the determination of Parliament to deal with the Income Tax as rapidly as the state of the national finances would allow; and that its reduction should not be rendered a matter of impossibility by frittering away every surplus as it arose. I believe that, without interfering with the credit of the country, dealing with the existing surplus, without attempting to alter or reduce other taxes, in the course of this year a reduction of from one-third to one-half in the amount of the Income Tax might safely and beneficially be effected. I was desirous that Parliament should, by some resolution, pledge itself to the gradual reduction of the Income Tax with a view to its final abolition; and I should have been prepared, if the duty had devolved upon me, to recommend to Parliament to grant only such a renewal of that tax as would reduce its amount by one-third or one-half; and I should have been prepared to pledge myself that any surplus revenue that might arise should in the first instance be applied towards the further reduction and final extinction of that tax."*

In these remarks Lord Stanley clearly pointed out the character of the new phase upon which the Income Tax was about to enter. It may, perhaps, be thought that he insisted a little too strongly upon the argument that the pledges of former Ministers had made the extinction of that tax a matter affecting the good faith of Parliament. Many of those who supported its renewal in 1845, and still more of those who did so in 1848, looked upon it as something more than the merely temporary impost which it had appeared in 1841; and in 1848, at all events, the language of Sir Charles Wood was sufficiently

---

* Lord Stanley's speech in the House of Lords, Feb. 28, 1851.

Financial Policy.

frank to exonerate him from any imputation of breach of faith in proposing a further continuance of the tax in 1851. Still, there can be no doubt that the budget of 1851-2, and the arguments by which that budget was supported, showed a greater disposition than any Chancellor of the Exchequer had yet manifested, to substitute direct taxes on property for a considerable portion of the indirect taxes on consumption. True, Sir Charles Wood did not exactly propose such a substitution; he proposed only to retain the Income Tax while the process of revising indirect taxation was incomplete; but it was plainly seen that this process, as he described it, was likely to be a very protracted one; and there were never likely to be wanting pleas for further reforms, which would indefinitely prolong the existence of the instrument by the aid of which they were to be accomplished.

Three main objections were urged against Sir Charles Wood's proposals. The Conservatives, as has been said, objected to the retention of an Income Tax for the purpose of further reducing indirect taxation; Mr. Hume and his friends, on the contrary, highly approved of the principle of using an Income Tax for this purpose, but contended that the existing frame of the tax was

Cha p.II.
1851.

Different views respecting the Income Tax.

inequitable, and that it ought not to be renewed as it stood, but ought to be altered, so as to make it bear more heavily upon fixed incomes derived from realized property, and more lightly upon industrial and temporary incomes. Lastly, the same gentlemen objected to the Chancellor of the Exchequer's retaining so large a surplus; and contended that the balance of revenue not required for expenditure would be much more profitably applied to the reduction of taxes pressing upon the industry of the people than to the redemption of debt, or, as they expressed it, to the purchase of Consols at 96. It is possible that a skilful tactician might, under certain circumstances, have so combined these objections as to have destroyed both the Budget and the Ministry; but it is evident, on close examination, that the objections themselves were so curiously complicated as to place the objectors pretty nearly in the situation of the embarrassed stabbing-party in the *Critic*. The Radicals could not join the Conservatives in demanding the extinction of the Income Tax; for they did not want to see it extinguished, but extended. The Conservatives could not join the Radicals in demanding its amendment; for to amend it implied a purpose of perpetuating it. But the Conservatives could point to the objections urged against the framework of the tax as an argument against continuing to use it as a substitute for other imposts; and the Radicals were embarrassed in pressing these objections by the fear of making out a case so strong as to destroy the tax altogether. Again, when the Radicals demanded that a larger proportion of the surplus should be given up to the remission of taxation, the Conservatives could not fail to perceive that such a step would still further delay the attainment of that equilibrium in the finances which would render the repeal of the Income Tax possible; and so, for one reason or another, when the Government found themselves pressed hard by one set of antagonists, it was not difficult for them to obtain assistance from the other set, and combined action against them was rendered impossible.

It is, however, probable that the Conservatives would have found themselves the masters of the situation, had not the financial question been complicated with the question of agricultural protection. The triumph of the Free-trade party was still recent; and it was doubtful whether they were even yet secure against a reverse. The sufferings of the agricultural popu-

Position of the Conservatives.

lation had been, and still were, severe; and the great party which had resisted the repeal of the Corn-laws were not prepared to admit that they had been mistaken, or to accept their defeat as final. The knowledge that a partial return to Protection was likely to follow the accession of this party to power incited the Free-traders of all shades of political opinions to resist them; and not only deterred the Radicals from attempts which they might otherwise have made to overthrow the Government, but alienated the friends of Sir Robert Peel from the great Conservative party at the critical moment when the reins of power were within Lord Stanley's grasp. They felt, as Sir James Graham expressed it, the necessity of "closing their ranks" to resist an attempt at reaction against the commercial policy of the last nine years; and in doing so they gave a decided and powerful impulse to a system of financial policy with respect to the prudence of which they might, perhaps, under other circumstances have seen reason to hesitate.

Budget again brought forward, Apr. 4. The Ministerial crisis having passed over, and the Government of Lord John Russell having resumed office, Sir Charles Wood, on the 4th of April, again brought forward his budget, in nearly the same form as before. He made,

Financial Policy.

however, an alteration of some importance in the framework of his proposed House-tax. His original plan had been to distinguish between old and new houses; or rather between houses already built and already subject to the Window-tax, and houses to be built thereafter. Upon the former class he meant to charge a House-tax equal to two-thirds of the amount actually paid as Window-tax. Upon the latter class he proposed to charge 1*s*. in the pound upon the value of simple dwelling-houses, and 9*d*. in the pound upon that of houses partly used as shops. The tax was only to apply to houses of the value of 20*l*. a-year and upwards. In his new plan he made no distinction between old and new houses; but laid an uniform tax of 9*d*. in the pound upon dwelling-houses, and of 6*d*. in the pound upon houses partly used as shops; still limiting the tax to houses of the annual value of 20*l*. and upwards. The first plan would have produced a revenue of 1,155,000*l*., and have afforded a relief, as compared with the Window-tax, of 701,000*l*.; the second plan would produce a revenue of 720,000*l*., and afford a relief of about 1,136,000*l*.

By this plan, not only was a considerable amount of relief to be given in the whole, but that relief was especially to be given to the lower

Chap. III.
1851.
Alteration in the House-tax.

classes of the community. Out of about 500,000 houses charged with the Window-tax, 100,000 were to be altogether exempted from the new House-tax; and, as the whole number of houses in the country was about 3,500,000, and only 400,000 of these were to be subject to taxation, Sir Charles Wood observed that it might be described as a property-tax upon houses of the class most able to bear taxation. In the course of his argument in support of it he quoted with approbation a sentence of Mr. John Stuart Mill's, to the following effect :—

" A House-tax, if justly proportioned to the value of the house, is one of the fairest and most unobjectionable of all taxes. No part of a person's expenditure is a better criterion of his means; or bears, on the whole, more nearly the same proportion to them. A House-tax is a nearer approach to a fair Income Tax than a direct assessment on income can easily be."

It might, perhaps, have been inferred, as a logical consequence of this doctrine, that the Chancellor of the Exchequer, who was at the same moment imposing a House-tax and renewing a direct Income Tax, ought so to have arranged the incidence of the two imposts respectively as to obtain as much as possible from the

Financial Policy. 155

fairer of the two, and to depend as little as might be upon that which is the less fair. An attempt to impose a House-tax, and especially a heavy House-tax, must always, as a matter of course, be hazardous for a finance minister; but it is impossible not to see that at this particular conjuncture a bolder step might have been taken, and with a better prospect of success, than at almost any other time that can be pointed to; for both the Window-tax and the Income Tax were extremely unpopular; and a scheme of taxation, framed with a view to extinguish the former, and to reduce and ultimately to abolish the latter, would have met with a great amount of support; even though the imposition of a larger House-tax than was actually proposed had been a necessary ingredient in it.

This alteration in the form of the proposed House-tax was the most important change made in the second edition of the budget. Sir Charles Wood adhered to his proposal for the reduction of the timber-duties, and of the coffee-duties. He withdrew, however, the proposal respecting the duties on agricultural seeds, and that respecting the transfer of the expense of the lunatic paupers from the County Rates to the Consolidated Fund. He now estimated the surplus for the year at 924,000*l*., of which 568,000*l*. was to arise from the uncollected balance of the Window-duty. This surplus he thought it necessary to retain, in order to meet contingencies; a view in which, he said, he was fortified by the circumstance that, even since the first introduction of the budget, the breaking out of a new Kafir war had been announced; thus illustrating the uncertainty under which a finance minister must always labour with reference to the expenditure of the year. He concluded by justifying the course he had taken with regard to the Income Tax; and by urging the importance of renewing it, for the purpose of continuing the process of reducing and amending other taxation, which had now been carried on with so much advantage for nine years.

It was upon this last point that the first attack was made upon the budget. Upon the report of the resolution for the renewal of the Income Tax,* Mr. Herries proposed the following resolution by way of amendment:—

" That it is the opinion of this House that the respective duties in Great Britain on profits arising from property, professions, trades, and

---

* April 7, 1851.

Financial Policy.

offices, and the Stamp-duties in Ireland, granted by two Acts passed in the sixth year of Her present Majesty, and which have been continued and amended by several subsequent Acts, were granted for limited periods and to meet temporary exigencies. That it is highly expedient to adhere to the declared intentions of Parliament when these duties were granted and continued; and, in order to secure their speediest practicable cessation, to limit the renewal of any portion of them to such an amount as may be sufficient in the existing state of the Public Revenue, to provide for the Expenditure sanctioned by Parliament, and for the due maintenance of the public credit."

The meaning of this amendment of course was, that the surplus now at the command of the Chancellor of the Exchequer should be applied rather to the reduction of the Income Tax, with a view to its ultimate and gradual abolition, than to the reduction of the Window-duty.*

---

* The phrase " reduction of the Window-duty " is used instead of " remission of the Window-duty," because, although it was proposed to abolish that tax altogether, it was proposed partially to replace it by another tax of a cognate description. The new tax might, of course, have been so arranged as to produce the same amount of duty as the Window-tax. The loss sustained by the revenue, which rendered the renewal of

The Income Tax was at that time producing about 780,000*l.* of revenue for every penny; and Mr. Herries was of opinion that the Chancellor of the Exchequer should have reduced it from 7*d.* to 5*d.*, thereby giving up about 1,560,000*l.*, or about 425,000*l.* more than the proposed reduction of the Window-tax; and, at the same time, securing the ultimate abolition of the Income Tax, of which he saw very little hope if the present policy of the Government were to be pursued.

This amendment was lost by a majority of 48.* The Government had the support of the friends of Sir Robert Peel; and the minority consisted almost exclusively of the Conservatives, though one or two Liberals voted with them.

Mr. Disraeli's amendment. Claims of the Agricultural interest.

The propriety of continuing the Income Tax having thus in general terms been affirmed, the Government, deferring for the present the consideration of the term for which, or the form in which, the renewal should take place, proceeded to introduce their measure for the abolition of the Window-tax, and the substitution

---

the Income Tax at its full amount necessary, must be measured by the difference between the produce of the Window-tax and the estimated produce of the House-tax.

* 278 to 230.

of the House-tax; and here they were met by another amendment, proposed by Mr. Disraeli,* to the effect that, in any relief to be granted by the remission or adjustment of taxation, due regard should be paid to the distressed condition of the owners and occupiers of land in the United Kingdom.

In support of this amendment, Mr. Disraeli referred to the passage in the Royal Speech at the commencement of the session, in which Her Majesty had lamented the continuance of agricultural distress; he pointed out that the Government had included in their first budget two proposals;—that relating to pauper lunatics, and that for the remission of duty on seeds, calculated, in their opinion, to confer a benefit upon the agricultural classes;—but that in their second budget they had entirely withdrawn them; and, after dwelling upon the extent of the distress which unquestionably prevailed, he indicated certain measures for relieving the land from local burdens, which he thought well deserving the attention of the Government. This amendment also was lost, but by a smaller majority than had been recorded against that of

* April 11, 1851.

Mr. Herries.* In the course of the debate to which it gave rise, Mr. Gladstone, who had voted for a somewhat similar motion in 1850, but who now voted against this amendment, explained his views with regard to the whole scheme of finance proposed by the Government. He did not object, he said, to the renewal of the Income Tax for the purpose of effecting large reductions of taxes upon industry, such as had been made in 1841 and 1845; but he was much dissatisfied at a proposal to renew it for the purpose of making such small remissions as those proposed upon coffee and timber, amounting only to 400,000*l*. He thought the substitution of a House-tax for a Window-tax a very proper measure; but he thought also that, looking to the uncertainty which must attend the permanence of the Income Tax, and the necessity which we might experience of relying upon a House-tax for a considerable portion of our revenue, the Chancellor of the Exchequer was committing a great error in now placing that tax upon so narrow a basis. He considered that should Parliament once sanction a tax confined to houses of 20*l*. value, from which those under

---

* 263 to 250. Majority 13.

Financial Policy.

20*l.* should be exempt, it was unlikely that that exemption would ever be revoked; and this circumstance would, he thought, render a future expansion of the tax a matter of the greatest difficulty. Upon this point Sir Charles Wood said in reply, that, even starting from houses of 20*l.* in value, he had brought under taxation some 25,000 or 30,000 houses which were exempt from the Window-duty; and that, had he carried the tax as low as to 10*l.* houses, he must of course have brought in a much larger number, while the whole amount of revenue which he would have gained thereby would only have amounted to 40,000*l.*

Hitherto the Government had been successful in carrying the chief measures in their budget; but, when the Income Tax bill was in committee, Mr. Hume* moved and carried † an amendment to the effect that the duration of the tax should be fixed at one year, instead of at three years; alleging as his reason that he wished to institute an inquiry by a Select Committee into the mode of assessing and collecting it, and into the possibility of removing or greatly

Mr. Hume's amendment, limiting the Income Tax to one year.

---

* On the 2nd of May, 1851.
† 244 to 230. Majority 14.

modifying the injustice of levying the same rate of charge upon terminable as upon perpetual annuities, and upon fluctuating and varying incomes from trades and professions as upon fixed incomes from real property. The debate upon this amendment was very animated, but was remarkable for a good deal of what is called crossspeaking; Mr. Hume himself being a warm supporter of an Income Tax as compared with indirect taxation, and being desirous to amend the framework of the existing tax with a view to prolong it, and to use it as an instrument for further financial reforms; while many who voted with him were anxious to put an end to the tax as speedily as possible, and had, not very long before, voted with Mr. Herries in that sense; on the other hand, some of Mr. Hume's closest political friends, more particularly Mr. Cobden, while condemning the structure of the tax as strongly as he did himself, opposed his amendment, under the impression that to adopt it would be to play into the hands of their adversaries and to bring about the destruction of the tax.

Mr. Hume, a few days after his success in carrying this amendment, proceeded, in accordance with the intention he had announced, to

Financial Policy. 163

move for the appointment of a Select Committee of inquiry; and his motion was agreed to, though not without a protest on the part of Mr. Gladstone, who strongly objected to the appointment of the Committee, and refused to serve on it; as did also the other leading friends of Sir Robert Peel. Mr. Hume experienced great difficulty in making up the Committee; and the debate upon the names of those who were to compose it was twice adjourned. The Committee was, at last, named on the 13th of June; but, though it began to sit at once, it had not time to complete its inquiry before the close of the session, and was reappointed in the following year.

The appointment of this Committee marks an important epoch in the history of the Income Tax. Looking at it in conjunction with the rejection of Mr. Herries' motion for the application of the surplus to the reduction of that tax in preference to the remission of any other, we may consider it as an indication that the House of Commons was anxious to retain it if possible, but felt that in its present shape its pressure was very severe, and that, if it was to be retained, it must be put, as it were, into a crucible, its ore extracted, and its dross purged away. It

CHAP. III.

1851.

Select Committee on the Income Tax appointed.

would, perhaps, be going too far to say that the Income Tax has ever been popular; but there have certainly been many persons who have looked with favour, and with something more than favour, not, indeed, upon the real concrete Income Tax embodied in the measures passed by Mr. Pitt and Sir Robert Peel, but upon a kind of abstract and ideal Income Tax, existing nowhere but in their own minds, and who have thought it a simple and straightforward matter to substitute this excellent impost for the coarse and clumsy one which has usurped its name, and which has, as they consider, brought discredit upon the idol of their imaginations. The essentially practical spirit which generally animates the House of Commons had hitherto led to the rejection, by large majorities, of all proposals for replacing the actual by the ideal Income Tax; but a Committee was now appointed; its doors were opened to all the world; and the actuaries, the political economists, and the other experts, who had long been declaiming against the ignorance or the indolence of Sir Robert Peel and his successors, and professing their readiness to solve the problem which our statesmen had found too difficult, were now taken into council, and encouraged to submit their plans for examination.

Financial Policy. 165

This is not the place to analyse the proceedings of the Committee. A great deal of evidence was taken, and some of the actuaries submitted an elaborate plan for ascertaining the capitalised value of incomes, and for levying the tax upon that, instead of upon the basis of the income itself; but the proposal was generally felt to be impracticable, and the Committee ultimately separated without making any recommendation at all; more than one of its members proclaiming themselves converted from their belief that a readjustment of the tax was possible, and the difficulties attending such readjustment having undoubtedly been exhibited in a very forcible light.

The adverse vote upon this question of the Income Tax was not the only defeat sustained by the Government upon financial matters in the course of the session. Lord Robert Grosvenor again carried his motion for the repeal of the Attorneys' and Solicitors' duty; and Lord Naas, by the aid of the Speaker's casting vote, again carried his resolution with respect to the mode of levying the duties on home-made spirits in bond; but neither of these successes were followed up. Lord Robert Grosvenor's Bill never came to a second reading; and that of Lord Naas was thrown out when it reached that

CHAP. III.
1851.

Other defeats of the Government.

stage. A resolution, moved by Lord Duncan, and carried by a majority of one,* calling upon the Government to subject the expenditure of the Office of Woods, Forests, and Works, to the control of Parliament, by paying the gross instead of the net revenue into the Exchequer, and voting the necessary expenses of the department in the estimates, belongs to a question (that of the management of Public Monies) which will be treated in a separate chapter.

A review of the proceedings of the session of 1851 would be incomplete without a notice of the discussion raised by Mr. Disraeli upon the occasion of the House going into Committee upon the Inhabited House-duty Bill on the 30th of June. In this discussion Mr. Disraeli and Mr. Gladstone concurred in blaming Sir Charles Wood for commuting so large and important a branch of our revenue as the Window-tax for a House-tax upon a narrow and unsatisfactory basis, at a time when the Income Tax was on its trial, and when its renewal in the following year could not be reckoned on with anything like certainty. Mr. Disraeli declined to enter upon any general inquiry into the comparative

---

* 120 to 119.

Financial Policy. 167

merits of direct and indirect taxation, saying that he felt persuaded that, in a country like England, the greater the number, and the more various the means of supply, the easier would be the task of raising a large amount of revenue; and upholding, as " the golden rule of all Chancellors of the Exchequer," that they should " beware that no tax, whatever form it may take, whether that of a customs' duty, an excise duty, or a direct impost, should, in its nature, be excessive." But, he argued, the principle upon which all our taxation, as well direct as indirect, should rest is, that it should be general in its application; for direct taxation, if accompanied by a system of large exemptions, limiting it practically to a single class, is nothing more or less than a forced contribution levied upon that class. The Income Tax, therefore, founded as it was upon a system of large exemptions, could not be regarded as a fit element of the permanent taxation of the country, however legitimate it might have been as a temporary impost designed to accomplish a temporary purpose. The Government, however, had now not only virtually adopted the principle of converting the Income Tax, with all its faults untouched, from a temporary into a permanent source of revenue;

but had carried the same vicious principle, of placing a direct tax upon too narrow a basis, into their new plan for the House-tax. Objectionable as this course was in itself, it was rendered doubly so by the circumstances of the time. Mr. Disraeli referred to the appointment of Mr. Hume's Committee, to the general feeling of dissatisfaction at the construction of the Income Tax, and to the equally general consent of "every man of authority upon financial subjects," that the "odious features of the tax cannot by any means be removed or modified." The conclusion at which he arrived from these considerations was, that the financial scheme of the year involved the sacrifice of an amount of revenue which, under the circumstances, it was most imprudent to put in peril.

Mr. Gladstone pursued a somewhat similar line of argument. He complained that the House-tax was now to be reimposed "without the slightest qualification of those great anomalies in the imposition of the tax, which, he would venture to say, were the sole cause of its abolition in 1834 . . . . But even if he were to overlook this flaw, he could not commend the plan of a House-tax which exempted altogether from the operation of the tax something like six-sevenths

Financial Policy.

of the House property of the country. . . . . It seemed to him the most obvious and unexceptionable of the permanent resources of the country; and he, for one, could not prevail upon himself to give a vote which would greatly prejudice, under ordinary circumstances, the interest of the country with respect to an impost so important. But the position in which the House now stood with regard to the Income Tax seemed to him to add tenfold importance to the consideration." He then proceeded to argue, as Mr. Disraeli had done, that the renewal of the Income Tax at all had now become a matter of uncertainty; and that, should it be abandoned, the greatest embarrassment would arise in the attempt to supply the deficiency of the revenue, from the unfortunate course now about to be taken with regard to the House-tax.

Sir Charles Wood made very little answer to these arguments, except in the way of pointing out inconsistencies between some of Mr. Disraeli's votes on other occasions and the views at present expressed by him. The House, however, supported the Government upon a division; and the order for going into Committee was carried by a majority of 113.*

---

* 242 to 129.

CHAP. III.
―――
1851.

1852.
Change of
Government.

It is curious to remark the coincidence, upon this occasion, of the views of Mr. Disraeli and of Mr. Gladstone, destined as they were, within less than eighteen months, to bring forward, as successive Chancellors of the Exchequer, budgets of their own, in which they would have to meet the difficulties which they plainly saw must arise from the course of financial legislation of 1851. We shall shortly see how the agitation against the Income Tax, and the framework of the House-tax, affected their respective proposals; and the difference between their methods of attempting to solve the embarrassing problem presented to them both.

A change of Government took place early in the session of 1852; and Lord Stanley (now Earl of Derby) was called to the head of affairs; Mr. Disraeli taking the office of Chancellor of the Exchequer. The new Ministers announced their intention of advising the Queen to dissolve Parliament after the necessary business of the session should have been completed; and there was, in consequence, a general disposition to put off all measures which were not of a pressing character, and to be content, as regarded finance, with an arrangement that should suffice for the year.

Financial Policy.

The Budget was brought forward on the 30th of April. Mr. Disraeli drew a very favourable picture of the condition of the revenue, and showed that the estimates of his predecessor had been far more than realized. Sir Charles Wood had founded his calculations for 1851-2 upon an estimate of revenue amounting to 52,140,000*l.*, of which he had proposed to sacrifice 968,000*l.* in remissions of duty on windows, coffee, and timber, leaving an anticipated surplus of 925,000*l.*; but, in point of fact, the income, after all the remissions had been made, had reached 52,468,000*l.*, or considerably more than Sir Charles had calculated it at before the remissions; and the surplus, instead of being 925,000*l.*, was 2,176,998*l.* With regard to the year 1852-3, Mr. Disraeli stated that he estimated the expenditure (including a sum of 660,000*l.* for the Kafir War, and a vote of 350,000*l.* for the newly-revived Militia force) at 51,163,979*l.* To meet this he was unable to reckon on an income of more than 49,038,000*l.*, as the Income Tax, which had been voted for a single year, had now expired, and there was only a balance of 2,600,000*l.* due in respect of the last half-year's payments which had not yet been collected.

CHAP. III.
1852.
Budget, April 30.

Mr. Disraeli then proceeded to point out the difficulties attending each of the three great modes of taxation open to a Chancellor of the Exchequer, namely, the increase of Customs'-duties, of Excise-duties, and of direct taxation. He admitted with great frankness the benefits which the country had derived from the large remissions which had been made in the Customs' tariff, showed the improbability of the House of Common's reversing the policy which had led to the recent reductions in both Customs' and Excise duties, and went on to state, at some length, the difficulties attending the increase of direct taxation also; but it is unnecessary to recapitulate them here, as they were in the main those which he had pointed out in the debates upon the House-tax at the close of the preceding session. In conclusion, he expressed his conviction that it was becoming necessary for the House to review the whole system of taxation, and to endeavour to form some clear and decided opinion on the principles upon which the public revenue should be raised. He looked, he said, with great apprehension to the opinions prevalent in the House, which seemed opposed to all the great sources of income in the country; and he considered that nothing could be more injurious than rashly and rapidly to reduce the sources of indirect taxation without having come to some general conclusion as to the principles upon which direct taxation should be levied. But, considering the shortness of the time for which the new Government had held office, he found it quite impossible to attempt, on the present occasion, to deal with this large and difficult question ; and he, therefore, contented himself with proposing, by way of a provisional arrangement, that the Income Tax should be renewed for one year more, which would convert the anticipated deficiency of 2,125,000*l.* into a surplus of 462,000*l.* This proposal was adopted. No other important financial business was done during the remainder of the session.

A dissolution of Parliament, and a general election took place in the autumn, and the new Parliament met in the month of November, when Mr. Disraeli took the earliest opportunity[*] of stating that it was not the intention of the Government to propose any measures for the reversal of the recent Commercial Policy of the country. He said, however, that believing our financial system to require revision, in order to

---

[*] In the Debate on the Address, Nov. 11, 1852.

CHAP. III.
1852.

bring it more into harmony with our commercial system, it was their wish to bring forward their financial proposals as soon as possible. The arrangements necessary for the funeral of the Duke of Wellington stood in the way of proceeding at once with any other business; and after those had been completed, and the funeral had taken place, several days were spent in discussing the terms of a resolution, moved by Mr. Villiers, and intended to express the sense entertained by the House of the benefits derived from Free-trade;* so that it was not till the 3rd of December that the Budget was introduced.

The Budget, Dec. 3, 1852.

Difficulties of the Government.

In framing this Budget the Government of Lord Derby were beset by difficulties of no ordinary magnitude. In the first place, they had to deal with a very large deficiency in the revenue. Mr. Disraeli had estimated the expenditure for 1852-3 at 51,163,000*l.*; and there was no reason for supposing that it would be materially less in 1853-4 and subsequent years. The revenue,

---

* Mr. Villiers' motion was set aside by a majority of 80 (336 to 256), in favour of an amendment, to the same effect in substance but more general in its terms, which was moved by Lord Palmerston. The amended resolution was then adopted by 468 to 53.

apart from the produce of the Income Tax, he had calculated at 46,438,000*l.*, or 4,700,000*l.* below the amount of the estimated expenditure. There would, of course, be a half-year's yield of the Income Tax to help the finance of 1853-4; but even this would leave a deficiency for that year of more than two millions; and in succeeding years that deficiency would amount, as we have seen, to more than four millions and a-half. Now Sir Robert Peel, in 1842, had dealt with a deficiency of two millions and a-half; but then Sir Robert Peel, in 1842, had been placed in more favourable circumstances than was Mr. Disraeli in 1852. Sir Robert Peel, in 1842, was at the head of a party commanding a large majority in Parliament, and which placed implicit confidence in him; whereas Mr. Disraeli, in 1852, was not sure of a majority upon any question, and, least of all, upon questions in any degree connected with commercial policy. Moreover, when Sir Robert Peel undertook to re-establish a balance in the finances, he was able to lay his hand upon a tax amply sufficient for his purpose, which the country was willing to bear, as a strictly temporary burden, for the sake of attaining a great object. But it was scarcely possible for a

Finance Minister, in 1852, to use the Income Tax again exactly as it had been used in 1842. The House of Commons, expressing in this respect a sentiment very general in the country, had, in the preceding year, distinctly refused to renew the tax in its existing shape, except as a provisional measure for a single year. Mr. Disraeli had no reason to suppose that the new House would consent to reverse the decision of its predecessor in this respect. But even if such a step on the part of Parliament were to be regarded as probable, the Minister himself had serious objections to the framework of the tax, considered as a permanent element of our system of taxation. Direct taxation founded on extensive exemptions was, as he said, only another phrase for confiscation. This opinion he had very forcibly expressed in the year before his accession to office; and it was a necessary consequence of it that, if he proposed a continuance of the Income Tax, he ought to remove some of its objectionable features by extending the area of its incidence. But to prolong the existence and extend the operation of the tax, without paying any attention to the complaints of those who had been remonstrating against the inequality of its pressure upon different classes of

Financial Policy.

incomes, was obviously a task of the highest difficulty, and one from which any Minister might be pardoned from shrinking. It was a task which Mr. Gladstone, indeed, did in the following year attempt, and in which he succeeded; but Mr. Gladstone had then some advantages which Mr. Disraeli had not, and was free from the peculiar difficulties which beset the latter.

The position of the Income Tax question was not the only embarrassing feature of the situation in which the Ministry found themselves. They had long been pleading the cause of certain classes which had recently been, and perhaps still were, suffering from the effects of recent legislation; for though that legislation had on the whole been productive of much general benefit, it had, at the same time, undoubtedly been accompanied with temporary inconvenience to certain interests. The shipowners, the sugar-planters, and the farmers, had all been undergoing distress; which they attributed,— and, in the opinion of Lord Derby's party, rightly attributed,—to the effects of the recent commercial policy. This circumstance seemed to render it incumbent upon the Government to propose some measures for the relief of these

CHAP. III.
1852.

Main features of the Budget.

classes. But that relief could not be given in the form of a return to protective duties; for the country at large had pronounced itself adverse to such a step. It could only be given in the form of a remission of burdens; and a remission of burdens implied a sacrifice of revenue, and, of course, an increased deficiency, which would have to be supplied by new taxation. It will be seen at once that the conditions of the problem were exceedingly difficult.

As the Budget of December, 1852, was not adopted by Parliament, it is unnecessary to examine it with the same minuteness as ordinary budgets. It contained proposals for relieving the shipping interest from certain taxes from which they derived no benefit; for giving the sugar-planters the advantages of refining in bond; for remitting half the Malt-tax and half the Hop-duty; and for reducing the duties on tea from 2*s*. 2*d*., by several successive stages, to the rate of 1*s*. per lb. The Income Tax Mr. Disraeli proposed to renew for three years, extending it to funded property and salaries in Ireland, to industrial incomes of above 100*l*. a-year, and to incomes arising from property of above 50*l*. a-year; he further proposed to reduce the rate of taxation on Schedules B,

Financial Policy.

D, and E from 7*d.* to 5½*d.* in the pound. He estimated that these alterations would so far countervail one another as to leave the ultimate productiveness of the tax undisturbed. It being then necessary for him to find a source of revenue from which to supply the deficiency created by the reduction of the Malt, Hop, and Tea duties, he proposed to extend the House-tax to houses of 10*l.* annual value, and to increase its rate from 9*d.* and 6*d.* to 1*s.* 6*d.* and 1*s.* in the pound. He was of opinion that this alteration, besides placing the House-tax on a sounder basis, would produce a revenue sufficient to make up for the contemplated remissions. An incidental proposal to put an end to the Public Works' Loan Fund, and to carry the repayments of the advances made from that fund to the account of the revenue, was calculated to produce a surplus of about 400,000*l.* This proposal, which was afterwards very severely criticised, was undoubtedly objectionable in principle; as the monies constituting the fund had originally been borrowed, and their application to current revenue was tantamount to an addition to the National Debt. Had Mr. Disraeli's calculations, indeed, been fully verified, there would have been no necessity for applying this surplus revenue to expenditure at all; it would have gone into the Exchequer, and have been used, as other repayments of advances have since been, to strengthen the balances; or it would have been applied in quarterly instalments to the redemption of debt. But, in the event of any failure in his estimates, an addition to the debt might certainly have been occasioned by this arrangement, and no Chancellor of the Exchequer can be sure that his hopes will not be disappointed.

Budget rejected. Resignation of the Ministry, Dec. 15, 1852.

Apart, however, from this subordinate question, it is sufficiently evident that the Budget presented too many assailable points to have much chance of being adopted. Mr. Thomas Duncombe's attempt to dispose of it as a whole, on the question of the Speaker's leaving the chair, was indeed unsuccessful; but as soon as the House had gone into Committee, and the first resolution, that relating to the House-tax, had been proposed, all the elements of objection were readily combined in opposition to it. Those who disliked the extension and the increase of the House-tax, those who disliked the extension of the Income Tax, those who were hostile to the principle of its proposed modification, those who looked with jealousy on the reduction

of the Malt-tax, and, in short, all objectors of
all sorts found themselves able to join in defeating the ministerial scheme as a whole,
though differing among themselves as to the
merits of its several parts. After a debate of
four nights, in which most of the leading
speakers in the House took part, the Government
were defeated, on the 16th of December, by a
majority of 19,* and the immediate result was
their retirement from office, and the subsequent
formation of Lord Aberdeen's Administration.

---

* 305 to 286.

Chapter IV.

Chap. IV.
1853.
Financial importance of the year 1853. HE year 1853 is one of the most important, in a financial sense, of those which fall within the period I am considering. It marks, if not the final, at least the temporary close of the great controversy opened in 1851, and continued in the following year. We have seen how, in 1851, Sir Charles Wood had proposed to deal with the finances in a manner which would have rendered necessary the retention of the Income Tax for an indefinite time, while he made no attempt to alter its framework, though an alteration was loudly called for by a large section of the people; how the House of Commons had condemned that proposal in the vote which affirmed Mr. Hume's amendment; how, in 1852, Mr. Disraeli had endeavoured to solve the difficulty by

Financial Policy.

an amendment of the tax, in partial conformity with the popular demand; and now we have to see how, in 1853, Mr. Gladstone succeeded in stemming that demand, partly by showing the impossibility of satisfying it, and partly by holding out the hope of an eventual, though distant, termination of the whole tax.

The financial statement was made on the 18th of April. Mr. Gladstone began by stating that the results of the preceding year, 1852-3, had been far more favourable than Mr. Disraeli had anticipated; that the revenue was greater by 1,464,000*l*., and the expenditure less by 380,000*l*., than had been estimated when the Budget of 1852 was introduced; and that the surplus on the year was no less than 2,460,000*l*. He then proceeded to show that the expenditure for the coming year, 1853-4, would be greater than that of 1852-3 by about 1,400,000*l*., in consequence chiefly of the large additions made to the Navy and Ordnance estimates, the Militia estimate, and the estimate for Education.* Upon

---

* Addition to Navy estimate 617,000 £
„ Ordnance do 616,000
„ Militia do 180,000
„ Education do 100,000

the whole, he estimated the expenditure at 52,183,000*l.*, from which sum he thought he might deduct 100,000*l.* on account of the gain he anticipated from the conversion of 3 per cent. Stock which he was then attempting to effect, and which will presently be described. This would reduce the probable expenditure to 52,083,000*l.*; while the revenue, including the Income Tax, might be taken at 52,890,000*l.*, so that there would be a surplus on the year of 800,000*l.* Of this surplus, however, 215,000*l.* arose from occasional payments, which could not be looked upon as ordinary revenue; namely, 135,000*l.* from repayments made to the revenues of the Crown in consequence of a Metropolitan Improvement Act, and 80,000*l.* from the extinction of the old Merchant Seamen's Fund, and the transfer of its capital to the Government.

In this estimate Mr. Gladstone, as has been said, assumed the continuance of the Income Tax, but the Income Tax had now legally expired; and the questions whether it should be renewed, and, if so, in what form it should be renewed, had to be answered before he could present his plan for the year. To these questions, then, he proceeded to address himself in a speech of unusual power, which not only obtained

Financial Policy.

universal applause from his audience at the time, but changed the convictions of a large part of the nation, and turned, at least for several years, a current of popular opinion which had seemed too powerful for any minister to resist.

He began by asking the House to consider whether or not it would make efforts to part with the Income Tax at once. " I do not say," he observed, " that such an alternative is impossible. On the contrary, I believe that by the conjunction of three measures, one of which must be a tax upon land, houses, and other visible property, of perhaps 6*d.* in the pound; another, a system of licences upon trade, made universal, and averaging something like 7*l.*; and the third, a change in your system of legacy duties; it would be possible for you at once to part with the Income Tax. But Her Majesty's Government do not recommend such a course. They believe, in the first place, that such a system would, upon the whole, be far more unequal, and cause greater dissatisfaction than the Income Tax; they believe, likewise, that it would arrest other beneficial reforms of taxation; and they believe that it would raise that difficult question, in regard to the taxation of the public funds of this country, in a form the most incon-

CHAP. IV.

1853.

Mr. Gladstone's argument with regard to the Income Tax.

venient." Mr. Gladstone then set forth in glowing terms the services rendered to the country in time past, and again in recent days, by the Income Tax. He showed its value as a financial reserve in time of war, and as an instrument of fiscal and commercial reforms in time of peace; and he expressed his own opinion, and that of the Government, that the time was not yet come for laying it aside. At the same time he stated his individual belief that it was not a tax well adapted for a permanent portion of our ordinary financial system. This belief he held, independently of the question whether it were possible to remove its inequalities; but he felt that all persons were agreed, that, if the tax were to be made permanent at all, it could only be so on condition of its being reconstructed with a view to their removal. He then proceeded to inquire into the possibility of a satisfactory reconstruction. He showed, by a careful analysis of the schedules, and by an examination of the system of assessment, that the profits of trade were not, as was assumed, taxed at an equal rate with the profits derived from land and houses, but that where trade paid 7d. in the pound, land paid 9d. He exposed the unfairness of the proposal to tax classes upon the average value of their incomes, which had been suggested as a mode of escaping from the extreme difficulty of taxing individuals upon the exact value of each man's income. He touched upon the evils attending the system of self-assessment, and upon the frauds to which it gives rise; he dwelt at great length upon the case of the fundholders, and not only showed the injustice which would be done to the public creditor, and the consequent injury that would be inflicted upon the credit of the nation in the money-market of the world, by imposing a higher tax upon incomes derived from the public funds than upon incomes from other kinds of property; but also pointed out the absurd consequences which would follow from the step; since an enormous proportion of the debt was in the hands of persons whom it would, for one cause or other, be necessary, after all, to exempt from paying the higher rate of tax. He admitted that the tax bore hardly upon the incomes of professional men, but he pointed out the difficulty of drawing a distinction between professional men and traders; and, in like manner, he showed how a great number of other cases, which might be regarded as cases of hardship, shaded off by imperceptible tints into others which could hardly be distinguished from them, until it was plain that no point could be found at which a stand could properly be made and a broad line of demarcation intelligibly drawn between incomes that should be taxed lightly and incomes that should be taxed heavily.

He summed up the case in these words:—
"The general views of Her Majesty's Government, with respect to the Income Tax, are, that it is an engine of gigantic power for great national purposes; but, at the same time, that there are circumstances attending its operation which make it difficult, perhaps impossible, at any rate, in our opinion, not desirable, to maintain it as a portion of the permanent and ordinary finances of the country. The public feeling of its inequality is a fact most important in itself. The inquisition it entails is a most serious disadvantage; and the frauds to which it leads are an evil which it is not possible to characterize in terms too strong.

"One thing I hope this House will never do; and that is, nibble at this great public question. Don't let them adopt the plan of reconstructing the Income Tax to-day, and saying,—'If that doesn't work well, we'll try our hands at it again to-morrow.' That is not the way in which the relations of classes, brought into the nicest competition one with another, under a scheme of direct taxation, are to be treated. Depend upon it, when you come to close quarters with this subject, when you come to measure and test the respective relations of intelligence and labour and property, in all their myriad and complex forms, and when you come to represent those relations in arithmetical results, you are undertaking an operation of which, I should say, it was beyond the power of man to conduct it with satisfaction; but, at any rate, it is an operation to which you ought not constantly to recur; for if, as my noble friend [Lord John Russell] once said with universal applause, this country cannot bear a revolution once a year, I will venture to say that it cannot bear a reconstruction of the Income Tax once a year.

" Whatever you do in regard to the Income Tax, you must be bold, you must be intelligible, you must be decisive. You must not palter with it. If you do, I have striven at least to point out, as well as my feeble powers will permit, the almost desecration, I would say, certainly the gross breach of duty to your country, of which you will be guilty, in thus putting to hazard one of the most potent and effective

CHAP. IV.
1853.

among all its material resources. I believe it to be of vital importance, whether you keep this tax, or whether you part with it, that you either should keep it or should leave it in a state in which it will be fit for service on an emergency; and that it will be impossible to do if you break up the basis of your Income Tax."

But if the tax could not be amended, was it then to be renewed and perpetuated without amendment? To this question, Mr. Gladstone's answer in substance was, It shall be renewed, but it shall not be perpetuated. It shall be renewed for what appear good and sufficient considerations; it shall be renewed for the purpose of effecting desirable and important fiscal and commercial reforms; but it shall be renewed in a form which will show that it is not intended to be a permanent part of the financial system of the country; and at the same time arrangements shall be made which will have the effect of placing it within the power of Parliament, at a certain definite period, to dispense with its aid.

Skilful arrangement of this speech.

It is almost impossible to condense this portion of Mr. Gladstone's speech; so consummate is the skill with which the topics are arranged and presented to his audience. Wholly apart from the merits of the scheme he proposes, the speech

Financial Policy.

itself, and especially this part of it, will repay the most careful study as a specimen of persuasive reasoning. There is, first, the hint thrown out as to the possibility, if Parliament were so minded, of dispensing with the Income Tax altogether,—a hint sufficient to relieve his audience from any sense of inevitable and oppressive necessity, and to bring them into the frame of mind proper for men who are to brace themselves to a great task, as freemen and not as bondslaves. Then, lest the hint should work too strongly upon the imagination, he hastens to disclaim for himself and his colleagues the slightest intention of acting upon it :—" Such is not the recommendation of Her Majesty's Government." Then comes, in some stirring sentences, a picture of the tax, as " constant study " had impressed it upon the speaker's own mind; a glance at the greatness of Mr. Pitt's conception; a bold attempt to show that, had that conception taken place somewhat earlier, the country might, at that moment, have been free from the whole burden of the National Debt; and finally, a personification of the tax itself as a giant, who, after having shielded us in war, had been called forth from his repose to assist our industrious toils in peace. When a proper sense has thus been created of the greatness of the subject, by a sudden plunge he carries us into the midst of minute and careful calculations, and appears to test by his analysis every element of the tax. He points out the flaws in the reasoning of the advocates for its reconstruction; exposes the injustice which would ensue from the attempt in some cases, and the embarrassments which it would cause in others; and succeeds, not only in clearly showing many of the difficulties which must attend the process, but, what for his immediate purpose is even more important, in raising a vague and indefinite sense of danger to be apprehended from the mere touching of the tax, danger such as that which attends any tampering with our very Constitution. Yet he does not withal deny the weight of the objections against the framework of the tax. Having in his own mind a plan for the ultimate extinction of the impost, he is not careful to conceal his sense of those objections. He has now his audience with him, and he can afford to make large admissions; to accept, as a matter of feeling at least, the doctrine that " the Income Tax bears, upon the whole, too hard upon intelligence and skill, and not hard enough upon property, as compared with intelligence and skill;" and yet, making these admissions, he can venture to ask, not only for a renewal of the tax for a term of seven years, but for permission to levy it upon incomes of as little as 100*l.* a-year, and to extend it to Ireland, a country which had not yet felt its pressure.

CHAP. IV
1853.

Mr. Gladstone offered the House two inducements to accept his plan. First, he proposed so to adjust taxation as to render possible the extinction of the tax in 1860; secondly, he proposed to make with its aid some immediate and extensive remissions of indirect taxation. The details of the plan are as follow. The Income Tax in its existing shape, with some slight amendments, mentioned in the note below,* was to be renewed at 7*d.* in the pound for two years; the rate was then to be reduced to 6*d.* in the pound for two years more; and then again to 5*d.* in the pound for a final period of three years, ending on the 5th of April, 1860,

Plan for the extinction of the Income Tax.

---

* Mr. Gladstone proposed to extend to professions the system of commutations hitherto confined to the case of trades. He proposed also to allow persons insuring their lives, or purchasing deferred annuities, to deduct the premiums paid by them from their income before ascertaining the amount to be charged with the tax, provided the amount did not exceed one-seventh of the whole income.

CHAP. IV.
1853.

when the tax would altogether cease, unless the Parliament of 1860 should see fit to renew it. Incomes of between 100*l.* and 150*l.* a-year were for the first time to be taxed, but only at the lower rate of 5*d.* in the pound; they were to continue to be charged at this rate throughout the seven years. The tax was to be extended to Ireland for the same term, and under the same conditions, as those assigned to it in England and Scotland. The estimated result of these changes was an increase of revenue in the year 1853-4 to the amount of about 295,000*l.** making the total produce of the tax 5,845,000*l.* Having thus dealt with the Income Tax, Mr. Gladstone next proposed to extend the Legacy-duty; and to make it apply to real as well as to personal property, and to successions under settlement, as well as to bequests by will. The immediate effects of this change upon the revenue for the year would be an addition of

Succession-duty.

	£
* Tax as existing, estimated at	5,550,000
Deduct for Life Insurances (half year) .	60,000
	5,490,000
Add, extension below 150*l.* (half year) .	125,000
Extension to Ireland (half year) . . .	230,000
	5,845,000

Financial Policy.

500,000*l*.: it would ultimately, he said, realize as much as 2,000,000*l*. He raised also the duty upon Scotch and Irish spirits, bringing the former up from 3*s*. 8*d*. to 4*s*. 8*d*., and the latter from 2*s*. 8*d*. to 3*s*. 4*d*. per gallon;* at the same time he conceded the principle for which Lord Naas had, in former years, contended, and upon which he had several times obtained majorities against the Government, that allowance should be made to the distiller for the waste of spirits in bond. The net gain from this change would be 436,000*l*. Finally, he announced a proposal for the revision of certain licences, involving an increase in the revenue of 113,000*l*. By these several additions he reckoned on obtaining an increase in the revenue amounting to 1,344,000*l*., which, added to the surplus of 807,000*l*. already estimated, gave a fund of 2,151,000*l*. available for the remission of taxation. Upon this fund he proposed to draw by remissions, which should not take full effect at once, but which would amount in the current year to 1,656,000*l*., leaving 1853-4 with a surplus of 493,000*l*. In the following year, the revenue would sustain, in consequence of the remissions, a further loss

marginalia: Chap. IV. 1853. Scotch and Irish spirit duties. Revision of trade licences. Surplus available for the remission of taxes.

---

* The duty on English spirits was 7*s*. 10*d*. per gallon.

of 1,087,000*l.*; but the new Succession-duty would produce about 700,000*l.* more than in 1853-4; the Income Tax extensions, about 295,000*l.* more; and there would be a gain upon the reduction of the interest upon the three-and-a-quarter per cent. Stocks* amounting to 312,000*l.* Thus there would be an increasing revenue more than sufficient to meet the prospective reductions; and, in like manner, when the rate of the Income Tax should begin to decline, the loss which that decline would occasion would be supplied by the increasing produce of the Succession-duty, the gradual revival of the Customs' and Excise revenue under the influence of diminished duties, and the diminution in the interest of the debt; until at length, in 1860, the Income Tax would legally expire at the same time with the falling in of the Long Annuities, amounting to 2,146,000*l.*; and, reckoning increased revenue from other sources, and diminished charge for the debt, on the one side, to amount to 5,959,000*l.*, while the loss of the Income Tax, on the other side, would be 6,140,000*l.* Mr. Gladstone showed that the balance on the whole transaction would be a loss to the

---

* Arising from Mr. Goulburn's arrangements in 1844.

Exchequer of only 200,000*l.* Thus, should his calculations be verified, the Parliament of 1860 would be in a position to dispense with the Income Tax altogether, if it should choose to do so.

CHAP. IV.
1853.

The remissions proposed were of a very extensive character. First came a boon to Ireland, no less an one than the remission of the whole debt of 4,500,000*l.* due from Ireland to England for the advances made in the time of the Irish famine. This measure, which involved a sacrifice of revenue amounting to 245,000*l.* a-year, was to be regarded as a set-off against the extension of the Income Tax, and the increase of the Irish spirit duties. Then came the repeal of the soap duty; the reduction of the tax on life assurances from 2*s.* 6*d.* to 6*d.* per 100*l.*; the substitution of an uniform penny stamp on receipts for the old system of graduated stamps; a reduction in the amount of the attorneys' and solicitors' certificate duty; a reduction of the advertisement duty, and of the newspaper stamp duties; a reduction of the hackney carriage duty; a reform in the whole system of the Assessed taxes, including the abolition of progressive duties, of compositions, and, as far as might be, of exemptions; an amendment of the post-horse

Remission of sum due from Ireland.

Soap duty repealed.

Various stamp duties reduced.

Hackney carriage duty and Assessed taxes reduced.

CHAP. IV.
1853.

Tea duties,

and other Customs' duties reduced.

duty; and an extension of the facilities given for the redemption of the Land-tax. Under the important head of the Customs' revenue, the first great reduction was to be upon the tea duties,—(for upon wine Mr. Gladstone said he could not see his way to a change),—and here he proposed to follow the plan of Mr. Disraeli, and to bring the duty down from 2*s.* 2¼*d.* to 1*s.* per lb. by successive stages of descent, the last to be reached in April, 1856. A large number of other duties of Customs were also to be dealt with: on 123 articles they were to be entirely remitted, on 133 they were to be reduced; protective and discriminating duties were to be abandoned to a great extent; and rated duties were, as far as possible, to be substituted for duties *ad valorem*. The account of the remissions in 1853-4 would then stand thus :—

	Gross loss or relief to the tax-payer.	Net loss allowing for recovery in consumption.
	£.	£.
Excise	786,000	771,000
Stamps	417,000	200,000
Post-horses	27,000	27,000
Customs	1,338,000	658,000
Total	£2,568,000	£1,656,000

Financial Policy.

		£.
In the next year would come		
Further loss on Tea duties	. . . .	510,000
,, Soap duties	. . . .	340,000
,, Post-horses	. . . .	27,000
,, Assessed taxes	. . .	170,000
,, Colonial postage*	. .	40,000
Total	. . .	£1,087,000

CHAP. IV.

1853.

Such are the outlines of the great Budget of 1853—a budget remarkable in many ways. The contrast which it presents to its most distinguished predecessors, the budgets of 1842 and 1845, can hardly fail to strike the most superficial observer. We miss in it the caution, which is perhaps the most striking feature of the financial plans of Sir Robert Peel; while in its place we meet with a boldness of conception, a love of effect, and a power of producing it, such as we do not find even in the remarkable budget of 1842. Yet it would be unjust to Mr. Gladstone to find fault with him on this account. When we look at the circumstances of the case, we cannot but feel that it was of the utmost importance to the financial prosperity of the country that a stand should be made against

General character of the Budget.

---

* The proposed reduction in the rate of Colonial postage was independent of the budget, but involved the probability of a loss of revenue.

that of which Mr. Disraeli had so justly complained—the tendency of the leaders of public opinion to decry and render impossible every mode of raising the necessary revenue; and, looking to the failure of Mr. Disraeli's own plans, and to the remarkable complications arising out of the state of parties, and out of the doctrines to which most of their chiefs had committed themselves, we may well believe that nothing less than a striking scheme like that which Mr. Gladstone brought forward would at that time have sufficed to save the finances from the most serious confusion. Nor should it be forgotten that the scheme, though bold, was founded upon experience; and that Mr. Gladstone could point to the results of the past ten years in justification of many of the assumptions on which it rested. In point of fact, had not events occurred which led to a large increase of our expenditure before the arrival of 1860, his calculations would have been nearly or quite verified; that is, provided the House had abstained for the whole seven years from demanding any new remissions of taxation. His great error consisted in not making a sufficient allowance for the uncertainty of all human affairs; and perhaps in a want of sagacity to discern the signs of the times It is proverbially much easier to see these signs after the events which they forebode have happened than before; still Mr. Gladstone ought, perhaps, to have remembered that within two years two millions had been added to the estimates; and to have foreseen that further additions were likely to be demanded, which would materially disturb his prospective arrangements. This he might have reckoned on, without reference to the question of the coming war with Russia, in which he probably did not yet believe, though he must have begun to feel some uneasiness on the subject.

The renewal and extension of the Income Tax was, as Mr. Gladstone expressed it, the keystone of his budget; and it was upon this point that the first discussion was taken. On his proposing the resolutions bearing upon it,[*] Sir E. Bulwer Lytton moved the following amendment:—"That the continuance of the Income Tax for seven years, and its extension to parties heretofore exempt from its operation, without any mitigation of the inequalities of its assessment, are alike unjust and impolitic." The debate upon this amendment was carried

---

[*] On the 25th of April, 1853.

on for four nights, and it was ultimately rejected on the 2nd of May by a majority of 71.* The discussion took rather a wide range, and the whole scheme of the budget was subjected to criticism. Many of the speeches delivered are well worthy of perusal, particularly those of Sir E. B. Lytton, Mr. Cobden, Mr. Henley, and Mr. Disraeli.

This question having been thus disposed of, the Income Tax resolutions were proceeded with. Some of the Irish members opposed the extension of the tax to Ireland, and very warm language was used upon this point; but the proposal of the Government was carried by a large majority. Another amendment, which led to a division, was moved by Mr. Palmer, the member for Berkshire, who proposed that allowance should be made under Schedule A for the cost of repairs, and that the tax should be levied upon net instead of gross income. This amendment was lost by a majority of 75.† A good many amendments of smaller importance were moved in the course of the progress of the bill, but they were for the most part defeated, and the bill passed its third reading without material alteration.

---

* By 323 to 252.   † By 276 to 201.

Financial Policy.

As soon as the Income Tax resolutions had been adopted, those relating to the new Succession-duty were brought forward. On the 12th of May Mr. Gladstone explained the principles of his measure. He stated that his object was to provide that a tax should be laid upon all successions to property taking place in consequence of death. Hitherto the Legacy-duty had been applicable only to personal property descending either by bequest or inheritance. Personal property passing under the trusts of a settlement, and real property, whether passing by settlement, inheritance, or devise, had been exempt from duty. This state of things, said Mr. Gladstone, was too anomalous to be permanent. There might be reasons for exempting real property from taxes imposed upon other kinds of property; for it was admitted, or at all events it was argued, that real property bore an undue proportion of local taxation, and was more heavily rated to the Income Tax than personalty, besides having to pay much more in the form of stamp duties on the occasion of its transfer; but there could be no such reason for exempting personal property passing under settlement from a charge to which the like property passing in another manner was subject; and, even as regarded real property, he pointed out that the reason assigned for the exemption was wider than the exemption itself; and that, if it were on account of its peculiar burdens that freehold property was to be allowed to escape, leasehold and copyhold property would have an equal claim to indulgence, which however they did not enjoy. He proposed, therefore, to abolish the existing distinctions, and to charge the Succession-duty upon successions of all kinds. But, recognizing the claim of certain kinds of property to consideration, on account of the peculiar burdens borne by them, he proposed to establish a new distinction between what he called rateable and non-rateable property; and to charge the former less heavily than the latter. This, however, he said he would do, not by making a difference in the rate of the duty, but by charging it upon a different principle. In the case of successions to non-rateable or invisible property, the successor would have to pay according to the interest he took. If he succeeded to an absolute interest, he would pay the per-centage upon the whole property; if to a smaller interest, he would pay upon the value of that smaller interest only; but a successor to rateable property should never be charged with the duty upon any higher interest than a life interest. Even though he should succeed to the absolute ownership of an estate, he should be charged only upon an amount ascertained by computing the annual value of the estate, and his own expectation of life.

It may be collected from Mr. Gladstone's speech that, in making this proposal, he was actuated, not only by a desire to relieve rateable property from some part of the pressure of the Succession-duty, but also by a desire to avoid bringing about a mischievous interference with the laws of entail and settlement. It was obviously impossible to tax the succession to a life interest upon the value of the perpetuity. Persons succeeding to life interests under entails and settlements, therefore, could only be taxed upon those interests. They would thus have been more lightly taxed than persons taking similar property by descent or by wills unencumbered with trusts. Hence, on the one hand, there would have been an inducement to the owners of estates to entail them, when they would not otherwise have done so; and, on the other hand, as the distinction would have told greatly in favour of the large proprietors, amongst whom the practice of entailing property generally prevails, and against the small proprietors, with whom it is less common, it might have led to a contest between classes, and to a movement against the law of settlement. It was obviously desirable to avoid in a simply financial arrangement any step which would either give a new inducement to persons to entail, or a new argument to the opponents of entails.

A similar desire to abstain, as far as possible, from interference with social arrangements appears to have dictated the mode in which successors to encumbered estates were dealt with. The amount of income which the possessor of a heavily-mortgaged estate has to pay away in the form of interest, usually bears a much larger proportion to the whole amount of income arising from the estate, than the principal of his debts bears to the capital value of the property; because the interest he pays is fixed at a higher rate than the rate of profit derived from land. His margin of income, after paying the encumbrancer his interest, is consequently much smaller in proportion than would be his margin of capital if he sold his estate and paid off the encumbrance altogether. To lay the tax on the margin of capital, therefore, would in many cases be, to force the proprietor

Financial Policy. 207

to sell his property; but, however advantageous it might perhaps be that he should do so, Mr. Gladstone thought it would be wrong to make a financial arrangement the means of forcing him to take the step; and he accordingly decided to lay the tax in such cases upon the margin of income only; but with the proviso that, if the successor should at any time afterwards sell the estate, he should make up the difference to the Government.* This proviso, however, was afterwards abandoned.

A scale of duties was to be so arranged as to press much less heavily upon successions in the direct line than upon successions of remote kinsmen or of strangers. The tax upon the direct succession of a child to a parent was to be 1 per cent., and that upon the succession of an entire stranger in blood 10 per cent. Intermediate rates were fixed for successions within certain degrees of consanguinity. It would seem that Mr. Gladstone did not at the time fully

---

* Thus, if an estate worth 500,000*l.*, with a net rental of 14,000*l.*, were charged with debts to the amount of 300,000*l.*, and with interest thereupon of 12,000*l.*, the tax would be levied, not on the 200,000*l.* margin of capital, but on the capitalized value of the 2,000*l.* margin of income. But should the estate afterwards be sold, the difference would have to be paid.

appreciate the financial operation of this provision. He then expected that his new duty would, in course of time, add 2,000,000*l.* to the revenue. This expectation has been entirely disappointed. In the year 1852 the Legacy-duty produced 1,380,000*l.*; in the year 1860-61 the Legacy and Succession duties together produced 2,169,000*l.* The increase, instead of being 2,000,000*l.*, is only 711,000*l.*; and of this only 605,000*l.* is due to the Succession-duty, for the old Legacy-duty produced, in 1860, 1,562,000*l.** Mr. Gladstone, in his budget-speech of 1860, attributed this disappointment mainly to the fact that " by the usual course of succession real property goes in the direct line in a much greater number of cases than personal property, so that if 100,000,000*l.* a-year in real and settled property came under the Succession-duty, that amount would not yield the same average of duty as if it had been personal property." It should be observed, however, that this explanation by no means meets the case. It is true that of the whole amount received for Legacy-duty in 1860-61, nearly 33 per cent. was derived from legacies to strangers, paying

---

* See 5th Report of the Commissioners of Inland Revenue.

10 per cent. duty, and only 22 per cent. from legacies to children, paying 1 per cent. duty; while of the whole amount received for succession duty 31 per cent. was derived from the successions of children, and only 28 per cent. from the successions of strangers: but even had these proportions been reversed, the amount of the succession duty would have fallen far below Mr. Gladstone's estimate. That estimate assumed that the new duty on successions would be far more productive than the old duty on legacies. The old duty was producing about 1,400,000*l*.: the new duty was to produce about 2,000,000*l*. As the rates of duty were nearly the same in both cases, this result could only be expected on the supposition that the property which would become liable to succession duty would be more valuable than the property liable to legacy duty. Now, if all the property that paid legacy duty in 1860, and all that paid succession duty, had alike passed directly from father to son, and had paid the same rate of duty, viz., 1 per cent, the legacy duty would have amounted to 613,000*l*., while the succession duty would only have amounted to 279,000*l*. In other words, the value of property subject to legacy duty in 1860 was

about 61,000,000*l.*, while the value of property subject to succession duty was only 28,000,000*l.*, or considerably less than half the value of the property subject to legacy duty; and it is in this fact, rather than in the small difference between the proportions in which they respectively pass to direct descendants, that we find the real explanation of the disappointment of Mr. Gladstone's calculations.

Mr. Pitt's plan of legacy and succession duties.

In the debates to which the proposed succession duty gave rise, frequent reference was made to the plans of Mr. Pitt in the year 1796. In that year, it will be seen on reference to Parliamentary history, Mr. Pitt proposed two measures, or one measure in two bills. The first was a legacy duty on personal property, the second a duty on successions to landed estates. The duty was not to apply to direct descents, but was to vary from 2 to 6 per cent. upon legacies or devises to collateral relations and strangers in blood. The bill imposing the duty on personalty was passed by a considerable majority. The other bill also passed through its earlier stages by large majorities; but, when it came to a third reading, Mr. Francis denounced it in the strongest language as a measure "immoderately increasing the influence of the

Financial Policy.

Crown, and full of danger in its obvious conse- CHAP. IV.
quences to the constitution and freedom of the 1853.
country!" His reasons for this view were, that,
as the tax would not affect present possessors,
members of Parliament would be reckless as to
the amount of burdens they might be asked to
lay upon posterity, and that all check upon extravagance would be removed. Whether this
was the argument by which the members of the
Opposition were influenced does not appear;
but the motion that the bill be " now " read a
third time was lost by a majority of two. Mr.
Pitt then proposed that it be read a third time
" to-morrow," for which Mr. Sheridan desired
to substitute the words " this day three months."
Mr. Pitt on this occasion succeeded by a majority of one, and the word " to-morrow" was made
part of the question; but, when the question
itself came to be put, there was an equal division, and the Speaker gave his vote against proceeding to the third reading; upon which Mr.
Pitt withdrew the bill.*

More fortunate than Mr. Pitt, Mr. Gladstone Success of
succeeded in carrying his measure through all Mr. Gladstone.
its stages. The discussion to which it was sub-

---

* May. 12, 1796.

jected in Committee was very full, and a large number of amendments were moved; but none were carried which materially affected the principle of the bill. In the course of the debates Mr. Gladstone intimated his intention of proposing, as a complement to the duty on individual successions, a duty on corporate property; but no measure with this object was introduced, nor has the case of corporate property ever been dealt with in this respect.

Increase of the Irish spirit duties.

Amongst the other important features in the budget, we must not omit to notice the addition made to the Irish spirit duties. This was another point upon which it was Mr. Gladstone's good fortune to succeed, where some of his most eminent predecessors had failed. Twice before, in 1830 and in 1842, had attempts been made to raise these duties, and twice those attempts had failed. Lord Wallace's Revenue Commission in 1822, Sir Henry Parnell's Excise Commission in 1833, Lord Althorp in 1834, and Mr. Goulburn in 1843, had all borne testimony to the fact, that advances of duty were uniformly followed by extension of illicit distillation, by loss of revenue, and by increase of crime. The addition of 6*d*. per gallon made in 1830, therefore, had been followed by a reduction of 1*s*.

per gallon in 1835; and the additional 1*s*. per gallon imposed in 1842 had been taken off in 1843. Mr. Gladstone, however, not discouraged by these failures, made one more attempt in 1853; and, as the result has shown, he achieved entire success. The point at which he was aiming was, the ultimate equalisation of the spirit duties in all parts of the United Kingdom. "It is very doubtful," he said, "whether [equalisation] will ever be entirely attained; but such an approximation to it as would stop smuggling might perhaps at some time be reached. It is quite plain that such an equalisation cannot be attained without some reduction of the spirit duties in England. We must lower the English duties at a fitting time to some point up to which the others may be raised."* His anticipations, as will be seen from the foregoing extract, were far from sanguine; but in the following year he was so much encouraged by the results of his experiment that he proposed a further advance of duty; and again, in 1855, Sir George Lewis proposed a third; at which time, instead of lowering the duty on English spirits, he raised it to 8*s*. a gallon, and succeeded in equalising

---

* April 18, 1853.

the English and Scotch duties at this high rate. At length, in 1858, Mr. Disraeli put the finishing touch to the work, by raising the duty on Irish spirits likewise to the common level of 8*s*.; and since that time Mr. Gladstone has further raised the duty in the whole of the three kingdoms to the rate of 10*s*. per gallon, or very nearly four times the duty paid on Irish spirits before 1853. The subjoined note shows the successive steps by which the present rate of duty has been reached, beginning with the year 1825, when (as the Board of Inland Revenue tell us in their Fifth Report) the existing system of levying the duty may be said to have commenced.*

The extension of the Income Tax to Ireland,

Year.	England.		Scotland.		Ireland.	
	s.	*d.*	*s.*	*d.*	*s.*	*d.*
1825	7	0	2	10	2	10
1830	7	6	3	4	3	4
1835	...		...		2	4
1840	7	10	3	8	2	8
1842	...		...		3	8
1843	...		...		2	8
1853	...		4	8	3	4
1854	...		6	0	4	0
1855	8	0	8	0	6	2
1858	8	0	8	0	8	0
1860	10	0	10	0	10	0

Financial Policy. 215

and the commencement of the equalisation of the spirit duties, are two remarkable features in the finance of the year 1853.

The last of Mr. Gladstone's proposals for increasing the revenue was not quite so successful as the first two. This was the proposal relating to a revision of licences upon certain trades, from which he had expected to gain 113,000*l*. The House never came to a vote upon this subject; but the representations made to Mr. Gladstone by persons affected by the plan were so strong, and he found it necessary to make so many deductions from the scale he had drawn up, that he was brought ultimately to the conclusion that he had better abandon the scheme altogether.*

Another point upon which he was compelled to give way related to the advertisement duty. Before the introduction of the budget, two motions on matters of taxation had been carried against the Government. The first was Lord Robert Grosvenor's motion for leave to bring in a bill for the repeal of the attorneys' certificate duty, which was carried on the 10th of March by a majority of 52.† The second was Mr.

CHAP. IV.
1853.

Failure of the plan for the revision of trade licences,

and for the readjustment of the advertisement duty.

---

* See his statements, June 20 and July 20, 1853.
† By 219 to 167.

Milner Gibson's resolution affirming that the advertisement duty ought to be repealed, which was carried, on the 15th of April, by a majority of 31.* Both these questions had been dealt with in the budget. Mr. Gladstone had proposed to lower both classes of duty, but not to take off either of them altogether. This proposal did not satisfy their respective advocates; and when the Stamp duties' bill, dealing with these and other matters, had made some progress, it was found necessary to divide it into two, in order to facilitate the passing of the unopposed portion, leaving the two knotty points referred to for separate discussion. The disputed bill was brought forward in Committee on the 1st of July, and Mr. M. Gibson moved an amendment upon it. The Government proposed to reduce the advertisement duty from 1s. 6d. to 6d.; Mr. M. Gibson moved to repeal it altogether. He was defeated by a majority of 10.† A fresh debate ensued; and, when the main proposal was put to the vote, Mr. Crau-

---

* By 200 to 169. At the same time two other resolutions relating to the newspaper stamp duty and the excise duty on paper, were defeated by majorities of 182 and 199 respectively.

† By 109 to 99.

furd moved to substitute the cipher o for the figure 6, which motion he carried by a majority of 9.* So that the House, having first rejected a proposal that the advertisement duty should be abolished, afterwards decided that it should be fixed at zero. This was, of course, a reversal of the former vote; but the Speaker, on being appealed to, decided that there was nothing informal in the proceeding; and the result was, that the Government abandoned the advertisement duty altogether. They were more successful in resisting Lord Robert Grosvenor's attempt to proceed with his measure for the repeal of the attorneys' and solicitors' duty, which they defeated on the 20th July by a majority of 84.†

The other measures of remission contained in the budget were passed without much difficulty. A large number of Customs' duties were swept away, in accordance with a principle to which Mr. Gladstone said he attached much importance, namely, that of levying our revenue upon the fewest possible number of articles. Sir Robert Peel had already acted upon this principle to some extent in 1845; and Mr. Gladstone himself has since carried it to a great

marginalia: CHAP. IV. 1853. Advertisement duty repealed. Repeal of attorneys' certificate duty defeated. Abolition of minor customs' duties.

---

* By 70 to 61.   † By 186 to 102.

CHAP. IV.
1853.

Soap duty.

Assessed taxes.

length in his arrangements for 1860. It may be as well to mention here that a doubt was thrown upon its soundness by Sir G. Cornewall Lewis in 1857. Some remarks of Lord John Manners', on the difference of saving in the cost of collection produced by the repeal of customs' duties and the repeal of excise duties respectively, are also worthy of attention.* The repeal of the excise duty on soap was an important boon to the lower classes, but involved no new or remarkable principle. The alteration in the assessed taxes, however, demands a few words of comment. The mode in which these taxes had previously been assessed was by imposing heavy progressive duties upon articles, of which more than one was kept by the same person. Thus, if a man kept one four-wheeled two-horse carriage he was taxed 6*l*. ; if he kept two such carriages he was taxed 6*l*. 10*s*. upon each; if three, 7*l*. upon each, and so on until the tax rose to a maximum of 9*l*. 1*s*. 6*d*. upon each carriage; the same was also the case with other articles. This is a mode of taxation which Mr. J. S. Mill,† upon abstract grounds, selects

---

* May 30, 1853.
† Principles of Political Economy, b. v. chap. vi. sec. 3.

Financial Policy. 219

for particular commendation, because the tax is thus made to fall chiefly upon luxuries. One carriage may be, and often is, a necessary of life to persons in certain positions; two or more carriages can only be regarded as luxuries. But however sound this argument may be in the abstract, it was found that the practical effect of the system of progressive duties was, to cause much inconvenience to trade, as well as many complications and even frauds arising out of the compositions and exemptions with which it was accompanied. Before the introduction of the budget, Sir De Lacy Evans had brought the subject under consideration, and had introduced a bill* in the interest of the carriage-builders, for simplifying the system and for substituting three uniform rates of duty upon three classes of carriages for the twenty-six different rates, ranging from 1*l.* 5*s.* to 9*l.* 1*s.* 6*d.*, to which they were previously subject. He pointed out very clearly the loss caused to the coachbuilders by the decline which had taken place in the number of carriages built within the last ten or twelve years; but he withdrew his bill on the promise of Mr. Glad-

---

* April 12, 1853.

stone to give the subject his favourable consideration.

It now only remains to notice an important financial operation, not directly connected with the budget, which Mr. Gladstone attempted in the session of 1853. This was the projected reduction of interest upon a portion of the 3*l*. per cent. Consols, and the creation of a 2*l*. 10*s*. per cent. Stock. Consols at this time were quoted at par, or even somewhat higher.* There was no longer any stock in existence bearing a higher rate of interest than 3*l*. per cent., except the New $3\frac{1}{4}$ per cent. Stock, which would in the course of another year be reduced to 3 per cent.; and this last could not again be meddled with till 1874. If therefore anything important was to be done in the way of reducing the interest of the national debt, it could only be done by an operation upon Consols.† But this great fund resembled a strong and unassailable fortress, compared with which all smaller stocks, which

---

* In December, 1852, Consols had stood at $101\frac{1}{4}$. In January, 1853, they had fallen to $99\frac{1}{4}$. In March, when Mr. Gladstone's proposal was made, they were at $100\frac{1}{4}$.

† There were in truth two distinct stocks, Consols and the Reduced three per cents, which could thus be operated upon; but for the sake of brevity they are here spoken of as Consols, that being the principal stock.

Financial Policy.

had in former times been dealt with, were but unimportant outworks. Its magnitude alone was enormous. Lord Bexley had operated on a capital of 152,000,000*l.* in 1822; Lord Ripon upon a capital of 77,000,000*l.* in 1824; Mr. Goulburn upon a capital of 153,000,000*l.* in 1830, and again upon a capital of 248,000,000*l.* in 1844; but the 3*l.* per cent. Consols amounted to 500,000,000*l.*, or more than double the largest stock that had yet been touched. This, however, was only one feature of the case. What was more important to consider was, that while it was a comparatively simple and easy matter to propose to the holders of a 5*l.* per cent., or of a 4*l.* per cent. stock, that they should submit to a reduction in a rate of interest considerably above that at which it was in the power of the Government to borrow, it was quite another thing to make the same proposal to the holders of a 3*l.* per cent. stock; for, "as far as the history of the world has yet gone," said Mr. Gladstone, we have never known a much lower rate than this prevail. Another and a still greater difficulty arose from the fact that the State is not free to deal with Consols as it is with other stocks. If the prevailing rate of interest were but 2 per cent., or if the Government could at this moment lay its

CHAP. IV.
1853.

hands upon 500,000,000*l.*, it would still not be at liberty to pay off the holders of Consols; because the bargain with them is, that they shall receive a whole year's notice beforehand; and no Government could venture on the bold step of giving such a notice, and taking the consequences which might ensue from a change of circumstances in the interval. These great advantages thus possessed by Consols had in former times assisted the Government in effecting the conversion of other stocks. Consols always bore a higher relative value than other and higher-priced stocks, on account of the magnitude of the stock, and its greater security from conversion. The value of a stock depends upon its being readily marketable; and a large stock, of which there is always an abundant supply, and which is invested by any circumstances with a character of permanence, must necessarily be more marketable than a small one, which may come to be held by a few persons, or than a high-priced one, of which the interest may some day be reduced. The existence of such a stock necessarily gives an advantage to a Government dealing with the holders of a higher priced, but proportionately less valuable, stock. At worst, it has always the resource of borrowing in the

Financial Policy. 223

lower-priced, in order to pay off the higher-priced. This advantage was of course lost when the question became that of dealing with Consols itself. What had been a source of strength now became an embarrassment. There was no fulcrum for the lever, by which the great operation was to be wrought.

CHAP. IV.
1853.

Nevertheless, Mr. Gladstone's courage did not fail him. He saw the impossibility of storming the fortress, but he thought he might induce it to capitulate. The terms he offered were as follow:—The holders of Three per cent. Stock (whether Consols or Reduced) were to be entitled to exchange it either for a New 3½ per cent. Stock, guaranteed against redemption for forty years, at the rate of 82*l*. 10*s*. of the new for every 100*l*. of the old stock; or, for a New 2½ per cent. Stock, also guaranteed against redemption for forty years, at the rate of 110*l*. of the new for every 100*l*. of the old; or for Exchequer bonds at par. These Exchequer bonds were in the first instance to bear interest at 2*l*. 15*s*. per cent. for not more than ten years, and then at 2*l*. 10*s*. per cent. for the residue of forty years from their first issue, and were finally to be redeemable at par; but whether at the option of the holders or at the option of the

Terms offered by Mr. Gladstone.

Government, was left to be determined thereafter, in order that Mr. Gladstone might be able to ascertain by actual experiment on what terms the holders of 3 per cent. Stock would accept them.

Those who accepted the first of these alternatives—the conversion of their 3 per cent. Stock into 3½ per cent.—would receive in respect of every 100*l.* stock an annuity of 2*l.* 17*s.* 9*d.*, guaranteed against reduction or redemption for forty years, instead of an annuity of 3*l.* as at present. At the end of the term of the guarantee the 3½ per cent. Stock so created would be redeemable by Parliament, while the capital of this portion of the debt would be reduced in consequence of the operation by 17½ per cent. Those who accepted the second alternative would receive in respect of every 100*l.* stock an annuity of 2*l.* 15*s.*, instead of an annuity of 3*l.* ; but the capital of this portion of the debt would be increased by 10 per cent.; and, though this portion also would at the expiration of forty years be redeemable by Parliament, yet, being only a 2½ per cent. Stock, it was not likely to be redeemed, as a 3½ per cent. Stock probably might be. It being thought probable that a great demand might arise for this 2½ per cent. Stock,

Financial Policy. 225

and that a considerable augmentation might thus be occasioned in the capital of the debt, Mr. Gladstone thought it prudent to limit the amount to be created; and it was provided that not more than 30,000,000*l.* of the new stock should be issued. In these two alternatives Mr. Gladstone only proposed terms similar to those which had been offered by his predecessors on former occasions; but the third alternative was of a more novel kind. He proposed to create a new security in the form of Exchequer-bonds, which were to be as easily transferable as Exchequer-bills, while they would have the advantage of bearing a rate of interest somewhat above that at which Exchequer-bills were usually issued,* and of having that rate secured for a long period. These bonds were to be issued to the extent of 30,000,000*l.* in exchange either for Exchequer-bills, or for 3 per cent. Stock. Mr. Gladstone, anticipating an objection which might be made to the exchange of Exchequer-bills, bearing interest at the rate of 1½ per cent., for Exchequer-bonds at 2¾ per cent.,

CHAP. IV.
1853.

---

* Exchequer-bills at this time bore interest at the rate of 1*d.* per diem, or 1*l.* 10*s.* 5*d.* per annum, but this was unusually low.

CHAP. IV.
1853.

showed that the state of the Exchequer-bill market was always extremely variable, "like a summer sky," and that when occasions had arisen which rendered necessary the funding of these securities, it had been effected at rates never below 3*l*. 6*s*. per cent., and sometimes as high as 4*l*. 6*s*. 8*d*. per cent.

The minor stocks.

Such were the main points in this scheme. A subordinate portion of it, which in the result, however, proved the most important portion, related to the liquidation of some small but time-honoured stocks, the debt to the South Sea Company, the old and new South Sea annuities, and the Bank annuities of 1720, amounting in the whole to about 9,500,000*l*. To the holders of these were offered the same alternatives as to the holders of Consols and of 3 per cents. Reduced, but with the difference that notice was given them, that in default of their accepting the terms, they should be paid off in money in January 1854.

Prevalent opinion as to approaching fall in the rate of interest.

It would seem, from the tone of the newspaper money-market articles, and of other indicators of public opinion, that the plan of the Chancellor of the Exchequer was very favourably received. The idea which appears to have prevailed, both within and without the walls of the House of Commons, was, that the terms were, if anything, too liberal; and that the 2½ per cent. Stock, in particular, would be greedily taken up. For some reason or other, there was a strong impression afloat that the time was at hand when a great and permanent reduction was to take place in the rate of interest. The stock of bullion in the Bank of England was undoubtedly very high, and the rate of discount unusually low. France was reducing her 5 per cent. rentes to 4½ per cent., and the East India Company was effecting a similar conversion of a portion of its debt. But the public were excited to a belief that much greater changes than these were about to happen. It was thought that the discoveries of gold in California and Australia would produce a revolution in the rate of interest; though why they should do so is a question more easily asked than answered. The rate of interest depends ultimately upon the proportion between the supply of capital and the demand for it. An influx of gold bullion may for the moment produce a great effect on the money-market; but gold, like corn or cotton, must be paid for; and the production of commodities to pay for it will create a demand for capital, which will probably be fully proportioned to the increased supply. There were indeed those who thought that the large discoveries of gold would reduce its value as a medium for the purchase of commodities. It is certainly possible that they may have this effect. Perhaps they have already to some extent produced it. But there seems no reason for concluding that an alteration in the relative value of gold and of other commodities would lead to a reduction in the rate of interest or to a rise of the funds. Indeed there were some who maintained, with a good deal of plausibility, that it would operate in precisely the opposite direction; for, said they, if the value of gold falls, the value of stock (which represents a right to receive a certain quantity of gold) will also fall; fewer people will buy stock; the funds will fall, and the rate of interest will rise. Few seemed to perceive that all this discussion as to the relative value of money and commodities had little or nothing to do with the question of the rate of interest. If, in a certain state of the market, 100*l.* will command 3*l.* a-year interest, there is no reason why those proportions should be altered, even though gold should become only half as valuable in relation to commodities as before; for the same circum-

Financial Policy.

stances which would reduce the purchasing value of the 100*l.* capital would reduce the purchasing value of the 3*l.* interest in exactly the same degree. The expectations of a great reduction in the rate of interest, founded on the discoveries of gold, therefore, seem to have been rather unreasonable. Other persons argued that the result in question was to be expected, because the value of money had for many years been progressively diminishing. But Mr. Gladstone himself pointed out the fallacy of this idea, showing that there had been a time (1739)* when the rate of interest was lower than in 1853; and that the 3 per cent. stocks had then stood at the high price of 107; that from that point they had gradually fallen to about 50,†and then had again risen till they now stood at par. There was, however, in this fall and subsequent rise no certain indication of the probability of a further rise. The rate of interest had been raised by an extraordinary demand for capital in connection with our long and expensive wars. That demand and its effects had now to a great extent passed away, and the rate

---

* June, 1737 (?).
† In June 1797, they fell to $47\frac{1}{2}$. This was at the time of the mutiny at the Nore.

of interest had returned to something like its original level. It did not follow that it would fall much below it. The national capital, indeed, was rapidly accumulating; but the demand upon it, arising out of the development of the national industry, was advancing with at least equal rapidity. More capital was seeking investment; but more investments were contending for capital. The public funds had to sustain the competition of railway debentures, joint-stock companies' shares, and a hundred other absorbents of capital; and this competition of course tended to keep up the rate of interest. The prevalent idea, in short, seems to have been somewhat of a prevalent delusion.

There was, however, this feature to distinguish it from other delusions,—nobody appeared disposed to act upon it. A small quantity of the $2\frac{1}{2}$ per cent. stock (3,007,672*l.*) was taken; and so was a trifling amount of $3\frac{1}{2}$ per cent. stock (240,746*l.*), and a very few bonds (418,300*l.*); but these last were chiefly in exchange, not for Consols, but for Exchequer-bills,* on which the Chancellor of the Exchequer was then reducing the interest. The South Sea Company dissented

---

* The amount taken in exchange for Exchequer-bills was 408,900*l.*

as a body from the terms proposed in respect of its stock and annuities, and demanded payment in cash to the extent of about 8,000,000*l*. It afterwards became a question whether the failure of the scheme did not result from the untoward events of the year, from the complication of affairs in the East, and the deficiency in the harvest; but it is to be borne in mind that this decision of the South Sea Company to dissent from the proposed terms was taken, as regards one portion of the annuities, as early as in May, at a time when there was no particular anxiety as to the state of foreign affairs, and when Consols still stood at 100¾.

It is necessary here to say a few words on another matter closely connected with the foregoing. When Lord Aberdeen's Government came into office, they found about 17,750,000*l*. of Exchequer-bills afloat, of which those dated in March bore an interest of 1½*d*. a-day, and those dated in June an interest of 1¼*d*. a-day. The premium on the March bills was very high; it had reached at one time from 70*s*. to 80*s*. per cent. When these bills came to maturity, Mr. Gladstone, who had large balances in the Exchequer to support him in case of need, reduced the interest to 1*d*. a-day, or 1*l*. 10*s*. 4*d*.

Reduction of the interest on Exchequer-bills.

per cent. per annum. This step he took in the face of an advance of the Bank rate of discount. It succeeded, however, and the whole amount of the March bills (about 8,500,000*l.*) were exchanged at the reduced rate. When the June bills came to maturity, a similar attempt was made, but not with the same result. Of the 9,250,000*l.* Exchequer-bills falling due in June only 5,890,000*l.* were exchanged at the reduced rate of interest; 408,900*l.* were exchanged for the new Exchequer-bonds; and about 3,000,000*l.* had to be paid out of the Exchequer balances. The effect of this was to reduce the amount of the unfunded debt, and to save the country a certain sum in interest, at the cost only of reducing the national balances, which were lying idle, and which were, as Mr. Gladstone thought, unnecessarily large. It would have been a better bargain for the country under other circumstances; but the necessity which speedily followed of again raising the rate of interest on the Exchequer-bills, and of issuing more of them in order to meet the claims of the dissentient South Sea fundholders, materially diminished the saving to the public; and, at the end of the financial year, the amount of Exchequer-bills was once more as large as at its commencement, and the interest upon them was 2*d*. instead of 1*d*. per day, while the balances in the Exchequer had been seriously drawn upon, and Deficiency-bills had been issued to a greater extent than had for some time been the case. What made this the more unfortunate of course was, that the country was then upon the verge of a serious war; and, although Mr. Gladstone maintained* that there was no inconvenience in raising 2,000,000*l*. or 3,000,000*l*. by Deficiency-bills, it will hardly be thought to be very desirable that a Chancellor of the Exchequer should be driven to this step just before the outbreak of war, and with a floating debt of more than 17,000,000*l*.†

Operations of the kind which have just been described must, after all, be judged by their result. There were many circumstances to be pleaded in mitigation of Mr. Gladstone's failure; and, if the harvest of 1853 had been good, and the dispute between Russia and Turkey had not occurred, and no other unforeseen event had disturbed the money-market, he might have succeeded in producing a sensible impression

---

* March 6, 1854.
† The amount of the Exchequer-bills was 16,437,000*l*. and there were Ways and Means bills unredeemed to the amount of 790,000*l*.

upon a great mass of the public debt. Had he done so, he would have deserved, and would have obtained, great credit for the accuracy of his judgment and the happy selection of his opportunity. As matters turned out, we have only to regret, as he himself afterwards regretted, that he attempted what proved to be above his power to accomplish. The slight saving which he actually effected by the transaction was not worth the cost at which it was purchased.

But whatever may be thought of this portion of the finance of 1853, and however inopportune may have been the steps which have been described, when a war was on the eve of breaking out, we should take a narrow view of the whole policy of the year if we failed to recognize the immense strength which it imparted to the country, and which enabled us to grapple successfully with the difficulties of the following period. The Government of Lord Aberdeen have sometimes been accused of incompetency, or of culpable negligence, for having brought forward such a budget as that of 1853 on the eve of a war which they ought to have foreseen. Whether they ought to have foreseen it or not, is a question not to be discussed here. Whether, if they had distinctly foreseen it, they would have brought forward exactly the budget they did, may be doubted; but the great features of that budget—the settlement of the Income Tax question, and, in a lesser but still in an important degree, the revision of our indirect taxation—mark it as a budget eminently calculated to strengthen the position of a country which was about to embark in a serious and expensive struggle. The declining condition of the revenue, which Sir Robert Peel arrested with a strong hand when he imposed the Income Tax and revised the Tariff in 1842, was not more perilous than was the state of things with which Mr. Gladstone had to deal in 1853. The discredit which had been thrown upon the Income Tax in 1851, and the reappearance in the policy of Lord J. Russell's Government of those symptoms of financial weakness which had characterized the Administration of Lord Melbourne, were indications of a growing evil, which, had it not been stayed, might have wrought fatal effects when the nation came to bear the burden of the Crimean war. That war, as we now acknowledge, revealed to us many imperfections in our military system; but the strain on our finances brought to light nothing but their soundness and their vigour.

Could we have borne that strain as we did, if it had not been for the life which Sir Robert Peel first infused, and which Mr. Gladstone afterwards renewed, in our fiscal system, and but for which 1854 might have found us struggling with an overwhelming deficiency, or inextricably entangled in the toils which must attend a reconstruction of the Income Tax? It was well for England that, in this respect at least, we had set our house in order before the day of trial came upon us.

Financial Policy.

Chapter V.

EFORE proceeding to the consideration of the general finance of 1854, we should take notice of an important change which was made, at the beginning of the session, in the mode of keeping the public accounts. This was a matter which had attracted the attention of Lord Derby's Government in 1852, and with which they had expressed their intention of dealing if they had remained in office. Mr. Williams had brought forward a motion on the subject in 1853, and Mr. Gladstone had promised to attend to it. In fulfilment of this engagement he introduced, on the 2nd of February, 1854, a measure intended to facilitate the proposed change.

As I hope to be able to devote a chapter to the subject of the Public Accounts, I shall con-

Chap. V.
———
1854.

Introduction of the system of paying the gross revenue into the Exchequer.

tent myself here with saying that the object of the change was, to bring the whole of the gross revenue of the country* into the Exchequer, and to provide for the expense of its collection by taking votes in supply on account of the revenue departments. Hitherto the practice had been, to pay all the expenses of collection out of the gross revenue, and to bring the net revenue or balance only into the Exchequer. Moreover, the growing revenue was charged, not only with the expenses of its collection, but with certain pensions and other payments wholly unconnected with it, which had from time to time been authorized by acts of parliament. Some of these pensions and payments Mr. Gladstone now proposed to buy up and extinguish; others he proposed to transfer to the Consolidated Fund: and others, again, were to be brought into the estimates, and voted like the rest of our expenditure. At the same time he proposed to bring upon the estimates some of the charges hitherto borne by the Consolidated Fund. The effect of these alterations will be seen in the comparison of the

---

* By this phrase the revenue from the Customs, Excise, and other taxes is intended. The revenue derived from the Crown lands stands on a different footing.

budgets of the years preceding and the years succeeding them. Since 1855 the revenue has appeared to be greater by about 4,000,000*l.* than it would have been if the accounts had been kept on the old system; but this apparent addition to the income of the country has been balanced by a corresponding addition to the expenditure, in the form of estimates voted for the collection of the revenue, and for the other charges to which I have already referred. The proportions of the Consolidated Fund charges and of the Miscellaneous estimates have also been altered.

The interest which attaches to the finance of the year 1854 is twofold. It was the test-year of the measures of 1853; and it was the first year of the Russian war. As regards the first point it appeared that, so far as the commercial policy of 1853 was in question, Mr. Gladstone's measures had been eminently successful. The customs, which in the year 1852-3 had produced 20,396,000*l.*, produced 20,703,000*l.* in the year 1853-4, notwithstanding a remission of taxation in this branch amounting to 1,483,000*l.* The excise, again, which in the year 1852-3 had produced 14,890,000*l.*, produced 15,263,000*l.* in the year 1853, notwithstanding an excess of taxes remitted over taxes imposed, which had

CHAP. V.
1854.

Financial character of the year 1854.

been estimated at 222,000*l.* The reduction of the Stamp-duties on receipts, too, had proved highly successful; and, instead of producing a loss to the revenue, had brought it up to an increased amount. The addition to the Irish spirit duty had not led, as it was feared it would, to smuggling or illicit distillation; and the addition to the revenue in consequence of that step had been somewhat greater than had been anticipated. On the other hand, a rather smaller increase than had been expected had been realized in Scotland; but this appeared to be more owing to moral than to fiscal causes. The extension of the Income Tax to Ireland, and to incomes of 100*l.*, had produced somewhat more than had been reckoned on. The Succession-duty had produced considerably less; but this was the only point upon which Mr. Gladstone's estimate of revenue had been materially disappointed.

Apart, then, from the questions connected with the management of the unfunded debt, and the conversion of the South Sea Stocks, the finance of 1853 had proved successful. With regard to these there was a great deal of controversy, the details of which are more than sufficiently intricate. The case of the Exchequer-bills was in substance simple enough. Mr.

Gladstone had reduced the rate of interest when the state of the money-market enabled him to do so. That he did not reduce it too far in March 1853, would appear from the fact that the lower rate was accepted by all the holders of bills. In June the circumstances of the money-market were less favourable; and a certain number of bill-holders would not submit to the reduction of interest, and preferred to present their bills for payment; but this alone would have caused no loss to the Exchequer, as it only involved the application of some 3,000,000*l.*, which were lying idle at the Bank, to the reduction of the floating debt. If reducing the balances weakens the Exchequer, reducing the floating debt strengthens it; and the one operation is a set-off against the other. In point of fact, Mr. Gladstone argued * that, even as things turned out, the country gained about 60,000*l.* by the transaction; that is to say, that the charge for interest on the Exchequer-bills of 1853 was less by 60,000*l.* than it would have been if the rate had been maintained at 1¼*d.* a-day throughout the year, and if no bills had been presented in June. But the conversion of the South Sea

---

* May 8, 1854.

Stock, or rather the redemption of 8,000,000*l.* of debt at par, was an unfortunate step, both in its effect upon the Exchequer-bill transactions, and in its general bearing upon the balances. A portion of this 8,000,000*l.* was undoubtedly taken out of balances which were lying idle; but a portion also was taken out of accruing surplus revenue, which would otherwise have been applied to the redemption of debt, not at par but at 90 or 91. Indeed, the fortunate dissentients, who received their money in full on the 5th of January, were able to reinvest it on the following day at a profit of nearly 10 per cent. But without entering into these details, we can see at once that for a government to employ such a sum of money as this in the purchase of 3 per cent. Stock at par, and then, within a few months or a year, to be obliged to borrow a much larger sum by the issue of Exchequer-bonds at 3*l.* 10*s.* per cent., and by loan in 3 per cent. Stock at 87 or 88, is a losing bargain. It is the weakest point in the finance of 1853.*

---

* It is curious to observe the relative values of the funded and unfunded securities in 1853 and 1854. In the beginning of 1853, Consols were at par, yielding an interest of 3*l.* per cent. Exchequer-bills were at 1¼*d.* per cent. a-day, or 1*l.* 18*s.* per annum, and these were at a premium. In Sep-

Financial Policy. 243

The budget for 1854-5 has now to be considered. It was brought forward, in the first instance, on the 6th of March; but the growing demands of the war rendered it necessary for Mr. Gladstone to introduce a second scheme on the 8th of May. The two plans will be described in their order.

On the 6th of March Mr. Gladstone estimated the revenue for 1854-5 at 53,349,000*l.* The charge for the debt he took at 27,546,000*l.*; the remaining expenditure, leaving out of consideration the extraordinary demands arising out of the war, would be 27,393,000*l.* To this he proposed to add a sum of 1,250,000*l.* as a special grant on account of the extraordinary expense of the expedition to the East. We were sending out a force of 25,000 men; it was, he said, uncertain what demands the war might occasion; and, as Parliament would be sitting for several months, there would be abundant time to ask for further grants if they should become

CHAP. V.
1854.

Budget of 1854-5, March 6.

---

tember 1854, Consols were at 94, yielding an interest of 3*l.* 3*s.* 10*d.* per cent.: but Exchequer-bills were at 2¼*d.* per cent. a-day, or 3*l.* 8*s.* 6*d.* per annum, and they were at par or at a discount. We see here one of the effects of the steps which alarmed the holders of Exchequer-bills, and which defeated the plan of reducing the amount of these securities.

CHAP. V.
1854.

necessary; all therefore which the Government now asked for was, a vote of 50*l*. per man, which was the smallest sum that would be required for sending the troops out and bringing them home again. This addition to the estimates brought them up to a total of 56,189,000*l*., or to 2,840,000*l*. above the estimated income of the year. It became, then, the question how this deficiency should be made up. Mr. Gladstone hoped it would not be by retracing the steps taken in 1853, by restoring the soap duty, or arresting the fall of the tea duty. About a million, he said, might be added to the revenue in this way; but it would be at the cost of a serious disturbance of trade and of great discomfort to a multitude of persons. Nor was he prepared to propose any present addition to our other indirect taxation; although he could not promise that, in the event of the war continuing, indirect taxation should not be increased. Neither would he ask the House to sanction a loan; such a step at that moment was neither required by the necessities, nor worthy of the character, of the country; but he would not confine himself to the present moment; he took the opportunity thus early, and, as it were, on the threshold of the war, to urge upon the House the importance of resolving that, so far as might be possible, they would meet the expenses of that war out of taxation, and not by the creation of debt. Having thus explained his objections to every other course that could be suggested for meeting the deficiency, he turned naturally to the Income Tax as the only remaining resource at his disposal, and proposed that it should be increased by one half, but that the whole amount of the addition should be levied in respect of the first moiety of the year;—in other words, that the Income Tax should be doubled for half a year. This would add 3,307,000*l.* to the revenue of the year, and would convert the deficit of 2,840,000*l.* into a surplus of 467,000*l.* This form of addition he proposed, in preference to altering the rate of the tax for the whole year, on account of the uncertainty then attending the probable course of events and the demands to be expected in connection with the war. If he had only added 50 per cent. to the amount of the tax for the whole year, it might afterwards have become necessary for him to come and make another demand for 50 per cent. more, in a form which would have involved a second alteration, and that, perhaps, a retrospective alteration, in the amount of the tax for the first

CHAP. V.
1854.

half-year. If, on the other hand, he had at once asked for a double Income Tax for the whole year, he would have been asking for that which might, after all, not be required. He was indeed making a budget rather for a half year than a whole year, and this addition to the first moiety of the Income Tax was in the nature of a provisional arrangement.

All Mr. Gladstone's budget speeches, (by which expression I wish to draw attention to the speeches rather than to the budgets they introduce,) are eminently characteristic. What makes them peculiarly interesting is, not so much the beauty of the language in which they are couched, as the breadth of the sentiments they express, and the comprehensiveness of the principles they set forth. The audience feel that the facts and the arguments laid before them are the outpourings of a well-stored and thoughtful mind,—not merely a stock of matter gathered together for the nonce. "*Suave est de magno tollere acervo.*" But that which thus gives these speeches an interest for the hearers is often productive of inconvenience, either at the moment or long afterwards, to the speaker. Mr. Gladstone seems to forget the wise man's caution,— "Let nothing be in excess." He is not satisfied with saying enough for his immediate purpose; he goes beyond it, and lays down broad principles, and commits himself to general doctrines, which he afterwards finds it would have been more prudent to have avoided touching upon. Mr. Sheridan once found fault with a budget speech of Mr. Pitt's, because the minister had, as he said, laid down his pencil and slate, and assumed the truncheon. There may be occasions upon which this is necessary. The budget of 1853 was perhaps a case in point. When a great object is to be accomplished a great effort must be made. But great efforts should not be made when they are not required. In March, 1854, Mr. Gladstone had a simple task to perform; and his reasons for resorting to the Income Tax rather than to a loan might have been very briefly stated. Instead of so stating them, however, he took occasion to enter into the general question of the mode in which war expenditure should be met; to impress upon the House the importance of raising in each year the supplies necessary for the year by taxation rather than by loan; and to support his argument by a reference not only to economical, but to moral considerations. "The expenses of a war are the moral check which it has pleased the Almighty to impose upon the ambition and the lust of conquest that are inherent in so many nations. There is pomp and circumstance, there is glory and excitement about war, which, notwithstanding the miseries it entails, invests it with charms in the eyes of the community, and tends to blind men to those evils to a fearful and dangerous degree. The necessity of meeting from year to year the expenditure which it entails is a salutary and a wholesome check, making them feel what they are about, and making them measure the cost of the benefit upon which they may calculate. It is by these means that they may be led and brought to address themselves to a war policy as rational and intelligent beings, and may be induced to keep their eye well fixed both upon the necessity of the war into which they are about to enter, and their determination of availing themselves of the first and earliest prospects of concluding an honourable peace." In making this appeal, Mr. Gladstone cannot be said to have been guilty of the precise fault with which Mr. Pitt was charged; for, when he laid aside his pencil and slate, it was certainly not a truncheon which he took up in their place. But however sound and just his argument may be in itself, and however weighty it would be in the mouth of an independent member resisting a proposal on the part of the Government to carry on a questionable war by the aid of loans, it was singularly unfortunate in that of a Minister who, with his colleagues, was at that very moment calling upon the nation to engage in a struggle, which was certainly not prompted by "ambition," or "the lust of conquest," and the speedy close of which was to be hoped for, rather from a display of energetic determination to spend and be spent in the cause, than from a deliberate and public adoption of the policy of so adjusting its burdens as to impose a "moral check" upon the ardour of the people. Mr. Gladstone's language upon this occasion was very liable to misconstruction; and it was in fact misconstrued, much to the detriment of his own influence, when at a later period he advocated the cause of peace. At the same time it did little to promote the particular object he had in view; for there was at that time a general agreement that recourse ought not then to be had to a loan; and when, a few weeks later, affairs became more serious, Mr. Gladstone himself was compelled to have recourse to the issue of Exchequer-bonds, that is to say, to loans in anticipation of taxes; and in the following year his successor, Sir George Lewis, was reduced to the necessity of raising a large sum by a regular old-fashioned loan, and Mr. Gladstone could say nothing but that he approved the step.

The second financial statement was made on the 8th of May. By that time it had been found necessary to frame new estimates, and to ask Parliament for a sum of 6,850,000*l.** more than had been contemplated on the 6th of March. To meet this demand Mr. Gladstone proposed, in the first place, to double the Income Tax for the second half of the year, thus making its total produce 12,832,000*l.*; and not only to double it for the nonce, but to provide for the continuance of the tax at the double rate, or 14*d.* in the pound, till the close of the war. He proposed also to raise the duties on Scotch and Irish spirits, the former by 1*s.*, the latter by 8*d.* a gallon. From this addition he expected to gain 450,000*l.* He further proposed a fresh plan for

---

* This amount was made up as follows:—

		£.
Supplementary Navy Estimates	. . .	4,550,000
,, Army ditto	. . . .	300,000
,, Ordnance ditto	. . .	640,000
,, Militia ditto	. . .	500,000
,, Vote of Credit	. . .	850,000

Financial Policy. 251

the classification of sugars, and a new scale of duties, intended at once to remove the injustice of taxing low qualities and higher qualities at the same rate, and to bring an amount of 700,000*l*. into the Exchequer. Lastly, he proposed to raise the malt duty from 2*s*. 8½*d*. to 4*s*. per bushel, by which step he expected to gain an additional revenue of 2,450,000*l*. These several sums would just make up the amount required to meet the addition of 6,850,000*l*. to the estimates, and would leave undisturbed the surplus already calculated on.

But although the sums thus to be provided would, when received, meet the expenditure to be incurred, it was to be borne in mind that a considerable proportion of them would not be received until after the close of the financial year, in consequence of the length of credit allowed to the payers of Income Tax and of the malt duty, while the expenditure would have to be provided for by immediate payments. To meet the demands of the year, therefore, Mr. Gladstone asked, and ultimately obtained, leave to issue Exchequer-bonds to the amount of 6,000,000*l*. in three series of 2,000,000*l*. each, payable respectively in 1858, 1859, and 1860. Mr. Gladstone had already, some days before making

CHAP. V.
1854.

Issue of Exchequer bonds.

CHAP. V.
1854.

this statement, viz. on the 21st of April, issued a notice calling for tenders for an advance upon securities of this description;* and the appearance of this notice had been the occasion of many remarks. On the 6th of March Mr. Gladstone had taken authority to issue Exchequer-bills to the amount of 1,750,000*l.* in anticipation of the first half of the doubled Income Tax. On the 11th of April, the day before the House rose for the Easter recess, he had stated that the Treasury had not yet issued nearly the whole of that amount, and that the amount issued fell short of the amount authorized by 1,174,000*l.* To this statement he had added that he had no present reason to expect that he

---

* The notice contemplated an exchange of Exchequer-bills for Exchequer-bonds as well as a direct advance of money. As, however, the Exchequer-bills so exchanged might have been re-issued, the transaction would have been in the nature of an advance of money.

The arrangement has some resemblance to that effected by Mr. Vansittart in 1814; when the holders of Exchequer-bills, which it was proposed to fund, were invited to contribute a further sum in money, and to receive in return debentures exchangeable for money or stock on the 5th of April 1815, or on the 5th of April in any subsequent year, on three months' notice being given. Perhaps, however, this plan more nearly resembles the amended Exchequer-bill system introduced in 1861.

should have to make any further demand for Exchequer-bills in the course of the session, nor even that he should have to issue the whole amount already authorized. Yet, on the 21st of April, before the conclusion of the recess, an advertisement calling for tenders for an advance upon Exchequer-bonds had appeared in the Gazette. This step was in accordance with precedent; but it was one certainly calculated to surprise the House of Commons, especially when considered in connection with Mr. Gladstone's recent strong language with regard to loans. When challenged with his apparent inconsistency in this respect, Mr. Gladstone justified himself by saying that an advance of money upon Exchequer-bonds redeemable in a few years' time was a different thing from a loan contracted in perpetual annuities, especially if the sum thus raised were only in anticipation of the produce of taxes already imposed. The distinction, though somewhat subtile, is in truth an important one; but it was obvious from the first that these Exchequer-bonds might very possibly not be redeemed when they came to maturity, but might be treated like Exchequer-bills, and renewed from time to time for an indefinite period. The result proves the correctness of these anticipations. They were therefore an addition, not indeed to the funded, but to the unfunded debt. Together with the 1,750,000*l.* of Exchequer-bills already sanctioned, they constituted an addition to the unfunded debt amounting to 7,750,000*l.*, or rather to 7,125,000*l.*, as a portion of the Exchequer-bills were exchanged for bonds. In some respects the new bonds were a more, and in others a less, convenient form of security than Exchequer-bills. The rate of interest upon them was fixed for the whole term they had to run; it was therefore necessary to make it higher than the rate at which Exchequer-bills could have been issued. On the other hand the Treasury was secure for a considerable time from the danger of having a large amount of securities presented for payment at a moment when the claim could not easily be met. The subject, however, is one which I need not pursue.*

---

* The public seem to have viewed them with little favour. Very few tenders were made in the first instance; the Treasury then published the reserved price for their issue, which was 98*l.* 15*s.*, with interest payable upon the whole bond from the date of issue, giving an advantage equivalent to a bonus of 15*s.* per cent. The bonds bore interest at 3*l.* 10*s.* per cent., and the investment at the reserved price was equal to nearly 3*l.* 11*s.* 6*d.* per cent. Exchequer-bills were at this time paying 3*l.* 8*s.* 6*d.*, and Consols 3*l.* 7*s.* 6*d.* per cent.

Financial Policy. 255

The running fight, which was kept up throughout the session of 1854, respecting the merits and the demerits of Mr. Gladstone's financial arrangements, is partly entertaining and partly perplexing. I remember a Londoner's advising his friend from the country to take his stand one thick November day in a certain part of the Park, where he could have "a good view of the fog." Any uninitiated person who might have a fancy for a good view of the intricacies of the English mode of keeping the public accounts would do well to plunge into the discussions of 1854, and try to comprehend them by the light of unassisted common sense. The proposition of Mr. Canning, that you may prove anything by figures, was never more completely illustrated than by the confusion of the arguments drawn from the Finance Accounts, and other authentic documents of the year, not by mere private members, but by Chancellors and ex-Chancellors of the Exchequer, Governors of the Bank of England, and men of business intimately connected with the transactions of the money-market. I do not attempt to conduct the reader into this maze of controversy. I could not hope to render it intelligible, or to do justice to the arguments on either side, without be-

CHAP. V.
1854.
Controversy respecting Mr Gladstone's financial arrangements.

ing intolerably tedious. The chief accusations against Mr. Gladstone were, that he had mismanaged the Exchequer-bill market in 1853; that he had emptied the Treasury by his injudicious attempt at converting the South Sea and other stocks; that he had made an improper use of the Savings' banks' monies to sustain his operations; that he had crippled the Bank of England, and through it the trade and commerce of the country, by drawing largely upon it for aid in the shape of Deficiency-bills; and that by the general tenor of his measures he had disquieted and weakened the money-market at a time when it was most important that it should be strong. Some of these charges were unfounded, and some exaggerated; but there was, no doubt, much truth in others. The cardinal error appears to have lain in the attempt to convert the South Sea and minor stocks in the then state of the money-market, whilst another great operation (that upon the Exchequer-bills) was actually in progress, and while the political horizon was not absolutely unclouded. By trying to do too much at once, Mr. Gladstone brought upon himself the necessity of emptying the Exchequer, of pressing hard upon the resources of the Bank, and of disturbing the money-market just before

Financial Policy. 257

the outbreak of a war. The use made of the
Savings' banks' monies was both legal and in accordance with precedent; but, though capable of a complete justification, it is a step which always provokes criticism, and it was unfortunate that Mr. Gladstone should have been compelled to have recourse to it in support of an operation of his own, which, as we have seen, was of doubtful advantage. As regards the Deficiency-bills, while it is quite true that Mr. Gladstone did not in reality overdraw the public account to the extent which his opponents represented, and that he generally had an Exchequer balance at the Bank much larger than the amount taken out by Deficiency-bills, the net result was certainly the withdrawal from the Bank of a very large sum of money which his predecessors had kept there, and the consequent diminution of the fund available for the discounting of commercial bills. In short, turn it how we may, it is impossible to spend one's balance and to keep it; and the balance, or the greater part of it, had been spent in paying off the dissentient fund-holders, greatly to their advantage, and, upon the whole, to the State's disadvantage. This appears to be the upshot of the case.

By far the most important of the questions

S

CHAP. V.
1854.

The question between taxes and loans.

raised by the discussions of 1854, however, was that relating to the mode in which the demands of a war should be met; that is to say, whether they should be met by taxes or by loans. Mr. Gladstone, as has been said, warmly advocated the former principle. He had, even in 1853, reproduced in his budget speech the argument of Sir H. Parnell,* that, had Mr. Pitt had recourse to the Income Tax at the commencement of the Revolutionary war, that war might have been carried on without any addition being made to the national debt; and in several of his speeches in 1854 he had strongly censured the financial policy pursued by Mr. Pitt in the earlier years of the war, contrasting it unfavourably with his later and nobler efforts to raise the supplies by the aid of the Income Tax. This censure had the effect of calling forth in 1855 a most interesting and valuable pamphlet by Mr. Newmarch,† containing an examination of Mr. Pitt's loans, and a spirited defence of his financial policy, as being that which the circumstances of the country forced upon him. His comparison of the effects of loans contracted

---

* See Sir H. Parnell's "Financial Reform," p. 272.
† "The Loans raised by Mr. Pitt during the first French War, 1793-1801, with some statements in defence of the methods of funding employed." London, 1855.

in high-priced and low-priced stocks respectively is peculiarly instructive. The statements and arguments of Mr. Newmarch seem to have had great weight with Sir George Lewis, and to have influenced the course taken by that Minister in his financial arrangements for 1855.

The question at issue between the advocates of loans and the advocates of taxes ought to be considered from two distinct points of view; that is to say, it should be considered as an abstract and as a practical question. If we regard it as an abstract question of political economy, it is by no means so clear as Mr. Gladstone seems to have thought it. Of course it is true that it would be a very good thing for the country at the present moment if we were not burdened with the 600,000,000*l*. of debt contracted by Mr. Pitt and his successors; that is to say, it would be a good thing provided we could be relieved of the charge without any other alteration in the circumstances of the nation. It is also evident that if our ancestors had raised the whole of the supplies necessary for carrying on the great war by taxation from year to year, we should at this moment be free from the debt to which reference has been made. But it does not necessarily follow that we should in that case be better off than we are; for we must pause to inquire whether excessive taxation fifty or sixty years ago might not have more seriously crippled our national resources at the present time than even the contraction of our enormous debt has done. If it be invariably more profitable to meet extraordinary expenditure by imposing taxes than by contracting debt, it would seem to follow that it must also be more profitable to apply a surplus revenue, when we have it, to the redemption of debt than to the remission of taxation. But this is a doctrine which modern statesmen have generally repudiated, or upon which, at all events, they have not acted. Mr. Gladstone's own practice in this respect has not always been in accordance with the doctrines he proclaimed in 1854. In that year he professed a desire to provide for the service of the war by taxation, and by taxation alone. He accordingly laid on taxes of an amount sufficient to raise a revenue adequate to the anticipated expenditure; but, inasmuch as their produce could not be realized immediately, he drew bills against them in the form of Exchequer-bonds payable at four, five, and six years' date. When the shorter-dated of these bonds came to maturity he was not in office, and cannot be held responsible for the manner in which they were dealt with; but

Financial Policy.

he was the Chancellor of the Exchequer in 1860, when the longest of them were presented for payment; and, instead of meeting them out of the income at his disposal, he preferred to apply that income to the reduction of the Wine duties and of the Paper duties. It may very possibly have been for the interest of the community to be relieved of taxes pressing upon commerce and industry rather than of a certain amount of debt; but if this was so in the days of Mr. Gladstone, it is at least equally probable that in the days of Mr. Pitt it was more for the interest of the country to incur a certain amount of debt than to overload and break down the springs of industry and commerce by an inordinate weight of taxation. The truth appears to be, that there are certain conditions of national existence, under which it is less injurious to part with capital than with earnings. When the capital of a country is accumulating with great rapidity, a certain part of it is annually lost in unwise speculations; and this part, at all events, may be safely drawn upon for Government loans. Undoubtedly the withdrawal of capital must always affect the interests of the labouring classes, because capital forms the fund which supports labour. But, unless we had a perfect system of taxation, pressing exactly as it should do upon every individual, it is probable that many of the labouring classes would suffer more from very heavy taxes, than from the withdrawal of a certain amount of capital from the market, since the pressure of taxation is unequal, while the pressure occasioned by the withdrawal of capital, being adjusted by a self-acting law, is comparatively speaking equal. Moreover, it must be remembered that a war absorbs not only capital but labour also, a circumstance which tends very much to mitigate the sufferings occasioned to the labouring classes by the diminution of the labour fund; and the contraction of trade, which is one of the consequences of war, must also have the effect of setting free a certain amount of capital, which may with advantage, or at least without disadvantage, be employed in the public service.

Viewed as a practical question, the proposition of Mr. Gladstone is even more doubtful. No war has ever in recent times been conducted without recourse to loans; and the attempts which have been made to maintain taxes in time of peace for the discharge of the debts contracted in time of war, have usually failed. In this respect Mr. Pitt and his contemporaries deserve honourable mention; for, though they were acting under a mistaken impression in trusting to a sinking fund supported by loans for the redemption of the debt, they had at all events a firm faith in its efficacy for the purpose, and they adhered to it, under the pressure of their greatest difficulties, with a tenacity which ought to be remembered in their favour when we reproach them with the immense load of debt which they have bequeathed to us. But, with this exception, the experience of many years shows that war taxation will not be borne a day longer than is absolutely necessary. Between 1798 and 1800 a sum of 56,445,000*l*. was borrowed, which was specially charged upon the Income Tax; and it was arranged that the tax should be retained after the termination of the war for a period long enough to extinguish this debt. Yet the first act of the Addington Ministry, upon the conclusion of the Peace of Amiens, was to take off the Income Tax and to leave the debt of 56,000,000*l*. to be discharged, like the rest of the national obligations, by the sinking fund. The rejection of the Income Tax in 1816, the agitation against the "War ninepence" in 1857, the renewal of the Exchequer-bonds of 1854, in 1858 and 1860,

CHAP. V.
1854.

are all symptoms of the national unwillingness to bear war taxation when spread over several years. But a nation, which will not bear such taxation in a diffused form, is still less likely to bear it in a concentrated form at a moment of severe national pressure. Much will be borne at such times, but not all. The instinct of the people teaches them that a war, if justifiable at all, is justifiable on account of its being waged for objects common to more generations than one; and that, although the main brunt of it ought to be borne at once, some aid at all events may not unreasonably be expected from succeeding ages, or at the least from succeeding years.

Change of Government.

Had it fallen to Mr. Gladstone's lot to introduce the budget of 1855, and to propose a loan, as he must have done, to meet a part of the expenditure of the year, he would probably have entered upon a discussion of this question, which could not have failed to be very interesting; but a change in the Administration, resulting from the appointment of the Sebastopol Committee, led to his retirement from office, and Sir George Cornewall Lewis succeeded him as Chancellor of the Exchequer.

Sir George Lewis brought forward his budget on the 20th of April, 1855. On the preceding Friday, (the 13th,) a notice from the

Financial Policy.

Chancellor of the Exchequer to the Governor and Deputy Governor of the Bank of England had been communicated to the members of the Stock Exchange, stating that the Government intended to contract a loan for the service of the year, and that contractors were invited to attend at the Treasury on Monday the 20th. At this meeting the terms of the loan were announced. They were as follow :—The sum required was 16,000,000*l.* ; for every 100*l.* subscribed in money the contractors were to receive 100*l.* in Consols, and a terminable annuity for thirty years, ending on the 5th of April, 1885. The biddings were to be made in the terminable annuity. The payments were required to be made in nine instalments; the first on the 24th of April, the last on the 18th of December. This loan was taken by Messrs. Rothschild at the price of 14*s.* 6*d.* terminable annuity for every 100*l.* stock; that is to say, at the rate of 3*l.* 14*s.* 6*d.* per cent. for thirty years, to be reduced to 3*l.* per cent. at their expiration. This was reckoned equivalent to a loan in Consols at 87⅝, which is the same thing as saying that the loan was contracted at 3*l.* 8*s.* 6*d.* per cent. The price of Consols had touched 92 on the day of the announcement of the intention to contract a loan; they had been but slightly affected by that an-

CHAP. V.
1855.
Budget of 1855-6, April 20.

Loan of 16,000,000*l.*

nouncement, but on the amount of the loan being made known, they fell to 90, and afterwards to a fraction lower. The scrip of the new loan was brought out at a premium of 1⅜. The bargain was generally considered a fair one.*

In bringing forward his budget Sir George Lewis stated that the income of the past year had exactly realized Mr. Gladstone's anticipations, but that the cost of conducting the war had been so large, that the expenditure had exceeded the estimates by 2,653,000*l.* Mr. Gladstone had calculated that the expenditure would exceed the produce of taxation within the year by 3,543,000*l*. It had actually exceeded it by 6,196,000*l*. As, however, Mr. Gladstone had issued Exchequer-bills to the amount of 1,750,000*l*. and Exchequer-bonds to the amount of 5,375,000*l*., the receipts of the Exchequer had amounted in the whole to 66,621,667*l*.,† or 928,705*l*. more than the expenditure.

---

* Such at least was the common opinion at the time. The mode in which the Loan was raised has, however, since been seriously criticised by Mr. Hubbard. See his Speech in the House of Commons, Aug. 13, 1860.

	£
† Produce of taxes	59,496,154
Exchequer-bills	1,750,000
Exchequer-bonds	5,375,513
	£66,621,667

Financial Policy. 267

For the coming year Sir G. C. Lewis estimated the expenditure at 80,899,561*l.*; besides which he had to provide 1,000,000*l.* to pay off Ways and Means bills, issued in the year preceding; and he added that he thought it prudent to take a vote of credit of 4,440,000*l.* for the service of the war. Adding these sums together, he found himself obliged to reckon the expenditure at 86,339,000*l.* To meet this he could only reckon on a revenue of 63,339,000*l.*, and he had therefore to meet a deficit of 23,000,000*l.*; which he proposed to do partly by the loan of 16,000,000*l.* already contracted for, partly by additions to taxation, amounting to 4,000,000*l.* receivable within the year,* and partly by the issue of 3,000,000*l.* of Exchequer-bills. The additions to taxation were to be as follow. The sugar duties were to be raised by 3*s.* per cwt.,† which would add 1,200,000*l.* to the revenue: the duty on coffee was to be raised by 1*d.* per lb.,‡ which would produce 150,000*l.*: the duty on tea was to be raised by 3*d.* per lb.§

---

* The new taxes were estimated to produce 5,300,000*l.* in the whole, but only 4,000,000*l.* would be received in the first year.

† *i. e.* from 12*s.* to 15*s.* per cwt.

‡ *i. e.* from 3*d.* to 4*d.* per lb.

§ *i. e.* from 1*s.* 6*d.* to 1*s.* 9*d.* per lb. The duty on tea

which would produce 750,000*l.* An addition of 200,000*l.* was to be made to the revenue from stamps by an alteration of the law relating to bankers' cheques.* The duties on Scotch and Irish spirits were to be increased, and were expected to produce a further addition of 1,000,000*l.* These several indirect taxes, therefore, would produce 3,300,000*l.* An addition of 2*d.* in the pound to the Income Tax would make up a further sum of 2,000,000*l.*; and the whole amount of the new taxes, when they should have come into full operation, would be 5,300,000*l.* Adding this sum to the amount of the revenue already estimated, we shall find that the taxation of the country was thus raised to 68,639,000*l.*† per annum, a sum largely in excess of any that had ever before been so levied; for, although the nominal revenue from taxation in 1815 was 72,000,000*l.*, a deduction of nearly 13½ per cent. must be made from that amount on account of the depreciation of the paper currency in which it was paid. The fol-

---

would by law have fallen to 1*s.* 3*d.* in the financial year 1855-6, but this fall had been arrested by an act passed early in the session.

* This proposal was afterwards abandoned, May 11.

† This sum represents the net revenue, and does not include the cost of collection.

lowing remarks of Sir George Lewis upon the ability of the country to bear this great strain are worthy of notice, and may suggest some important considerations:—

"To enable the country to bear the increased charge, the items of which I have now submitted to the Committee, all that is necessary is, that its resources should remain unimpaired, and that the vast creation of wealth which has been going on without interruption for some years past should not suffer any diminution in consequence of the vicissitudes of the war. Now, Sir, there is one cause of favourable anticipation to which I think hardly sufficient attention has been paid in this House, and to which, as it seems to me, scarcely sufficient credit has been given to the Government which preceded that of my noble friend near me,—I mean the measures they adopted with respect to trade with neutral nations. It is well known that during the late war a large portion of the disturbance of trade and interruption to manufactures was owing to the unwise retaliatory measures adopted by this country against the Berlin and Milan decrees. The orders in council then issued led to a great disturbance of the trade with neutral nations, and created an amount of loss and disturbance of commerce and industry, which it would perhaps be no exaggeration to say was equal to the entire detriment and suffering created by the increased taxes. From that cause of national loss the country has been fortunately saved by the wise measures which the late Government have adopted. In consequence of the measures adopted in former years by the legislature, as well as of the measures taken for the protection of our commerce since the war, hitherto with success, a sound state of commerce has been preserved, and it appears that a vast increase has taken place in the amount of our foreign trade. As a proof of the present power of the country to bear increased taxation, I will beg to draw the attention of the Committee to a comparison of our imports and exports in the year in which the French war broke out, in the year when peace was concluded, and in the present year. In 1793 the imports into the United Kingdom were valued at 17,850,000*l.*; in 1815 they were valued at 32,987,000*l.*; in 1853 they had risen to 123,099,000*l.* Our exports in 1793 were 18,486,000*l.*; in 1815 they were 58,629,000*l.*, and in 1853 they were 242,072,000*l.** These

---

* The figures here given show the *official* values of the imports and exports, which are founded on a wholly fictitious

Financial Policy.

figures, Sir, present incontestable proofs of the enormous increase of the trade of this country since the beginning of the French war, and since the last peace; and they prove that an enormous mass of wealth exists in the country, from which an additional amount of taxation can be raised to defray the extraordinary expenditure of the country."

The additional taxes imposed in this budget occasioned less discussion than did the loan. It was said by some that the Government should have contracted it in terminable annuities, rather than in a perpetual stock like Consols; by others, that they should have created a high-priced stock, which might afterwards be converted into a low-priced one, as had been done upon former occasions; and by others again, that they ought to have opened a subscription loan, like that which had recently been raised in France, instead of negotiating it through the agency of contractors. Much difference of opinion also

---

basis of calculation. The *declared* or real value of the exports of British and Irish produce in 1853, for instance, was only 98,933,000*l.* But as we cannot get the real value of our imports for the earlier years here compared with 1853, the official value is the only standard of comparison which can be set up; and it is a fair one, as showing the comparative quantities of goods.

prevailed with regard to a proposal made by Sir George Lewis, to introduce into the act sanctioning the loan a clause providing for the gradual extinction of the debt by means of a sinking fund. On the first of these points the answer of the Government was, that, while borrowing on terminable annuities is very convenient to the State, lending upon them is very inconvenient to capitalists, and that it would have been impossible to raise so large a sum as 16,000,000*l.* in that form unless at an enormous sacrifice. As to borrowing in a high-priced stock, the obvious answer was, that lenders would calculate the probabilities of a future reduction in the rate of interest as well as borrowers, and would take care to advance their money on such terms only as would secure them against any risk of loss. The arguments in favour of an open loan were specious rather than sound; and the case of France was not at all analogous to that of England in this respect. Mr. Baring* pointed out that in France there was in the aggregate a considerable amount of money in the hands of the small peasant proprietors, which, from feelings of distrust, they

---

* Speech of Mr. T. Baring, April 23, 1855.

Financial Policy. 273

either hoarded or employed at a very low rate of interest; and that the Government had been able to call out a good deal of this money by the offer of good security and upwards of 4½ per cent. interest;* whereas in England the holders of small sums generally invested them at a fair rate of interest, and were not likely to be tempted by an offer of 3¼ or 3½ per cent. for their money. Sir George Lewis also remarked † that to open a subscription-loan would create a demand upon the Savings' banks, and that the sale of Savings' banks' stock would bring down the price of the funds at the very moment when the loan was being contracted, and when it was therefore desirable that they should be kept up.‡ He further reminded the House that, if the

---

* The French loan was contracted in 3 per cent. rentes, at 65.25, or about 4*l*. 12*s*. per cent., but the discount allowed was such as to raise the interest very considerably above this rate. As moreover the ruling price of the funds was a good deal higher than 65, the investment was a tempting one.

† On the same day, April 23.

‡ The Government were at this very time censured for having had recourse to the sale of Savings' banks' stock in order to meet the demands of the war towards the close of the last financial year, and for having thus reduced the price of the funds just before contracting a loan. See upon this point the observations of Mr. Laing, and the answer of Mr. Gladstone, April 20, 1855.

T

Government had taken the course proposed, they must have fixed the price at which they would receive subscriptions, and must have kept the subscriptions open for a considerable time, so that they would have lost the advantage resulting from the competition of capitalists.

<small>Opposition to the proposed sinking fund.</small>

Upon these points of objection the Government appear to have satisfied the House of Commons; but the clause relating to the proposed sinking fund was not carried without serious opposition. Mr. Disraeli, Mr. Gladstone, Mr. Cardwell, Mr. Labouchere, Mr. Henley, Mr. Ricardo, and other gentlemen of various shades of political opinion, resisted the proposal on the ground that it was inconvenient and embarrassing to attempt to bind a future Parliament to a particular course in such a matter. Mr. Glyn, Mr. T. Baring, and other gentlemen of authority upon commercial questions, supported the Government, and the clause was carried on a division by a majority of 99.* It was generally admitted that the clause could not be held so binding on a future Parliament as to preclude its repeal if it should be found desirable to repeal it; but a great number of votes

---

* By 210 to 111.

Financial Policy. 275

were recorded in its favour with a view to "assert a principle;" the principle being, that the country should exert itself in time of peace to pay off debts contracted in time of war. Mr. Gladstone, however, expressed his fear that many of those who intended to give their votes on this ground "would be disposed to flinch from the maintenance of that principle, when they felt a strong pressure from without for the reduction of the hop, malt, insurance, or paper duties."

Although by the arrangements which have now been related, Sir George Lewis had made provision for raising more than 86,000,000*l*., and had anticipated that this amount would leave a surplus of more than 4,000,000*l*. above the estimated expenditure of the year, he found, as the session wore on, that still heavier demands had to be met, that "war did not consume according to rule and measure," and that his surplus of 4,000,000*l*. would be insufficient to meet the charges which would probably fall upon it. Accordingly on the 2nd of August he applied for power to issue, not 3,000,000*l*. but 7,000,000*l*. of Exchequer bills or bonds for the service of the year. On that occasion he stated that 6,135,444*l*. had been

CHAP. V.
1855.

Sir G. Lewis applies for power to issue more Exchequer-bills.

CHAP. V.
1855.

voted, as supplemental estimates, since the introduction of the budget in April. The effect of these additional votes was to raise the estimated expenditure of the year to 87,034,000*l.* The amount of revenue which he expected to receive from taxation within the year was, as has been said, 67,139,000*l.*, and there was therefore a deficit of 19,895,000*l.*, of which 16,000,000*l.* would be covered by the loan. Of the 7,000,000*l.* of Exchequer-bills, 1,000,000*l.* would be absorbed by the redemption of the Ways and Means bills created in 1854-5, and an unappropriated margin of 2,105,000*l.* would remain to meet contingent demands. This proposal concluded the financial arrangements of the year.

Sardinian and Turkish loans.

Notice ought here to be taken of two arrangements concluded in the course of this session with our allies, the Sardinians and the Turks respectively. On the 23rd of March Lord Palmerston moved a resolution, in pursuance of a convention with the King of Sardinia, by which the British Government had undertaken to advance one million immediately, and another million at the end of a twelvemonth, if the war should last so long, by way of loan to the Sardinian Government; the King of Sardinia on his side stipulating to keep on foot an army of 15,000 men for the service of the war. The loan was to bear interest at 3 per cent., and to be repaid by instalments of 1 per cent. per annum. This resolution was agreed to after a short debate without a division. The Government, however, had much more difficulty in obtaining the consent of the House to a convention, by which they undertook, conjointly with the Government of France, to guarantee a loan of 5,000,000*l.*, which the Turkish Government were about to raise at 4 per cent. The resolution adopting this arrangement was brought forward on the 20th of July, and after an animated debate was carried by a majority of only 3,* Mr. Gladstone, Mr. Disraeli, Mr. Ricardo, and Mr. Laing, taking the lead in opposing it. The objections taken to the guarantee were partly of a financial and partly of a political character. A good deal of warmth was displayed both in debate and out of doors, and on both sides of the question. The friends of the Government represented the opposition to the loan as an attempt of the Peace party to throw difficulties in the way of prosecuting the war. On the other hand, those who objected

---

* By 135 to 132.

CHAP. V.
1855.

to the measure described it as a first step towards the system of subsidies, which had proved so costly in the great wars with France; they considered that it would tend to destroy the independence of Turkey, and to weaken the spirit of self-reliance, which it was so desirable to confirm in her. They thought a direct subsidy would have been better, or at all events not worse, than this guarantee, which was in their view a subsidy in disguise; and they found fault with some of the arrangements connected with the loan, especially with that by which France and England were made jointly and severally responsible for the whole amount, instead of each being made separately responsible for one half of it.

Supplementary estimates again presented.

Ample as the provision made for the service of 1855-6 must have appeared at the time it was made, the result showed that the war was even more costly than had been expected. Early in the following session supplementary estimates amounting to upwards of a million and a-half were presented. At the same time the Chancellor of the Exchequer perceived that the revenue which he had calculated on receiving would not be realized. Accordingly, in the month of

Fresh loan of 5,000,000*l*.

February, tenders for a new loan of 5,000,000*l*. were called for. The loan was again negotiated

Financial Policy.

in 3 per cent. Consols. Baron Rothschild, the only person who tendered, made an offer of 100*l*. for 112*l*. 5*s*. stock; but this offer having been rejected, he accepted the Government minimum of 111*l*. 2*s*. 2*d*., which was equivalent to an issue of Consols at 90. On the 22nd of February Sir George Lewis applied to the House for a confirmation of this provisional agreement. He showed that the Customs' and Excise revenue was likely to fall much below the amount at which he had estimated it; partly on account of the diminished consumption of sugar, partly on account of the falling off in that of spirits. By the combined effect of the excess in the expenditure, and the deficiency in the revenue, the surplus of 4,000,000*l*., on which he had calculated in the preceding year, had disappeared; and he applied for authority to raise the loan of 5,000,000*l*., in order to replace the finances in the condition in which he had proposed that they should stand; at the same time he took power to fund 3,000,000*l*. of Exchequer-bills.

CHAP. V.
1856.

This statement was, however, of a merely provisional character. The budget itself was not introduced until the 19th of May, before which time the war had come to an end, and a definitive treaty of peace had been signed at Paris.

Budget of 1856-7, May 19.

In this statement Sir George Lewis reviewed the financial circumstances of the complete year 1855-6, showing that the ordinary expenditure had amounted to 88,428,345*l.*, and that, including the advance of 1,000,000*l.* to Sardinia, and the sum of 213,000*l.* applied to the redemption of hereditary pensions, it had reached 89,641,345*l.*; that the revenue from taxation had been 65,704,491*l.*; and that the deficiency of 23,936,854*l.* had been supplied by loans to the amount of 26,478,750*l.*,* the excess of which above the amount required to meet the expenditure had gone to strengthen the balances in the Exchequer. He then attempted to estimate the total cost of the war. He stated that the expenditure of the two years, 1854-5 and 1855-6, had in the whole amounted to 155,121,307*l.*; the expenditure of the two preceding years, 1852-3 and 1853-4, had been 102,032,596*l.* The difference, 53,088,711*l.*, was, he thought, the measure of the cost of the

---

	£
* By Loan of April, 1855	16,000,000
By Loan of Feb. 1856, part received	3,501,000
By Exchequer-bonds	977,750
By Exchequer-bills	6,000,000
	£26,478,750

Financial Policy. 281

war up to that time; a further sum of 24,500,000*l*. must however be added on account of the increased charge to be thrown on the estimates of 1856-7. This addition would make the whole cost of the war 77,588,711*l*. As far as that cost had yet been defrayed, the mode of meeting it had been as follows:—Additional taxation had produced 17,182,522*l*.; there had been added to the funded and unfunded debt 33,604,263*l*.; and there had been applied to the service of the war the surplus income above the expenditure during the last two years of peace,* being 5,985,427*l*.; " thus making the total sum applicable to war expenditure, over and above the sums applied to peace expenditure, 56,772,312*l*." Upon these results Sir George Lewis made the following observations :—

"Before I proceed with a detailed statement of the estimated expenditure of the year, I would beg leave to call the attention of the Committee

---

* Sir G. Lewis does not mean by this that the surplus revenue of those two years had been kept in the Exchequer, and applied to the service of the two following years, but that the taxes of the two years of peace, though lower by 17,000,000*l*. than the taxes in the two years of war, had been more than sufficient to meet the expenditure, and had left a surplus of nearly 6,000,000*l*., while the war taxes, though 17,000,000*l*. higher, had left no surplus.

to the peculiar character of the contest in which we have been engaged. By the modern inventions of machinery, by that acceleration of the means of locomotion which modern science and skill have devised, we have been able to crowd into a small space of time operations which in former years might have spread over a period of far longer duration. The American war lasted six years, and added 124,000,000*l.* to the national debt. The actual hostilities of the late war have lasted two years, and will add about 42,000,000*l.* to the national debt, funded and unfunded. We have, Sir, by the measures which have been adopted during the war, avoided those drains upon the industry and trade of the country, which have been so severely felt under the policy pursued by belligerents in previous wars. We have avoided incidental disputes arising from the exercise of the obnoxious right of searching neutral ships. We prudently waived our extreme rights as a belligerent power in maritime warfare at the commencement of the contest; and I trust that the convention lately concluded at Paris will set the seal to that concession, which was so wisely made, and which has been attended with most wholesome results during the late hostilities. . . . There is another

Financial Policy. 283

point also, which ought not to be left out of consideration with respect to the great expenditure for military and naval purposes during the late war. At the beginning of the war we found ourselves to a certain extent unprepared for the contest. During the last two years we have devoted large sums to extending and improving our naval and military establishments. Our military arsenals are now much fuller, our stores are greater, our guns more perfect, our troops armed with much more efficient weapons than was the case at the commencement of the war. Our navy is likewise more numerous, better appointed, and more efficient for all the purposes of war; and although the objects of a belligerent power are not those which we now seek, it is to be remembered that we are in possession of a much greater amount of articles for naval and military purposes than we had at the commencement of the war. It must not, therefore, be supposed that all our expenditure has merely been for the accomplishment of temporary purposes, for a considerable portion of it remains in a permanent form."

Perhaps I may be forgiven for remarking that the last sentence of the foregoing extract has been verified by subsequent events in a sense

Observations on the effect produced by the war on the National Expenditure.

which was probably not present to the mind of the speaker. He meant, it may be presumed, to say that England would to some extent be the richer for the outlay she had made, for that the results of a portion of that outlay would remain with her as a permanent possession. But though this is undoubtedly true, it is equally true that Sir George Lewis's words have been fulfilled in another, which is perhaps their literal, meaning. The expenditure upon naval and military services, which we learnt to make in the Russian war, has never since been unlearnt; and we may say with perfect accuracy that " a considerable portion of it still remains in a permanent form." This is not the place to discuss the general merits of that war; nor shall I attempt to inquire whether it was worth what it cost, either to mankind at large, or to England in particular. But there can be no doubt that among the results which have followed it have been these two; first, that it has stirred up in Europe a spirit of restlessness which has made all nations feel it doubly incumbent upon them to look to their means of defence; secondly, and as a consequence of the first result, it has set all the world to seek for the means of improving the instruments of attack and defence, and to add enormously and without stint or measure to the most unprofitable and the most unsatisfactory of all possible forms of expenditure. Nor is the mischief one for which it is easy, or perhaps even possible, to suggest a remedy. While the warlike preparations of other countries appear to threaten the safety of England, it is the first duty of English statesmen to take care that her preparations for defence are upon a corresponding scale; and yet, when England arms, other nations may justifiably hold the same language on their part, and thus warlike movements on the one side can hardly fail to beget warlike movements on the other. The mode of solving the difficulty must be left to the consideration of statesmen. The financier is deeply interested in its solution; but it is a task which lies beyond his province; and it would seem to be his duty frankly to acknowledge the difficulty in which it places him, and to endeavour to accommodate his financial measures to the circumstances which he cannot control, rather than fritter away his time, and perhaps endanger the resources of the country, by looking back with regret to the halcyon days of undisturbed peace and peaceful estimates, or forward to a time when those happy visions of the past may realize themselves again. If Sir George Lewis was right in saying that modern inventions shorten and so diminish the cost of wars, it is also true that they spread the cost of war over times of peace to a much greater extent than was formerly the case; and this, as it appears to me, is the main lesson we have now to learn from the period of financial history with which I am about to deal.

I proceed with the account of the budget. Sir George Lewis stated that, in consequence of the conclusion of peace, the original estimates for the military services of the year had been reduced from 54,874,000*l*. to 37,315,000*l*.; that he proposed, as a measure of precaution, to take a vote of credit for 2,000,000*l*. to cover any unforeseen expenses that might have to be met in winding up the transactions arising out of the war; and that the Government considered it right to make provision for advancing a second sum of 1,000,000*l*. to the King of Sardinia in order to give effect to the spirit of the convention of 1855; although, according to the literal construction of the instrument, the advance could not have been demanded, because peace had been made five or six days before the expiration of a twelvemonth from the date of paying the first instalment of the loan. The

Financial Policy. 287

expenditure for the year would therefore amount to 77,525,000*l*., or, including the cost of collecting the revenue, which was now for the first time brought to charge in the estimates, to 82,113,000*l*. To meet this expenditure the Chancellor of the Exchequer could reckon upon a gross revenue of 71,740,000*l*. The Income Tax would, he said, by law remain at the rate of 1*s*. 4*d*. in the pound for the coming year, and for the year following; the additional duties on tea, coffee, sugar, and molasses, would continue for the coming year only; and the additional duty on malt would cease on the 5th of July in the year then current.* There was thus a difference of 10,373,000*l*. between the estimated revenue and the estimated expenditure, against which, however, was to be set the sum of 1,500,000*l*. received within the current year

---

* The additional Income Tax was to continue " during the present war, and until the 6th day of April, which shall first happen after the expiration of one year from the ratification of a definitive treaty of peace." The war duties on tea, sugar, &c. were to continue until the 6th of April next after the ratification of a treaty of peace: and the war-duty on malt until the 6th of July next after such a ratification. The treaty of peace having been ratified on the 27th of April, 1856, the war rate of Income Tax would therefore expire April 5, 1858, the war tea duty, April 5, 1857, and the war malt duty, July 5, 1856.

from the loan of 5,000,000*l.* contracted in February. The deficiency was thereby reduced to 8,873,000*l.*, of which the Chancellor of the Exchequer proposed to supply 5,000,000*l.* by a further loan, and the remainder, if it should be necessary, by the issue of Exchequer bonds or bills. It was, however, as he observed, possible that the 2,000,000*l.* which he proposed to take as a vote of credit might not be required. The loan of 5,000,000*l.* had that morning been taken on very favourable terms by Baron Rothschild. The price tendered by the contractor had been 108*l.* Consols for 100*l.* in money; but this offer had been rejected as being above the reserved price fixed by the Government, namely 107*l.* 10*s.* 7*d.*, and Baron Rothschild had thereupon amended his offer, and agreed to the terms of the Chancellor of the Exchequer. This was equivalent to a loan contracted in Consols at 93, being 3 per cent. higher than the terms on which the previous loan in the month of February had been negotiated; and about 37 per cent. higher than those of the last loan at the close of the war in 1815. It was no slight proof of the extent of the resources of the country that applications amounting to 40,000,000*l.* had been forwarded to Baron Rothschild by

Financial Policy. 289

persons desirous of obtaining a share in the loan before the terms of the bargain had been settled, and that deposits to the extent of 4,000,000*l.*, in Bank of England notes or in gold, had been remitted to him, and were in his hands when he attended at the Treasury to negotiate on the subject.

Sir George Lewis took the opportunity of this statement to lay before the House of Commons some particulars respecting the state of the National debt at the close of the French war, and at the time at which he was speaking. The nominal capital of the funded and unfunded debt in January, 1816, had been 860,251,647*l.*; in January, 1856, it was 793,392,799*l.*, showing a reduction of 66,858,848*l.* The annual charge for the debt in January, 1816, had been 32,784,168*l.*; in January, 1856, it was 28,269,537*l.*, showing a reduction of 4,514,631*l.* per annum. In these statements, however, the additional debt contracted in 1856 is not included. Sir George Lewis also reviewed the general condition of our taxation, arriving at the conclusion that " the great obstacle to the improvement of our system of taxation is owing, not to any want of care on the part of Parliament, nor to any want of frequent revisions and sug-

CHAP. V.
1856.

Sir G. Lewis' remarks upon the state of the debt,

and on the pressure of taxation,

U

gestions elaborately carried out by successive governments, but to the necessity under which we are unfortunately placed of raising a large revenue to meet the expenditure of the country." He went on to argue that the rate of our expenditure in proportion to our population was not excessive when compared with that of other countries, if the charge we bear on account of the debt were set aside. The whole public expenditure of the country in the year 1853 had amounted to 1*l*. 19*s*. 6*d*. per head of the population. In France the amount in the same year had been 1*l*. 12*s*. 1*d*. per head; but the charge for the debt in France was much less than the charge for the debt in England; and if this charge were deducted in both cases, the rate of taxation in England would prove to be 19*s*. 10*d*. per head, while in France it was 1*l*. 3*s*. 1*d*. In Prussia, however, the whole expenditure amounted only to 19*s*. 3*d*. per head, or, excluding the charge for the debt, to 17*s*. 3*d*. Comparisons like these, however, require very careful examination before they can be admitted. I hope to be able to touch upon this question in a chapter which I propose to devote to the consideration of the financial policy of foreign countries in the period of which I am treating.

Financial Policy.

What is more material to notice at the present moment is the effect which the war had produced upon our own taxation. The sum of 1*l.* 19*s.* 6*d.* per head, being the amount of our whole expenditure in 1853, had risen in 1855 to 3*l.* 5*s.* per head; while, excluding the charge for the debt, the sum of 19*s.* 10*d.* per head in 1853 had risen to a sum of 2*l.* 5*s.* 4*d.* per head in 1855; that is to say, we had much more than doubled that portion of our expenditure which is required for the regular service of the country, without reference to the portion required for the discharge of the interest of the debt. It may be interesting to add that in the year 1861-2 the total amount of our expenditure, including the charge for the debt, was 2*l.* 2*s.* 8*d.* per head; and that the amount expended for current services, excluding the charge for the debt, was 1*l.* 11*s.* 7*d.* per head.*

In the course of the discussion which followed the introduction of the budget, Mr. Disraeli took occasion to impress upon the Government

Chap. V.
1856.

Mr. Disraeli's and Mr. Gladstone's

---

* Population, 29,049,540.

	£
Charge for Debt	26,142,606
Other Expenditure	45,943,879
Gross Expenditure	£72,086,485

CHAP. V.
1856.
remarks upon the necessity for economy.

the importance of giving their best attention to measures of " wise, but at the same time rigid, economy." He said, " I am convinced that that is the only spirit in which we can confirm the principles of finance upon which our system is now generally established, and that will enable us to prepare those resources for the future which, whenever an emergency arises, will enable us to show the same power we have recently displayed." He pointed out the mistake of supposing that the mischances and disappointments, which had marked the commencement of the late war, would be prevented on a future occasion by the maintenance during peace of an army much larger than the needs of the country required; and that the only result which we should reap from the support of unduly large military establishments in time of peace would probably be, that we should enter upon another struggle without those resources which, having been accumulated by the wise economy of former years, had enabled the country to pass through its recent difficulties with comparative ease, and the Chancellor of the Exchequer to present at the close of the war so satisfactory a report on its financial position. Mr. Gladstone, rising a little later in the evening, expressed his entire

Financial Policy. 293

concurrence with Mr. Disraeli in this respect; and then, referring to some observations which had been made with regard to remissions of taxation, went on to urge upon the Chancellor of the Exchequer the duty of holding very firm and decided language to prevent such incursions upon the funds at his command. " I trust," he said, " that whatever may be our differences of opinion, we shall not set the pestilent example of abolishing taxes and meeting the expenditure of the country with borrowed money." Mr. Gladstone expressed his regret that the Government had not done more than they had in the way of reducing the estimates, and his wish that the House had shown a greater disposition to press for a further reduction; and concluded by repeating his hope that the Government would firmly maintain the revenue until it should be in a position to propose those remaining reforms, which, he said, " I quite agree are yet to be accomplished in our system of taxation."

No other debate of general interest took place upon the financial arrangements of the year. The proposals of the Chancellor of the Exchequer were adopted; the revised estimates were accepted and passed; and the Parliament was prorogued on the 29th of July.

CHAP. V.
1856.

Prorogation of Parliament.

CHAPTER VI.

CHAP. VI.
———
1857.
Financial character of 1857.

HERE is not, in the whole period which I have undertaken to review, a more interesting time than the opening of the year 1857. The Treaty of Paris had put an end to the war with Russia in the spring of 1856; and the year following the ratifications of that treaty had been, in common parlance, a year of peace; but, financially speaking, it had been just as much a year of war expenditure as either of the years before it. It is at the close, therefore, and not at the commencement, of 1856, that we must consider the war to have terminated, and that we must put to ourselves the question,—Stands England where she did before the struggle?

As regards the material resources of the

Financial Policy. 295

country, it needs but a hasty glance to see that, while serious drafts had been made upon them, they had in no degree been impaired by the contest in which we had been engaged. The whole cost of the war was estimated* to have amounted to 76,398,000*l*. To meet this charge, about 40,362,000*l*. had been raised by additional taxation, and 41,041,000*l*. had been added to the debt. Thus about 5,000,000*l*. more had been raised than had been expended, and the balances in the Exchequer were the stronger by that amount. The net addition to our debt, after making allowance for the improvement in the balances and for the repayments due to us from Sardinia, was 32,361,078*l*.† Our trade

---

* By Sir G. C. Lewis, February 13th, 1857. The principle upon which his calculation was founded was that of comparing the expenditure of the three years 1854-1857 with that of the preceding three years, 1851-1854. But the cost of the war, if calculated on that principle, is still going on, for every subsequent year of peace since 1856-7 shows a much larger amount of expenditure than the years 1851-1854, which Sir G. C. Lewis took as his standard.

† Russian war loans, Funded debt :—

£
First loan . . . 16,000,000
Second ,, . . . 5,000,000
Third ,, . . . 5,000,000
Carried Forward ——— £26,000,000

and manufactures, again, were in a condition of great prosperity. The value of our exports, which in 1853 had reached the very large sum of 98,933,000*l*., had fallen in 1855 by little more than 3,000,000*l*., and had risen again in 1856 to no less than 115,890,000*l*., a sum much larger than any recorded in any previous year. The largest increase had taken place in the exportation of those articles which form the staple of our manufactures, namely, textile and metallic fabrics. The quantity of raw cotton imported and retained for consumption had also largely increased. In 1853 the quantity was 746,709,000 lbs.; in 1855 it was 767,406,000 lbs.; and in 1856 it was 877,814,000 lbs. The returns relating to the

	£
Brought Forward	26,000,000
Exchequer bonds	7,000,000
Exchequer bills issued	5,041,000
Ditto, funded	3,000,000
	£41,041,000
Increase in Exchequer balances between March 31, 1854, and March 31, 1857	6,679,922
	£34,361,078
Repayable by Sardinian Government in forty years	2,000,000
Net addition to Debt	£32,361,078

amount of shipping employed in our trade were equally satisfactory. In short, while Russia had been exhausted, and even France had felt herself seriously weakened, by the drain of the war, England had but just begun to put forth her strength, and was evidently in a position which would have enabled her, had it been necessary, to carry on the contest for a considerably greater length of time without distress.

But while the war had thus passed over without making any serious impression upon the material resources of the country, the moral effect which it had produced had been enormous. It had awakened that combative spirit which lies deep in the English character, and which is something distinct from the love of glory or the thirst for conquest which we notice in other warlike nations. It had rudely dispelled the dream of perpetual peace and uninterrupted tranquillity in which the nation had for some time been lapped. It had exposed the defects which our military system had by long disuse contracted, and it had not lasted for a sufficient time to enable us to show how much we had done towards supplying those defects, and making our army what it ought to

CHAP. VI.
1857.

Moral effect of the war.

be; so that we left off with an uneasy and dissatisfied feeling with respect to the state of our military power. It had compelled us, too, to spend our money freely, and almost recklessly, and had thus begotten in us a habit and even a taste for expenditure, such as it is much easier to acquire than to get rid of. The ease with which we had borne our burdens had, of course, greatly contributed to encourage this tendency to expense, and to make men listen impatiently to the cautious warnings of the economist. Yet, with all this, there was in the public mind a strong and very general desire, I should rather say a firm determination, to get rid of the burden of the war taxes. As Mr. Gladstone very happily said,* the country, while perfectly reckless with regard to expenditure, was jealous with respect to taxation. The addition which had been made to the Income Tax for the purpose of the war was the chief subject of attack. Associations were formed, and meetings held, to get rid of the " war ninepence," which it was feared the Government would attempt to retain for another year. The excitement upon this point was all the greater, be-

---

* February 3, 1857.

cause, according to the literal construction of the law, the additional impost had still to be borne for another year; and the dislike to the tax itself was enhanced by the dislike which an Englishman always feels towards what he calls sharp practice. Had the ratifications of the treaty of peace been exchanged on the day on which the treaty itself was signed (March 30), or even within five days afterwards, the tax would have expired on the 5th of April, 1857; but as the ratifications were not exchanged until the 27th of April, 1856, the duration of the Income Tax at the increased rate would by law extend to the 5th of April, 1858. This was a grievance which men were determined not to bear, and a formidable agitation against it was set on foot in the course of the recess.

But the recess was remarkable for other reasons. Not only had there been cause to apprehend that the new-made peace with Russia would be broken, upon a question of boundary, before it had well had time to consolidate itself; but troubles had sprung up in other quarters of the globe. There was a misunderstanding between Prussia and Switzerland, which caused some uneasiness; England and

France had broken off diplomatic relations with the King of the Two Sicilies, thus taking the first step in the direction of that moral intervention in the affairs of Italy, for which the foundation had been laid in the protocols of the Treaty of Paris, and which was destined in due time to bring about the Italian war of 1859; complications had arisen between this country and the United States in respect of the affairs of Central America; and in the East we had engaged in two new wars, a war with Persia, and a war in China. It was as though a self-sown crop of disturbances were growing up, after the great harvest of the Russian war had been gathered in.

Opening of the Session. Debate on the Address.

Under these circumstances, the debates upon the Address in answer to the Queen's Speech, at the opening of the Session of 1857, especially that in the House of Commons, were peculiarly interesting. The occasion of the Address is one which is frequently taken for raising a discussion upon questions of foreign policy; but it is seldom that so much of the financial element enters into those discussions as they this year contained. Even in the House of Lords, Lord Derby offered some serious observations upon the question of the

Financial Policy.

Income Tax; while in the House of Commons, Mr. Disraeli, Mr. Gladstone, and Lord John Russell, (who was not at this time a member of the Government), dwelt at considerable length upon the financial aspect of affairs, and upon the prospects of a reduction of war expenditure and of war taxation. Mr. Disraeli referred to the settlement which had been arrived at in 1853 with respect to the Income Tax, and expressed his alarm at the reopening of all those exciting topics of controversy which had then, he hoped, been settled for ever. He stated his intention of moving resolutions against the continuance of war taxes in time of peace, and in favour of adhering to the spirit of the arrangement of 1853, for the ultimate extinction of the Income Tax. " I cannot but believe," he said, " that if these Resolutions are carried, we shall witness some beneficial changes in the financial system of this country. I think we shall give a great impetus to salutary economy, and shall in a most significant manner express our opinion that it is not advisable that England should become what is called ' a great military nation.'" Mr. Gladstone agreed with Mr. Disraeli in thinking the state of things as regarded the Income Tax unsatisfactory, adding, "as long as you have an Income Tax you will never entirely get rid of that discussion, [of the question between temporary and permanent incomes,] and this conviction, and the political dangers of this tax, led me to the conclusion that the Income Tax is an admirable instrument for national purposes upon a great and adequate emergency, but that it is a dangerous instrument to retain in the time of peace. But," said Mr. Gladstone, "that which really governs the whole question of the Income Tax and of our other taxation, is the question of the amount of the expenditure which is to be maintained. This House cannot efficiently discharge its duties by looking only at taxation. . . . . I feel it my bounden duty first to lay hold of the proposed expenditure, and it is my conviction that, if it be the opinion of the Government that it is necessary to maintain a military establishment upon a scale at all approaching to that which I have named, we must grapple with the Estimates, not by nibbling at them here and there, but by a general motion, taking the sense of the House upon the expediency of saddling the country with such a charge." Lord John Russell, speaking later in the debate, and after Lord Palmerston

Financial Policy. 303

and Sir George Lewis, urged the Government to anticipate the proposed motions of Mr. Disraeli and Mr. Gladstone by bringing the state of the finances before the House at a very early period of the session. Referring to the question of our military establishments, he said, " Perhaps, if I might venture to recall old times, and refer to what he (Lord Palmerston) said the first time I made a motion in this House, which was in 1816, when I asked the Ministry to withdraw the Estimates, and propose reduced ones; and my noble friend, then Secretary at War, stated the grounds why considerable Estimates were necessary; I might observe that the reasons he then gave were not very dissimilar from those which he offered to-night, and I have no doubt were perfectly well grounded. All I should wish to prevent, as far my vote lies, would be the adoption of any new system with regard to our Naval and Military estimates. We have been accustomed, (and very great ministers,— ministers who knew what the country required,—have sanctioned the practice), to keep up low establishments in time of peace ; and though there has been always a complaint in the first year of war, that we have been very unprepared, and have not made sufficient provision for a period of war, somehow or other, after a time, we have generally found ourselves strong enough to meet our enemy with the establishment we possessed. Moreover, though the complaint I refer to has been made very recently, arising out of the events of the late war, I do not think that our experience during the last thirty years is at all adverse to the plan pursued. We have seen in France,—I believe almost ever since the accession of Charles X, and certainly since the accession of Louis Philippe,—that that country has been maintaining an immense army, and a considerable navy, and every year increasing its debt. We, on the other hand, have been keeping up establishments, thought by some persons too great, but which were, in fact, not very considerable; we have thus been enabled to secure a surplus revenue, to reduce taxes, and abolish customs' duties which pressed upon the energies and checked the industry of the people; we have enabled our population to grow rich; and we have seen in the last war what that wealth was able to effect; for when our enemy was exhausted, and our ally was so far weakened in its finances, that its war spirit flagged, the Government of this country found that, owing to our wealth, we had more than sufficient to pay for the large expenditure of the war; and the spirit of our people, if terms of peace had not been accepted, was such that for five, six, or ten years longer, if necessary, we might have made the exertions necessary for war. Now these are the things which produce good terminations of wars, and not large and expensive establishments, with generals and admirals growing so old that they are unfit for their duties when war comes. It is by moderate establishments, by rendering such establishments good and efficient, by attending to everything which cannot be easily originated or replaced,—it is by such a system, and by relying on the greatness of the country, and on the spirit of our people, that you will be most formidable in war, and not by any new-fangled system of increased Estimates during a time of peace."

Such were, at this juncture, the opinions of the three most eminent among the independent members of the House of Commons, of three statesmen usually differing very widely one from another upon most questions of policy, yet concurring upon this occasion as to the importance of reducing our large military estimates, and of returning as rapidly as possible to the level of an ordinary peace establishment. But the task upon which they thus urged the Government to enter was like the task of the husbandman, who, having dug a hole in a stiff soil, tries afterwards to replace the earth he has taken out in the pit from which it came.

> "In sua posse negabit
> Ire loca, et scrobibus superabit terra repletis."

Budget of 1857-8, Feb.13,1857. The Budget was brought forward on the 13th of February, 1857, and Sir George Lewis stated the estimated expenditure for the year at 63,224,000*l*., independently of the amount which would be required for the repayment of debt. There were Exchequer-bonds for 2,000,000*l*. to be paid off, and 250,000*l*. to be provided as a sinking fund on the last loan of 5,000,000*l*. These sums, added to the estimates already mentioned, would bring the expenditure up to 65,474,000*l*. The total amount of the Army and Navy Estimates* was

---

* Including the Militia, the Packet Service, and the Coast Guard. This last service (amounting to 486,000*l*.) ought to be excluded from the comparison, as it was now for the first time brought upon the Navy estimates, having previously been defrayed out of the Customs' revenue.

Financial Policy.

20,699,000*l.*, being about 17,000,000*l.* below the reduced estimates of the preceding year, but about 3,400,000*l.* above those of 1853. Sir George Lewis offered some explanation as to the causes of this increase, as well as of the increase which had taken place in the miscellaneous estimates also. Before proceeding to the question of the taxation for the year, he added some particulars respecting the engagements into which Parliament had entered for the repayment of the debt contracted during the war. There were 7,000,000*l.* of Exchequer-bonds to be redeemed by 2,000,000*l.* a-year; the last 1,000,000*l.* would fall due in 1860. There was 250,000*l.* to be paid by way of sinking fund in 1857, and afterwards there was 1,500,000*l.* a-year to be paid, till the debt contracted during the war should be discharged. Moreover, there was a considerable addition to the interest of the debt, arising from the recent additions to the principal, which it was necessary to take into account. The finance of the coming years, therefore, would be affected by the following additions,—

	£
1857. Capital debt to be redeemed	2,250,000
Increased annual charge	1,421,000
Total	£3,671,000

		£
1858.	Capital debt to be redeemed	3,500,000
	Increased annual charge	1,324,000
	Total	£4,824,000

1859.	Capital debt to be redeemed	3,500,000
	Increased annual charge	1,207,000
	Total	£4,707,000

1860.	Capital debt to be redeemed	2,500,000
	Increased annual charge	1,108,000
	Total	£3,608,000

These additions to the expenditure, said Sir G. Lewis, must necessarily be held to have disturbed the basis of the settlement of 1853, and to have left Parliament free to deal with the Income Tax as might appear best.

Sir G. Lewis' views as to the remission of taxes. Approaching now the question of the taxation for the coming year, Sir G. Lewis first disposed of the appeals which had been made to him on the subject of the Paper duties, the Wine duties, and the duty on Fire Insurance. Of the claims made in respect of the first he thought lightly; the Wine duties, he said, must be reserved for a more favourable moment; and as regarded the Insurance duties he came to the conclusion,—founded upon Mr. Coode's excellent and elaborate report upon the subject,—that there was no ground whatever for acceding to the propositions which had been made for their reduction. There is no quality for which Sir George Lewis is more remarkable than for a quiet courage, which emboldens him to give utterance from time to time, and sometimes without any apparent necessity for his doing so, to propositions of the most alarmingly unpopular nature. On the present occasion, besides going a little out of his way to apologise for the Paper duty, and to eulogise the Insurance duty, he proceeded to run a tilt against the doctrine of simplification which had for so many years been admitted to a place of honour in the fiscal creed of the country. In support of his view, he quoted the following passage from Mr. Arthur Young :—

" The mere circumstance of taxes being very numerous, in order to raise a given sum, is a considerable step towards equality in the burden falling on the people: if I was to define a good system of taxation, it should be that of bearing lightly on an infinite number of points, heavily on none. In other words, that simplicity in taxation is the greatest additional weight that can be given to taxes, and ought in every country to be most sedulously avoided."
"That opinion," said Sir George Lewis, "though

contrary to much that we hear at the present day, seems to me to be full of wisdom, and to be a most useful practical guide in the arrangement of a system of taxation."

This digression, which had really but little to do with the main action of the budget, brought down upon the Chancellor of the Exchequer a vigorous denunciation from Mr. Gladstone, and a gentler rebuke even from Lord John Russell. Mr. Gladstone treated the Chancellor of the Exchequer's language as a total condemnation of the principles by which Parliament had been guided during the last fifteen years; and Lord John Russell, while arguing that it was impossible that Sir G. Lewis could have intended to abandon those principles, mentioned this as a portion of his speech which he "should have been quite willing to have spared."

His proposal for the coming year.

To return, however, to the budget. Sir G. Lewis, having stated that it was his intention in dealing with the taxation of the current year to confine himself to those taxes which were imposed during the war, proceeded to say there was no reason for reducing the Spirit duties, and that the additional duty on Malt had already expired. The Income Tax he proposed at once to reduce to the rate of 7*d*. in the pound; but to fix it at that rate for the remainder of the term during which it had to run, that is say, until 1860. As regarded the duties on tea and sugar, he proposed to fix them at rates somewhat higher than those at which by law they ought now to have stood, but somewhat lower than those at which they had been temporarily maintained during the war. According to the arrangement of 1853, modified by the arrangements made during the war, the duty on tea ought to have fallen in April, 1857, to 1*s*. 3*d*. per lb., and in the following year to 1*s*. per lb. It had been maintained for the last two years at 1*s*. 9*d*. per lb. Sir G. C. Lewis now proposed to fix it at 1*s*. 7*d*. for the year 1857-8, at 1*s*. 5*d*. for 1858-9, at 1*s*. 3*d*. for 1859-60, and at 1*s*. per lb. from 1860 forwards. The case of the Sugar duties, and the mode proposed for dealing with them, was substantially the same as the case of the duty on tea. These arrangements would, he said, produce in the coming year a revenue of 66,365,000*l*., and would leave a surplus of 891,000*l*. above the expenditure, including in the expenditure the sum required for the discharge of debt.

CHAP. VI.
1857.
Income Tax reduced to 7*d*.

Tea and sugar duties fixed for three years.

"If the Committee," he continued, "should adopt the plan which I have proposed, I believe that sufficient revenue will be provided to meet the liabilities of the Exchequer for the payment of the Bonds due in the three years commencing from the 1st of April, for the extinction of the war sinking fund, and also for the payment of the increased interest on the debt; leaving some margin for any slight increase in the Army, Navy, or Civil Service Estimates. If the liabilities created by the 40,000,000*l.* of debt contracted during the war should be discharged according to the plan which has been laid down by Parliament, and according to that which I am now proposing for the next three years, and if further accruing liabilities should be met by a corresponding provision, I calculate that the entire debt created by the war will have been extinguished by the year 1877. More than half of the extraordinary expenditure of the war was defrayed from taxation, the remaining half by loans; and this portion, as I have just said, if the arrangement I propose is adopted, will be extinguished in about twenty years. It seems to me that such a state of things affords a favourable retrospect of the arrangements made during this war. It shows the greater providence of the present generation; and if our ancestors had treated us as well as we are, I hope, about to treat posterity, we should not, at the present time, be loaded with the burden of a debt of 800,000,000*l*."

CHAP. VI.
1857.

The Budget, as has been said, was brought forward on the 13th of February. On the following Monday, the 16th, Mr. Disraeli took occasion to give notice of his intention to move a resolution in the following terms :—

Mr. Disraeli's resolution.

" That in the opinion of this House it would be expedient, before sanctioning the financial arrangements for the ensuing year, to adjust the estimated income and expenditure in the manner which shall appear best calculated to secure the country against the risk of a deficiency in the years 1858-9 and 1859-60, and to provide for such a balance of revenue and charge respectively in the year 1860, as may place it in the power of Parliament at that period, without embarrassment to the finances, altogether to remit the Income Tax."

Immediately after this notice had been given, Sir George Lewis stated, by way of comment upon it, that in his opinion there was no risk of a deficiency in the two years which were to come; for that he estimated the revenue of 1858-9, after paying off the redeemable debt for the year, at 58,800,000*l*., and that of 1859-60 at very nearly the same sum, while the gross expenditure of the year 1853-4, the year immediately preceding the war, had been only 55,840,000*l*.; so that there would probably be a surplus of about 3,000,000*l*. to meet the increased expenditure of the years 1858 and 1859.

Mr. Disraeli brought forward his resolution on the 20th of February, on the question that the Speaker do leave the chair that the House may go into a Committee of Ways and Means. The line of argument which he adopted was substantially this:—If the expenditure of the two years 1858 and 1859 is to be upon the scale of that announced for 1857, there will, upon the proposed plan of finance, be a large deficiency at the end of the first, and a still larger one at the end of the second of those years, and the removal of the Income Tax in 1860 will be absolutely impossible; if, on the other hand, the expenditure of those two years is to be reduced to the scale of 1853, then there is no reason why the reductions which are anticipated in 1858 and 1859 should

Financial Policy.

not at once be made in 1857, and in that case there will be no reason why the Income Tax and the Tea duty should be kept at the war rates. In the Budget speech of the 13th, Sir G. Lewis had appeared to treat the expenditure of 1857 as being susceptible of little, if any, reduction in future years; while in the few words he had spoken on the 16th, he had appeared to hold up the expenditure of 1853 as the model for the time to come. As there was a difference of nearly seven and a-half millions between the two standards, it was certainly not unimportant to know which was likely to be the nearest to the truth; and Mr. Disraeli seems to have thought that by aiming a decisive blow at the war taxation he would put the matter to the touch, and force the Government to follow the more economical of the two courses before them. He referred to the success which had attended the protests against the Income Tax in 1816 and 1848, and urged the House to take the same course as had on those occasions led to a reduction of expenditure. If, said he in conclusion, the Government " will really adopt the policy which on Monday appeared to be in the ascendant, and take the Estimates of 1853 in the manner then set forth, I, for one, have no wish to embarrass them. .... I should not care even for the first year,—though I think increased taxation is unnecessary,—perhaps even for a further period, to meet as regards the Income Tax the views of the Government. If we saw that in 1860 we were to get rid of the Income Tax, —if we saw that there was to be no permanent increase of the duties on tea,—I would be disposed to make some sacrifice to meet the convenience of Government. But if the policy of the Government is this,—that, though we may make sacrifices by this increase of direct and indirect taxation, we are only in the end to be landed in a deficit, then, I think, the House of Commons cannot too speedily and decidedly interfere to prevent a result so calamitous. In the belief that, if the House will sanction this resolution, we shall be able altogether to avoid new taxation by wise and well-considered reductions, I now place it in your hands, and commend it to the impartial but earnest consideration of the House of Commons."

Sir George Lewis, in opposing this resolution, argued that it was impossible to foretell the expenditure of the two coming years, and that it was especially difficult to say how far reduc-

Financial Policy. 317

ions of the Military and Naval Estimates might be carried, as the Estimates for 1857 had not yet been discussed. It was, of course, obvious that their discussion would throw considerable light upon the question, how much of the increased charge for the Army and Navy was permanent, and how much of it arose out of the transactions connected with the close of the war. Sir G. Lewis expressed his belief that a considerable reduction might be made in coming years; at the same time he showed that we could not expect to go back to the standard of 1853, especially in respect of the Civil Service Estimates. He disputed the correctness of Mr. Disraeli's estimate of the revenue of 1858 and 1859, and, referring to the great difference between the expenditure now under consideration, and that which prevailed in the years before the war, he argued that there was no reason to think that that of coming years might not be brought within the revenue, especially as he considered that it would be perfectly legitimate to defer the operation of the Sinking Fund of 1,500,000*l*. until the Exchequer-bonds should have been redeemed. The main ground, however, upon which he took his stand was, that he had made ample provision for the supplies of the coming year, which was all that he was bound to do; and that as regarded future years, he was not increasing, but mitigating and lessening the difficulties attending the ultimate removal of the Income Tax and of the other war duties, by providing a considerable revenue, and discharging a portion of the encumbrances of the country.

Mr. Gladstone's speech.

Mr. Gladstone followed the Chancellor of the Exchequer in an eloquent and highly impassioned speech. His criticism, however, left the main argument between Mr. Disraeli and Sir G. Lewis nearly untouched. The real point at issue was this: shall taxation be refused in order to compel the Government to reduce expenditure, or shall it be kept up in order to enable the Government to meet expenditure? It may be observed, by anticipation, that the solution actually arrived at was the very worst that was possible; the expenditure was not reduced, and the taxation was not maintained. The country compromised the matter by reconciling itself to the abandonment of the attempt to reduce the debt. Looking back upon the budget of 1857, with the advantage of knowing how matters which were then in doubt

Remarks on the budget of 1857.

Financial Policy.

have since been cleared up, we cannot fail to see that when once it was shown, as it very soon was, that the House was not prepared to make an earnest effort to reduce expenditure, it would have been prudent to have adopted the plan of Sir George Lewis; to have resolved on maintaining our revenue so as to keep up a good surplus, which might have been applied to the payment of debt; and to have determined to postpone further remissions of our ordinary taxation, until after the war taxes should have been got rid of, and the scheme of 1853 should have been carried into effect. Of course, if Mr. Disraeli and Mr. Gladstone had been strong enough to compel the Government at once to cut down the expenditure, so as to bring it nearly to the standard of 1853, they would have done good service; and taxation might, in that case, have been safely and materially reduced. The misfortune was, that they were not strong enough to do this; and it is to be regretted that, having failed in the main object which they had in view, they did not accept the plan which Sir George Lewis was proposing in contemplation of the continued maintenance of high estimates. Some remarks of Mr. T. Baring's upon this point are worthy of notice. Speaking on the 6th of March, and referring to the rejection of Mr. Disraeli's resolution of the 20th of February, he described it as being in point of fact a resolution " to refer the original proposition for expenditure back to the Government, from a belief that it was only by such a course we could hope to enforce the acceptance of our own views. I confess I thought that reduction was not only desirable but necessary, and I gave my vote for it. The appeal was made to the House, and the House decided that the Estimates should not be sent back for reconsideration by the Government. . . . If that appeal had not been rejected, I believe that these estimates would have been much reduced without the country risking the loss of Her Majesty's Ministers. For my part, seeing the temper of the present House, I fear very much that there will be no great reduction in the Estimates; and that being the case, I am of opinion that it would be the very worst species of economy to run the risk of a deficiency in our revenue."

Among the observations to which Sir George Lewis had laid himself open, there was one which Mr. Gladstone did not fail to urge, and to urge with great force. We were at

Financial Policy.

that time engaged in two wars, one in Persia, the other in China. The budget for 1857-8 contained no provision for meeting the expense of either of them. A sum of 260,000*l*. had been taken to defray the charge of the former up to the end of the financial year 1856-7, but nothing was proposed to be taken for the year 1857-8. There was, of course, much uncertainty as to what would ultimately be required to meet the demands occasioned by these operations; and the uncertainty was fully sufficient to justify the Chancellor of the Exchequer in declining to estimate the expenditure of future years; but it would have been better if, under those circumstances, he had abstained from hinting at a reduction to something like the standard of 1853, a standard which he must have felt it would be impossible to return to, or even to approach, without a complete change in the line of policy with regard to expenditure to which the Government of which he was a member had committed itself.

CHAP. VI.

1857.

Expense of Persian and Chinese wars.

The debate on Mr. Disraeli's resolution was adjourned till the 23rd of February, on which evening a very excellent speech was made by Lord John Russell, justifying, to a considerable extent, the proposals of Sir George Lewis, but

Speeches of Lord J. Russell,

Y

adopting the substance of Mr. Disraeli's charge; namely, that, according to the scale of the expenditure proposed for 1857, there must be a considerable deficiency in 1858, and that, if it were possible to avert that deficiency by a great reduction in 1858, that reduction ought to be commenced in 1857. He referred to the case of the Estimates of his own Government in 1848, which he had been obliged, in consequence of the general feeling of the House, to abandon, although they were less by five millions than the Estimates now under consideration; and, comparing the circumstances of 1848 with those of 1857, he said he could not help thinking that some reductions might be made in the latter. He thought, however, that the House ought to go at once into Committee of Supply and to consider the Estimates most carefully and vigilantly; and he was, therefore, not willing to vote for Mr. Disraeli's resolution. Mr. Cardwell took up somewhat the same line of argument. There was, undoubtedly, an appearance of logic in the conclusion which both he and Lord John Russell drew from the premisses which they laid down; and, if it were really possible for the House of Commons to cut down the estimates of a government by

Financial Policy.

discussions upon each separate vote in Committee of Supply, it would certainly be a very sensible and constitutional course to take. But Mr. Milner Gibson suggested what appears the true answer to this theory. "No doubt," he said, "the honourable member for Lambeth (Mr. Williams) would be gratified by finding among his small minorities the names of the noble lord and the right honourable member for Portsmouth (Sir F. Baring), and perhaps with great exertions he might succeed in reducing the salary of a chaplain in the Bahamas, or in knocking off the odd shilling upon some other particular vote. But if the House was in earnest, if it wanted to obtain a practical result, it must take its stand at once. During his experience in Parliament he had never known a successful effort to bring about a reduction of expenditure in any other way than by leaving to the Government the responsibility of proposing the reductions, by informing them generally that the scale of expenditure and taxation which they proposed did not meet the approval of Parliament."

The resolution of Mr. Disraeli was ultimately lost by a majority of 80.* This decision in

CHAP. VI.
1857.

and of Mr. Milner Gibson.

Resolution defeated.

---

* By 286 to 206.

CHAP. VI.
1857.

Defeat of the Government on Mr. Cobden's motion respecting China.

favour of the Government was, in effect, conclusive as to the policy of the House of Commons; and it may be presumed that, but for the political crisis which shortly afterwards occurred, the Budget would have been accepted without any important amendment. But on the 3rd of March the Government were defeated upon Mr. Cobden's motion, condemning their proceedings with regard to the dispute in China; and, in consequence of that defeat, they resolved upon winding up the business of the session and dissolving Parliament as speedily as possible. Under these circumstances, it was obviously proper for them to abstain from calling upon a Parliament, in the last weeks of its existence, to legislate for the finance of three years to come; and Lord Palmerston accordingly, on the 5th of March, announced that they would ask for the regulation of taxation for one year only, while with regard to the Estimates they would take votes on account sufficient to carry on the public service till the new Parliament should be in a condition to provide for it.

Financial measures in anticipation of a dissolution.

On the following day (March 6th) the Government proposed to go into Committee of Ways and Means. Mr. Disraeli and Mr. Gladstone had both given notice of amendments which they intended to move upon parts of the Government scheme. Mr. Gladstone proposed to move for the reduction of the Tea and Sugar duties; Mr. Disraeli, for the reduction of the Income Tax to the rate of 5*d.* in the pound. The latter began by appealing to the Government not to proceed with their financial measures, but to leave them over till the new Parliament should meet; but Sir George Lewis pointed out that in that case the Income Tax would continue to be levied at the war rate of 16*d.* in the pound, that being the amount directed by the law as it stood. The House, therefore, went into committee; and, the resolution with regard to the Tea duties having been proposed first, Mr. Gladstone moved that the rate be 1*s.* 3*d.* instead of 1*s.* 5*d.* per lb. This amendment was lost, after a warm discussion, by a majority of 62.* Mr. Gladstone said that, after that decision, he would not press his amendments with regard to the Sugar duties, but would allow them to be negatived without a division. The Income Tax bill was brought forward at the next sitting of the House, and

---

* By 187 to 125.

CHAP. VI. 1857.

Mr. Disraeli then stated that, in consequence of the evidently growing demands of the China war, he should not propose the reduction of which he had given notice. Votes on account were afterwards taken in Committee of Supply with very little discussion; but upon the report of the Committee being brought up,* Mr. Gladstone moved an amendment to the effect that a further revision and reduction of expenditure was necessary. He reviewed the growth of the estimates, both Military and Civil, in an interesting speech, but did not press his amendment to a division. Parliament was dissolved on the 21st of March.

Estimates brought forward in new Parliament.

It will not be necessary to give any lengthened account of the discussions connected with finance which took place in the first session of the new Parliament. The Estimates for the year were voted, after full and interesting statements on the part of the Ministers charged with the duty of introducing them. Sir Charles Wood brought forward the Navy Estimates on the 18th of May; Lord Palmerston himself brought forward the Army Estimates on the 25th; and Mr. Wilson brought forward the Miscellaneous Civil Esti-

* March 10.

Financial Policy.

mates on the 12th of June, on which occasion he took the unusual course of making a general statement with respect to them, similar to those made by the Ministers introducing the Military estimates. These three speeches may be looked upon as furnishing a point of departure from which to calculate the progress we are making in our expenditure. It may be worth mentioning, as a matter of curiosity, that among the reasons given for our increasing our outlay upon dock accommodation, was the arrival of the new American frigate the Merrimac—the vessel which has since given us the opportunity of testing the value of iron-cased ships, and which on this occasion gave us a lesson of another kind, being found to be so much larger than any of our own frigates, that there was scarcely a dock in the country which could have received her.

On the 17th of July Sir George Lewis brought forward two supplementary estimates, the one for 500,000*l.* on account of the Persian war, the other for 400,000*l.* on account of the war in China. An additional vote for 100,000*l.* was at the same time taken for the navy. This was occasioned by the necessity which had arisen for sending a squadron to the Indian seas in

Supplementary estimates, July 17.

consequence of the breaking out of the mutiny. Sir George Lewis then proceeded to give information respecting the condition of the Exchequer. He said that the year 1856-7 had closed much more favourably than he had anticipated when he made his budget speech in February, and that the result of that year had been better by 1,860,000*l.* than had then been reckoned on. The receipts from Customs' duties in the current year had been about half-a-million more than had been expected, and so had the Excise revenue from malt. There had thus been a gain of 2,860,000*l.* to the Exchequer; against which, however, were to be set the charge for the redemption of the Sound dues, the supplementary estimates for the Persian and Chinese wars, and the dowry of the Princess Royal, which together amounted to 2,210,000*l.* He considered, therefore, that the finances were in a satisfactory position.

Tea and sugar duties fixed for three years, Aug. 12.

The last financial measure of the session was the revival on the 12th of August of Sir G. Lewis's original proposal to fix the rates of duty on tea and sugar for a period of three years. This proposal he made for the convenience of merchants, in order to obviate the uncertainty which would otherwise have attended their

Financial Policy. 329

transactions in these articles. The measure was adopted without opposition, Mr. Gladstone remarking that the adoption of the estimates of the Government, and the approval that had been given to their foreign policy, had entirely altered the circumstances under which he had acted in the early part of the year when he resisted the budget.

Sir George Lewis took this opportunity of stating that there would be no occasion for the Imperial Government to offer any present assistance of a financial kind to the East India Company. The mutiny was then at its height; and the difficulties of the Company were of course very great; but they were not of a financial character.

This was the last financial business transacted this session. Parliament was prorogued on the 28th of August. The autumn which ensued was a very gloomy one. The Indian mutiny continued to excite the gravest alarm, though by degrees the ultimate result became more and more certain. Combined, however, with this cause of uneasiness, was another of a scarcely less serious character. Failures of an unprecedented amount were taking place in the United States, and Europe was suffering in consequence. Some of the most eminent commercial houses

CHAP. VI.
1857.

Circumstances of the autumn of 1857.

Commercial pressure.

in this country were involved in the ruin of their American correspondents. A drain of gold set in, for money was needed as much in France and Germany as in England and America. The necessity of sending large sums of silver to the East, to meet the demands occasioned by the mutiny and by the Persian and Chinese wars, added to the mischief. The Bank raised its rate of discount in six weeks from 6 to 10 per cent.; but even so it was unable to maintain its reserve. By the 11th of November the stock of coin and bullion had fallen to 7,675,000*l*., and the reserve of notes to 957,710*l*.; these being points considerably below the lowest which had been reached in the great panic of 1847, when the stock of coin and bullion had fallen to 8,760,000*l*., and the reserve of notes to 1,547,000*l*. The demands to which the Bank was liable, moreover, were greater than in the earlier year; the amount of the private deposits being 12,935,000*l*., while in 1847, it had been only 8,580,000*l*. On the other hand, the amount of accommodation it had given to the public was far greater, the bills under discount and other private securities being 26,115,000*l*., while in 1847 they had only amounted to 19,467,000*l*. The severity of the distress and the greatness of the alarm may be measured by the estimated amounts of the failures which took place. The liabilities of five banks which stopped during the panic, were stated at 24,000,000*l.*; and those of about forty-five private firms were stated at 14,000,000*l.* The amounts given were, no doubt, exaggerated; but they were those which were generally believed in, and which affected the public mind.*

Under these circumstances, the Government took the same step as had been taken ten years before. They recommended the Bank directors to take upon themselves the responsibility of issuing notes upon securities beyond the limit prescribed by the Bank Charter Act; and they undertook to call Parliament together, and propose a bill of indemnity for this breach of the law. In the letter conveying this recommendation, the Treasury expressed their opinion that, in order to prevent the temporary relaxation of the law being extended beyond the actual necessities of the occasion, the Bank terms of discount ought not to be reduced below the rate at which they then stood, namely, 10 per cent.

---

* Ann. Register, vol. xcix.

This letter had considerable effect in calming the mind of the public; but it did not, as had been the case in 1847, at once put an end to the crisis. The demands for assistance continued to increase, and the bullion to decrease; for, though the high rate of discount had stopped the foreign drain of gold, the commercial failures in this country had only just begun, and the stoppage of two banks in Scotland, and the alarm in Ireland, had rendered it necessary to send a large quantity of specie to those parts of the kingdom. The Bank had to avail themselves of the authority given by the Treasury letter to the amount of 2,000,000*l*., and they increased their advances to the public until the 21st of November, when the amount of the "other securities," under which terms are included the discounts and advances to the public as distinguished from those made to the Government, was upwards of 31,000,000*l*. The stock of coin and bullion had at that time fallen to about 6,500,000*l*., and the reserve of notes was 1,148,000*l*. This was the turning-point of the pressure, and a gradual recovery then took place. By Christmas, the stock of bullion and the amount of the bank-note issues once more bore to one another the proportion prescribed

Financial Policy.

by the Bank Charter Act; the rate of discount was reduced, and by degrees matters returned to a satisfactory condition.

In the meantime, Parliament had been called together on the 3rd of December; and the Indemnity bill was passed; and a Select Committee was appointed to inquire into the operation of the Bank Acts. This last step was opposed by Mr. Disraeli, who maintained that Parliament was already in possession of all the information necessary to enable it to come to a conclusion upon the merits and defects of the law, and that it would be more proper to legislate, if any change were intended, than to spend more time in inquiry. The appointment of the Committee was, however, decided upon by a majority of 178.*

No other business of a financial character was transacted before the House rose for the Christmas recess. On its reassembling in February the public attention was engaged by the bill relating to conspiracies, which had been introduced in consequence of the recent attempt on the life of the Emperor of the French. The defeat which the Government

CHAP. VI.
1857.

Meeting of Parliament; Committee on the Bank Acts.

Defeat of the Government on the Conspiracy Bill, Feb. 19, 1858.

---

* By 295 to 117.

CHAP. VI.
1858.
Change of Government.

Estimates for 1858-9 brought forward.

sustained upon the 19th of February, upon Mr. Milner Gibson's amendment to the second reading of that bill, led to their resignation, and to the formation of Lord Derby's second administration, in which Mr. Disraeli again took the office of Chancellor of the Exchequer.

The Estimates for the service of the year 1858-59 had already been framed when the new Government came into office; and, as it was the 12th of March when the House met again after the re-election of the ministers, it was necessary to proceed at once with some votes in Supply. Votes on account were, therefore, taken for the Army and Navy Services on the 12th, and for the Revenue departments on the 15th of March; and the Government at once proceeded to make a careful review of the estimates which their predecessors had prepared, in order that they might introduce the budget without unnecessary delay. On the 12th of April, Sir John Pakington stated the alterations which he had made in the estimates for the Navy, and which involved reductions to the amount of about 300,000*l*. It was found that the Army estimates could not be reduced. The Civil Service estimates were still undergoing examination, when Mr. Disraeli

Financial Policy.

on the 19th of April brought forward his budget.

Circumstances had undergone a great change since the introduction of the budget of the preceding year. It had then seemed possible to reduce the military establishments of the country to the level at which they ought to stand in time of peace; and, although there was some difference of opinion as to the extent to which the reduction could be carried, and the rapidity with which it could be made, there was probably an unanimous expectation that the estimates would be gradually lowered, and that the reductions of 1857 would be carried further in 1858. Two disturbing causes, however, had defeated this expectation. The China war, though disapproved by the majority of the House of Commons, had been sanctioned by the voice of the country, and had assumed larger dimensions than the Government which undertook it had been willing to foresee. The formidable mutiny which had broken out in India had also led to a considerable addition to our expenditure; for, though the first charge, incurred in suppressing it had fallen upon the Indian, and not upon the English Treasury, yet it had rendered necessary an increase in our

CHAP. VI.
1858.
Budget, April 19.

CHAP. VI.
1858.

home force to supply the demands upon it occasioned by the large reinforcements sent to the East; and we had been compelled to maintain a larger naval force in the Indian seas, and to supply a greater amount of transport for troops, than we should otherwise have done. The consequence was that the Army and Navy estimates for 1858-59, instead of falling below those presented in 1857-8, exceeded them by more than a million.* But while the hopes that had been entertained of a material reduction of expenditure had thus been disappointed, the ability of the country to bear heavy taxation had, at the same time, been considerably diminished by the commercial crisis and the calamitous failures of the past autumn ; nor was it possible to say whether we had yet seen the last of the consequences of these misfortunes, or to predict what effect the disturbances in India might have upon the prosperity of England. A wonderful recovery had, indeed, taken

* This refers to the estimates as originally presented, but it was found necessary to vote large supplementary estimates for 1857-8, so that in reality the amount of supplies voted for 1858-9, was somewhat less than the amount voted for 1857-8. The whole amount voted for Army and Navy Services for 1857-8 was 22,749,208*l.*; the whole amount voted for 1858-9 was 22,297,253*l.*

place since the commencement of 1858; the revenue, which had seriously fallen off before the close of December, had increased with great rapidity in the quarter ending the 31st of March, and had actually exceeded Sir George Lewis's estimate by a million and a-half; confidence had revived; money had become abundant; and the rate of interest had fallen to a very low point. But the time was, nevertheless, one in which it was obviously of the highest importance to press as lightly as possible upon the resources of the country.

CHAP. VI.
―――
1858.

These considerations ought to be borne in mind when we come to examine the budget of the year. Mr. Disraeli began by estimating the expenditure for the ordinary services of 1858-9 at 63,610,000*l*. To this, he said, must be added the sums of 1,500,000*l*. for the war sinking fund, and 2,000,000*l*. for the redemption of Exchequer-bonds. The whole amount to be provided by the Treasury would therefore be 67,110,000*l*. To meet this charge he reckoned on a revenue of 63,120,000*l*. This estimate was made on the assumption that the Income Tax should be allowed to fall to 5*d.* in the pound, as it was provided by the Act of 1853 that it should do, and on the assumption that

Budget of 1858-9.

the revenue from the Customs and Excise, the Stamp duties and the Post Office, would be considerably larger than in the past year. It may be observed in passing that, although Mr. Disraeli's estimates were much cavilled at, and were regarded as excessively sanguine, they were fully justified by the result; he reckoned upon receiving from the four sources of income which have just been mentioned 53,050,000*l.*; he actually received from them 53,225,712*l.*

From this statement it of course follows that the deficiency for which Mr. Disraeli had to provide amounted to 3,990,000*l.* Of this 3,500,000*l.* was occasioned by the obligation to redeem debt. The question then arose, shall taxation be increased, or shall war taxation be kept up in time of peace, in order to redeem debt contracted in time of war? It is difficult to see how debts contracted in time of war can ever be paid off in time of peace without keeping up what may be called war taxation. All taxation beyond what is required for the regular service of the year, that is to say all taxation applied to the redemption of a debt, or even to the discharge of the interest of a debt, contracted for the purposes of bygone wars, may in a certain and very definite sense be called war taxation. It cannot, therefore, be laid down as a general rule that war taxation ought not to be kept up in time of peace for the purpose of redeeming debt. But there were circumstances peculiar to 1858 which undoubtedly involved the question in some difficulty. It was disputable whether the year could, strictly speaking, be called a year of peace, for war was going on in China and in India. The phrase which has lately become popular had not then been invented, but we should probably now describe it as an "exceptional" year. Then the amount of debt to be redeemed was too large to be redeemed all at once in any but an exceedingly flourishing year, which this was not. Again, and this perhaps was the most important consideration of all, it was not merely a question whether a certain amount of taxation should be levied, but whether a certain tax, which the public wished to put an end to, should be continued or not. It was the critical moment for deciding whether the scheme of 1853 should or should not be carried into effect. The choice lay between the extinction of the debt, and the extinction of the Income Tax. Whether the Government acted rightly or not in deciding upon the latter alternative, there can be no doubt

CHAP. VI.
1858.

that their decision met with very general acquiescence both in and out of Parliament. Indeed, as they did not command a parliamentary majority, they were not in a position to carry any measures which did not command such acquiescence. The nerves of the country were not sufficiently braced for the greater effort, which perhaps under other circumstances it ought to have made.

Repeal of War Sinking-fund Act.

Postponement of Exchequer-bonds.

Abandoning, then, the attempt to pay off any portion of the three millions and a-half of debt, Mr. Disraeli proposed to repeal the Act relating to the war Sinking-fund, and to re-borrow the amount of the Exchequer-bonds. By this means he reduced the deficit to somewhat less than half-a-million, for which he provided by raising

Equalisation of the Spirit duties.

the duty on Irish spirits to the level of the English and Scotch spirit duties, thus putting the finishing hand to the great work of equalisation, upon which so many Chancellors of the Exchequer had, for so many years, and with such unequal success, been engaged. "At this moment," said Mr. Disraeli, "the only differential duty that remains between Ireland and Great Britain is the differential duty on spirits. I am sure my Irish friends, who are always demanding justice for Ireland, and who define that justice to consist in an identity of institutions, of rights, and of duties, cannot on reflection consider the position in which they are placed by this differential duty on spirits with any other but feelings of indignant humiliation. I remember once, when I was at Bristol, a ship came in from Ireland, and to my great surprise I saw it boarded instantly by custom-house officers, and the crew treated just the same as a parcel of foreigners. All this was to see if there were any Irish spirits in the hold, which, if they had come in undetected, would have paid a duty of 6s. 2d. instead of 8s. Was that a position for high-spirited Irishmen to be placed in? How much better will it be for the Irish to have the command of the English market, and not only of the English but of the British market; how much better for them to enter into active competition with English and with Scotch spirits, and instead of confining themselves to the supply of a mere provincial demand, to be entitled to pour in their admirable products,—which I am told the French now prefer even to their own brandy; how much better for them to pour their spirits into this country, and through this country into the continent, and thus give a great stimulus to trade."

CHAP. VI.
1858.

Discussion of the Budget.

The equalisation of the Spirit duties was expected to equalise the revenue with the expenditure. In order to get a surplus, Mr. Disraeli proposed to lay a penny stamp on bankers' cheques,—a measure by which he hoped to gain a revenue of 300,000*l*. This proposal completed the arrangements for the year.

In the discussion which followed the introduction of the budget, a very general approval of its principal features was expressed by nearly all the prominent members of the House. Mr. Cardwell was almost the only person who objected to the arrangement for deferring the payment of the Exchequer-bonds. He asked how, if they could not be paid in the current year, when six millions were to be received from the Income Tax, it would be possible to pay them off in 1862 or 1863, when the Income Tax would have ceased; and he intimated that, in his opinion, they should have been paid off before the Income Tax was reduced. "He was very glad that he could generally concur in the proposals of the right honourable gentleman; but if he thought that his views would have any influence in the matter, he should have recommended the bolder course of taking the additional 2*d*. upon the Income Tax for one year,

Financial Policy.

which would have furnished 2,000,000*l.* for the liquidation of the Exchequer-bonds." Sir Francis Baring, on the other hand, while admitting that Mr. Cardwell was "financially right," thought the course proposed by the Chancellor of the Exchequer preferable, as tending to keep faith with the nation in the matter of the final extinction of the Income Tax. This appeared to be, upon the whole, the general opinion.

A more serious debate, however, upon the principles of the budget was raised on the 3rd of May, when the Exchequer-bonds' bill came on for a second reading. Sir George Lewis availed himself of that opportunity, in the first place, to justify his own financial policy,—which he thought had been misrepresented,—and in the next place to criticise the plans of Mr. Disraeli. He objected particularly to the renewal of the Exchequer-bonds, and to the abandonment of all attempts to reduce the debt. Referring to Mr. Disraeli's argument that we were bound to make an effort to part with the Income Tax in 1860, he asked whether prospective engagements for the remission of taxation were to be held sacred while prospective engagements for the payment of debt were to be held worthless. He offered some observations in defence of the In-

CHAP. VI.
1858.

Debate on the Exchequer-bonds' Bill, May 13.

come Tax, which he thought had been too much abused, and declined to be held bound to remit it at any particular time. In conclusion, he spoke strongly upon the necessity of regulating our taxation by the amount of our expenditure, and pointed out the numerous forms in which increased expenditure was now pressed upon the Government. He admitted that it was, with rare exceptions, an expenditure of a just and useful nature that was called for; and that it was occasioned by the vast number of plans for public improvement, and for putting things into as perfect a state as possible; but it was not the less an expenditure which rendered the remission of taxation impossible, and made it extremely dangerous for the House to fetter itself with rash obligations.

Mr. Gladstone replied to Sir George Lewis, and disputed some of his calculations. He defended the course taken by the Chancellor of the Exchequer in renewing the Exchequer-bonds, and said that Sir G. Lewis himself was responsible for their not being paid off as they ought to have been out of the last instalment of the war Income Tax. He denied that any one had asserted that there was a positive engagement that the Income Tax should cease in 1860; but he protested against the view which Sir G. Lewis appeared to take, that it was a tax which was a convenient part of the ordinary financial system of the country. Hitherto it had been asked for in order that great ends of policy might be obtained by its temporary employment. If a transition was now to be made from that system, and the tax was to be made permanent, that transition ought not to be made in the dark. "No doubt," said Mr. Gladstone, "the Income Tax has a great many recommendations as part of the permanent revenue of the country, but there are also great objections against it. One is a moral objection; for I believe it does more than any other tax to demoralise and corrupt the people. . . . . Another objection is, that so long as you consent, without a special purpose, to levy the Income Tax as part of the ordinary and permanent revenue of the country, so long it will be vain to talk of economy and effective reduction of expenditure. It is a source so productive, an engine so convenient,—it is so easy to lay on 1*d.* or 2*d.* at a time; it is so easy to come down to the House like my right honourable friend (Sir G. Lewis) and show that the difference between 2*l.* 1*s.* 8*d.* and 2*l.* 18*s.* 4*d.* is, after all, so very contemptible a sum that we need make no difficulty about paying it,—that, so long as you have the Income Tax a part of your ordinary revenue, you need not think of effective and extensive economy."

The discussion was continued by Mr. Cardwell, Mr. T. Baring, Mr. Bright, Mr. Disraeli, Mr. Wilson, and other members. Mr. Baring spoke with great force on the advantage of making some regular provision for the payment of debt, and lamented the abandonment of the Sinking-fund. Mr. Bright attacked the expenditure of the country, and the mode in which, as he said, the rich were for shifting the burden of taxation from themselves to the poor. Mr. Disraeli agreed with Mr. Bright in deploring the great expenditure upon armaments, but protested against his doctrine that we were throwing an undue proportion of taxation upon the poor. Upon the main question raised by Sir George Lewis he observed, that nobody now maintained that it would be possible to keep up the Sinking-fund; but he admitted that he had felt the greatest regret when he found himself compelled to defer the payment of the Exchequer-bonds. That was, however, a purely financial arrangement, while " the engagement with respect to the Income Tax was not merely based upon financial considerations, but also upon several other considerations, and those of high policy."

It would have been a great convenience to the Government of 1858, if Sir George Lewis's original budget of 1857 had been adopted, and the Income Tax retained at 7*d*. in the pound for three years. There would then have been no collision between financial maxims and those more general considerations of policy which were allowed, and perhaps unavoidably allowed, to overrule them in the year 1858.

The financial results of the year 1858-9 were so satisfactory that there is little doubt that, if no fresh occasion for expenditure had arisen in the following year, the hopes of Mr. Disraeli would have been realized, and that the 5*d*. Income Tax would have been sufficient, without any additional taxation, for the service of 1859-60. The surplus upon the year was 813,000*l.*; and the balances in the Exchequer were sufficiently strong on the 31st of March, 1859, to enable Mr. Disraeli to pay off the 2,000,000*l.* of bonds that fell due in the month of May, without calling on Parliament for any assistance. The income of the year had reached nearly 65,500,000*l*. A portion of this was due to the balance of the 7*d*. Income Tax remaining over

Financial results of 1858-9.

from the previous year; but even after deducting this, Mr. Gladstone, in bringing forward the budget for 1859-60, in the month of July, estimated the ordinary revenue for the coming year at 64,340,000*l.*; and it actually amounted to 65,969,000*l.** The expenditure of 1858-9 was 64,664,000*l.*; and of this 782,000*l.* was due to the Chinese and Russian wars. The proper expenditure of the year therefore was somewhat below 63,000,000*l.* If this rate of expenditure could have been maintained in 1859-60 there would have been a surplus of three millions at the close of that year. The falling in of the Long Annuities would have brought the expenditure of the following year down by more than two millions, and taxation to the amount of five millions might therefore have been remitted. This would not quite have sufficed to take off the Income Tax, which was then producing 5,600,000*l.*; but the difference would have been so small that an effort would probably have been

---

* Mr. Gladstone estimated the income at 64,340,000*l.* His additions amounted to the estimated sum of 5,220,000*l.*, making 69,460,000*l.* in all. But the actual produce was 71,089,000*l.* or 1,629,000*l.* more than the estimate. The revenue, therefore, without any addition would probably have been 65,969,000*l.*

Financial Policy. 349

made to pare down the expenditure so as to render the operation possible. At the same time an addition, such as has since been made, to the Spirit duties, a curtailment of the malt credit, and the general elasticity which would have been imparted to the revenue by the remission of the Income Tax, would have enabled the Chancellor of the Exchequer to take off, either at once, or by two instalments, the war duties upon tea and sugar.

CHAP. VI.
1859.

These hopes, however, were rudely dispelled by the necessity which arose in the year 1859 for adding enormously to the naval and military estimates. The disturbed state of Europe, and the great naval preparations of France, were the causes of this addition. In 1858 the estimates for the army and navy, including the packet service, had been taken at 21,610,000*l.*; in 1859 they were taken at 26,082,000*l*. showing an increase of no less than 4,472,000*l*. There was at the same time an increase of about 600,000*l*. in the miscellaneous estimates; and when, after the change of Government, Mr. Gladstone brought forward the budget in the month of July, he had to inform the Committee of Ways and Means that there was an estimated deficiency of 4,867,000*l*. to be provided for.

Necessity for increased Estimates in 1859.

The measures by which Mr. Gladstone proposed to supply this deficiency were two. In the first place he proposed to shorten by six weeks the credit of eighteen weeks previously by law allowed to maltsters; and thus to bring into the Exchequer, before the close of the financial year, a sum of about 780,000*l*., which would otherwise not have been payable until after the 1st of April, 1860. Secondly, he proposed to add 4*d.* in the pound to the Income Tax, but to levy the whole of that 4*d.* on the first half-yearly payment, or, in other words, to collect the Income Tax for the first half of 1859-60 at the rate of 13*d.* instead of 5*d.* in the pound. By this addition he expected to gain 4,340,000*l*.; and the effect of these two measures would be to convert the deficit of 4,867,000*l*. into a surplus of 253,000*l*.

The actual result was much more favourable than he anticipated. The expenditure indeed somewhat exceeded the amount on which he had reckoned, and reached the sum of 69,502,289*l*. This was owing to the breaking out of the third China war, and to the consequent necessity for supplementary estimates in the beginning of 1860. But the income, which Mr. Gladstone had estimated at 69,460,000*l*., reached the large sum of 71,089,669*l*. and the surplus on the year was therefore 1,587,380*l*.

I have thus brought this sketch of the financial policy of recent years down to the year 1860. I find it so difficult and even impossible to enter at any length upon a discussion of the budgets of 1860 and 1861, that I shall not make the attempt. I have endeavoured to criticise the policy of the years I have been describing fairly and impartially. If I were to go on with the history of the two years in the struggles of which I have myself had occasion to take part, I should try to avoid all conscious unfairness, but I could hardly hope to write without a greater amount of bias than I should like to show. I shall therefore content myself with giving a bare outline of the measures of the two years, referring the reader to the Table of Budgets given in the Appendix* for more compendious information.

Mr. Gladstone introduced the budget of 1860-1 on the 10th of February, 1860. Two events had occurred since the close of the preceding session which had a material influence upon his calculations. In the first place, the war, which had

---

* See Appendix A.

again broken out in China in the course of the recess, had rendered it necessary to present a supplementary estimate of 850,000*l.* for the year 1859-60, and of course to make some additional provision for the naval and military service of 1860-1. In the second place, a commercial treaty had been concluded with France, by which the English Government had pledged themselves to propose to Parliament large remissions and reductions of duty on French produce. The alterations required by the treaty involved a remission of Customs' duties to the amount of 1,737,000*l.* which Mr. Gladstone considered would involve a loss to the revenue of 1,190,000*l.* Besides these remissions, Mr. Gladstone also proposed that other duties of Customs to the amount of 1,039,000*l.* should be repealed or reduced, thus causing a further loss bf 910,000*l.* to the Customs' revenue; and he proposed to repeal the Paper duty and to reduce some other Excise duties, causing a loss of 990,000*l.* within the year to the revenue from the Excise. The total amount of the Paper duty was 1,200,000*l.* or 1,300,000*l.*; but its repeal was not to take place until an advanced period of the year, so that the whole loss would not be felt immediately. These reductions would have involved a total

Financial Policy. 353

loss of nearly three millions ; but Mr. Gladstone proposed to lay some small charges upon imports, exports, warehousing, and other operations of trade, and to impose one or two minor taxes, as, for instance, one upon chicory, and some stamp duties on certain documents; and these were estimated to reduce the total loss to about 2,100,000*l.*, that is to say, to about the amount which the country was to gain by the falling in of the Long Annuities.

CHAP. VI.
1860.

The expenditure of the country was estimated in the month of February at 70,014,000*l*. including a vote of credit of 500,000*l.* for the operations in China. To bring the revenue up to this level Mr. Gladstone reimposed the Income Tax at the rate of 10*d.* in the pound for one year, combining with this reimposition a provision for bringing three-fourths of the tax, instead of one-half only, into the Exchequer within the financial year. He also again shortened the Malt and the Hop credits. The Tea and the Sugar duties he reimposed, also for a single year, at the rates at which they had stood since the war. With these additions, he estimated that the revenue would amount to 70,564,000*l.*, thus leaving a surplus of 464,000*l.* It should be observed that in his estimate of

A A

revenue he included about 250,000*l.* to be received from Spain in repayment of an old debt to this country. A like amount had already been received in the preceding year. It should also be noticed that he renewed the 1,000,000*l.* of Exchequer-bonds falling due in May, 1860.

Amongst the articles which were entirely set free from Customs' duties by this budget the most important were, silk manufactures, gloves, artificial flowers, watches, and all other manufactured articles upon which any duties were still in force; also butter, cheese, tallow, oranges, eggs, nuts, and a number of articles of food. In fact, Mr. Gladstone stated that whereas, in 1842, the number of articles subject to duty had been 1052, which had been subsequently increased by Sir Robert Peel's first reform of the tariff to 1163, and had afterwards been brought down by several stages to 419, that number would now be reduced to no more than 48, of which 15 only would be contributors of any importance to the revenue. These fifteen are as follow:—spirits, sugar, tea, tobacco, wine, coffee, corn, currants, timber, chicory, figs, hops, pepper, raisins, and rice. The chief reductions of duties, besides the total remissions, were in the cases of wine, brandy, timber, currants, and dried fruits.

Financial Policy.

The budget was met on the 21st of February by a resolution proposed by Mr. Ducane, and couched in the following terms:—" That this House, recognizing the necessity of providing for the increased expenditure of the coming financial year, is of opinion, that it is not expedient to add to the existing deficiency by diminishing the ordinary revenue, and is not prepared to disappoint the just expectations of the country by reimposing the Income Tax at an unnecessarily high rate." This resolution, after a debate of three nights, was rejected on the 24th of February, by a majority of 116.* The main principles upon which the budget was founded having thus been affirmed, the only point of detail upon which any serious resistance was afterwards offered, was the question of the repeal of the Paper duty. When the Paper duty repeal bill came on for a second reading (March 12), Sir William Miles moved the following amendment:—" That as it appears the repeal of the duty on paper will necessitate the addition of 1d. in the pound to the Property and Income Tax, it is the opinion of this House that such repeal is, under such

CHAP. VI
1860.
Mr. Ducane's resolution, Feb. 21,
rejected Feb. 24.
Opposition to the repeal of the Paper duty.

---

* 339 to 223.

circumstances, at the present moment inexpedient." The second reading was, however, carried by a majority of 53.* The bill was again opposed at the third reading, on the 8th of May, and was then carried by the diminished majority of 9.† It was ultimately thrown out in the House of Lords, on the 21st of May, by a majority of 89.‡

On the 16th of July, Mr. Gladstone found it necessary to propose a large addition to the Vote of Credit which he had announced would be required for the war in China. The sum originally named was 500,000*l.*; the sum finally asked was 3,800,000*l.*; of which, however, 450,000*l.* was for the purpose of closing an old account with the East India Company, arising out of the first Chinese war. At the same time, Mr. Gladstone explained some other changes that had been made in the financial position of the country since the first introduction of the budget. An error of more than 200,000*l.* had been discovered in the estimate for the collection of the revenue. Several of the minor charges upon trade had been

---

* 245 to 192. † 219 to 210.
‡ 193 to 104.

abandoned or modified, and about 180,000*l.* of anticipated revenue had thus been lost. On the other hand, about 900,000*l.* had been saved by the rejection of the bill for the repeal of the Paper duty. The result of these various operations was, that a sum of 2,336,000*l.* remained to be provided. In order partly to meet this deficiency, Mr. Gladstone proposed to raise the Spirit duties to 10*s.* per gallon, a measure by which he reckoned on obtaining 1,050,000*l.* within the current financial year, leaving a deficiency of 1,286,000*l.* to be paid out of the balances in the Exchequer. This was the position in which the financial arrangements were left at the close of the Session of 1860; for the money raised in terminable annuities for the purpose of defraying the expense of the fortifications which were commenced this year did not form part of the regular supplies, and was excluded from all Mr. Gladstone's calculations.

The actual result of the year 1860-1 was even more unfavourable than Mr. Gladstone had anticipated. The income, mainly through the failure of the Excise revenue, fell short of the estimate by upwards of two millions; and, though the expenditure also fell short of the amount at which it had been taken, the deficiency, instead of being 1,286,000*l.*, proved to be 2,558,385*l.* Of this, as Mr. Gladstone explained,* a sum of 288,000*l.* properly belonged to the finance of 1859-60, having been paid as drawback upon the stocks of wine in the hands of the merchants at the time of the reduction of the duties. If, however, this deduction from the deficit is to be allowed, we must, on the other hand, add about an equal amount for the excess of naval and military expenditure above the sums included in Mr. Gladstone's statement, as the exact expenditure had not then been ascertained, and the charge for the excess had afterwards to be made good. The real deficiency, therefore, on the year 1860-1, was, as nearly as possible, 2,550,000*l.*

Budget of 1861-2, April 15.

The budget for the following year (1861-2), was brought forward on the 15th of April. Mr. Gladstone then estimated the expenditure at 69,900,000*l.*, or at nearly three millions below that of the preceding year, the difference arising from the termination of the Chinese war; and the revenue, (including 750,000*l.* of anticipated receipts from China), at 71,503,000*l.*, suppos-

---

* April 15, 1861.

Financial Policy. 359

ing the Income Tax to be renewed at 10*d.* in the pound, and the Tea and Sugar duties also to be renewed at the same rates at which they had stood since the war. This would have given a surplus of 1,900,000*l.*, and Mr. Gladstone thought this would enable him to reduce the Income Tax to 9*d.* in the pound, and to take off the Paper duty. The produce of a penny in the pound of Income Tax is about 1,100,000*l.* a-year, and the produce of the Paper duty was about 1,300,000*l.* The full amount of the proposed reductions, therefore, was equal to about 2,400,000*l.* per annum. But this amount would not all fall upon the current year; one quarter of the 10*d.* Income Tax had still to be collected, which would reduce this item of loss to 850,000*l.*; and the repeal of the Paper duty was put off till the 1st of October, so that Mr. Gladstone estimated that upon this head the first loss would not exceed 665,000*l.* He reckoned, therefore, on a surplus of 388,000*l.* in the year 1861-2, and on such a reduction of expenditure and such elasticity of resources in 1862-3 as would enable that year to bear the further loss which would be thrown upon it by the final cessation of the Paper duty.

Considerable doubts were expressed by mem-

CHAP. VI.
―――
1861.
Financial results of 1860-1.

bers of the Opposition, whether the expected payment of 750,000*l.* would be received from China. The result justified those doubts; the amount actually received, after making the necessary payments to the merchants who had claims on the indemnity, was only 266,000*l.* The repeal of the Paper duty also caused a greater loss to the revenue of the year than had been anticipated by Mr. Gladstone; and, instead of costing only 665,000*l.*, cost between 900,000*l.* and one million. The whole amount of revenue received was 69,674,479*l.*, or 588,000*l.* below the anticipated amount. The expenditure, swelled by the preparations required by the aspect of American affairs, reached 71,116,000*l.*, or 1,340,000*l.* more than had been reckoned upon. The deficiency on the year was 1,442,000*l.*, without counting the sum of 970,000*l.* applied to the erection of fortifications within the year, which was raised by loan.

Mr. Horsfall's amendment on the Tea duty rejected, May 2.

The only important division taken upon the budget of 1861, was that on the 2nd of May, when Mr. Horsfall opposed the re-imposition of the Tea duty at 1*s.* 5*d.* per lb. and moved that it should be reduced to one shilling. Had this motion been carried, the repeal of the

Paper duty must have been abandoned; but Mr. Horsfall was defeated by a majority of 18.*

It is natural, at the close of such an inquiry as that which I have now completed, to turn back and ask :—What has been the general result, in a financial sense, of the whole policy which I have been reviewing; does the country stand better or stand worse in 1862 than in 1842; how do its accounts appear when we come to make them up?

In endeavouring to contribute some suggestions towards an answer to this question, I must guard myself by once more referring to the narrow point of view from which I am about to look at it. The great fiscal and commercial measures of the last twenty years have wrought a wonderful change in the circumstances of the country. A complete revolution has taken place in many parts of our moral, social, and political system, which may be directly traced, either wholly or in great part, to the effects of those measures. Our material wealth, too, has enormously increased ; our trade has developed; and our manufactures have been carried to great perfection. There have been seasons of tem-

---

* 299 to 281.

porary, local, and partial suffering, and the changes which have proved beneficial to the public have sometimes pressed hardly upon particular interests; but, upon the whole, it can hardly be questioned that the condition of every portion of the community has been greatly improved by the new policy.

But these are matters of which I have not undertaken to treat, and I therefore leave them on one side while I look at the mere financial question which I have already put. I am by no means sure that the answer to this question is as clear as many persons are inclined to think it. Of course, in a general way, it may be said that a country whose wealth has increased is better able to bear heavy financial burdens than it was before such increase. England, therefore, being richer in 1862 than she was in 1842, is, in a certain sense, better able to bear such burdens now than she was then. But it must not be forgotten, in the first place, that she is not only able to bear increased taxation, but is actually called upon to bear it. If her wealth has increased, so has her expenditure; and that, too, in a pretty equal degree. Mr. Gladstone, in his budget speech of 1860, pointed out that between 1842 and 1859 the wealth of the country had increased about 28¼ per cent. and the expenditure in the same time about 27 per cent. Now this is a serious consideration; and it is made the more serious when we remember that Mr. Gladstone at the same time showed that the increase in the expenditure had been advancing at a greatly accelerated rate of speed in the last six years of the term of which he was speaking, and that the portion of the public expenditure which is, so to speak, optional and subject to the control of the public, had in those six years risen by no less than 58 per cent. Nothing can be more natural than that a nation should, like an individual, increase its expenditure as its wealth increases; but it is to be borne in mind that while nothing is easier or pleasanter than to expand one's outlay upon the necessaries and conveniences of life, nothing is more painful or more difficult than to contract it; and that, should our prosperity encounter any check, the habit of large expenditure which we have allowed to gain upon us may prove a very inconvenient one.

But, it will be said, the increase of our expenditure has been occasioned by causes entirely independent of the fiscal policy of recent years; that policy has not caused the expenditure, it has only given us the means of meeting it. I am not sure that either branch of this assertion can be admitted—at all events, not without some qualification. Our fiscal policy has, perhaps, not directly caused us to spend more, but it has certainly encouraged us to do so. Many causes have been at work to lead to increased expenditure; and so have many causes been at work to lead to increased prosperity; we assign to the fiscal and commercial policy of late years a very large share of credit for the prosperity, perhaps we do not sufficiently recognize its influence on the expenditure. The long peace, the progress of science, and its application to all the arts of life, the development of the railway system, the improvements in agriculture and manufactures, the discoveries of gold, the impulse given to colonisation, are the causes which have most manifestly led to our prosperity. Their effect has undoubtedly been much enhanced by the removal of restrictions which would otherwise have retarded the march of improvement; and the improvement may therefore, in a sense, be said to be due to that removal. But somewhat similar reasoning is applicable to the case of our expenditure. If we had not had so ready an engine as the Income Tax at our hand, we should have found it impossible to do all that we have

Financial Policy.

done in the way of spending. We could not have met the demands that have been made upon us for the education of our people, for the improvement of our judicial system, for the comfort or even the efficiency of our army and navy, and for hundreds of other objects of more or less importance, if our fiscal system had continued as inelastic as it appeared to be in 1840. When, in order to meet any additional expenditure, it was necessary to impose a new tax, the power of increasing our expenditure was greatly restricted. Now that additional expenditure can be met by the simple expedient of slightly adding to the rate of an existing tax, that restriction is nearly done away; and as the removal of the restrictions on commerce has promoted commerce, so the removal of the restrictions on expenditure has promoted expenditure.

But to what extent is it true that our present system of finance has increased our means of meeting expenditure? We now experience about the same amount of difficulty in meeting an expenditure of 70,000,000*l.* as twenty years ago we found in meeting an expenditure of 55,000,000*l.** Apparently, then, we can sup-

---

* This sum is arrived at by adding the cost of the collec-

port an expenditure greater by fifteen millions than we formerly could. This is a matter which requires a little illustration. In 1842 Sir Robert Peel, before making any change in our system at all, estimated the income for the year at 48,350,000*l*.,* the expenditure at 50,819,000*l*., and the deficiency at 2,469,000*l*. These figures show, or at least enable us to form an approximate idea of, the relation of our ordinary income to our expenditure before the Income Tax was imposed. In the year 1853, after Sir Robert Peel's reforms had borne their fruit, and when Mr. Gladstone's measures were in the first year of their trial, the ordinary income, that is to say, the income without the produce of the Income Tax, was 48,657,000*l*.,† the expenditure was 51,250,000*l*., and the amount by which the latter exceeded the former was 2,593,000*l*. The close correspondence between these figures and those of Sir Robert Peel's estimate is very curious. But in the year 1861 the net ordinary

---

tion of the revenue to the other expenditure, so as to make a fair comparison.

* The average income of the three years, 1839, 1840, and 1841, had been 48,343,000*l*.

†. The average income of the three years 1850, 1851, and 1852, without the Income Tax, had been 47,496,000*l*.

income was about 55,300,000*l*.,* the expenditure was 67,387,000*l*.,† and the amount by which the ordinary income fell short of the expenditure was about 12,000,000*l*. While therefore we have increased our expenditure by about sixteen millions a-year,‡ we have brought up the productiveness of our ordinary sources of revenue by no more than about seven millions.§ When we say we support expenditure better than we did, we should bear in mind that we do so by making more use of the Income Tax. Now the Income Tax is generally regarded as the financial reserve of the country, which should be kept available for emergencies. What we are doing, therefore, is drawing on our reserve; and it is a grave question whether this is to be considered a proof of financial strength.

It seems to me that a broad distinction must be drawn between the policy pursued from 1842 up to the time of the Russian war, and that

---

* This sum is arrived at by deducting from 59,309,000*l*., which is the gross amount of the ordinary income, the sum of 4,000,000*l*., which I suppose to be about the cost of the collection of the ordinary revenue.

† Including the outlay on fortifications, but excluding the cost of collecting the revenue.

‡ *i.e.* from 50,819,000*l*. to 67,387,000*l*.

§ *i.e.* from 48,350,000*l*. to 55,300,000*l*.

which has been pursued since. The principles which appear to have guided Sir Robert Peel and Mr. Goulburn in their financial arrangements were,—first, the maintenance of a surplus of revenue over expenditure, with a view to keep up the credit of the country and to operate upon the National Debt; secondly, the repeal or reduction of taxes upon a settled plan, adopted with a view, so far as its financial aspect is concerned, to render the ordinary sources of revenue more productive by relieving trade and industry from unwise restrictions, and by improving the general condition of the taxpayer; and thirdly, the use of the Income Tax at a fixed rate, and for definite periods, with a view to enable them to give effect to their plans for remission of taxation without endangering the maintenance of an adequate surplus of revenue. The result of a steady adherence to these principles was, that in the five years of Sir Robert Peel's administration the unredeemed capital of the National Debt was reduced by 9,232,000*l.*, and the annual charge by 1,436,777*l.*; and though taxes to a very large amount were remitted, their productiveness was in no degree impaired; for, whereas the ordinary revenue had amounted before 1842 to 48,343,000*l.*, it amounted in 1846 to 48,341,538*l.* without including the produce of the Income Tax or the receipts from China. The aggregate amount of the surplus of income over expenditure in those five years was 11,161,879*l.* In the next seven years, 1847-1854, the principles of Sir Robert Peel were more or less exactly followed. An addition was unavoidably made to the debt in consequence of the Irish famine; but notwithstanding this addition the amount of the unredeemed capital was, in the course of the seven years, further reduced by 13,855,000*l.*, and the amount of the annual charge by 320,000*l.*; so that the total reduction in the capital of the debt between 1842 and 1854 was 23,000,000*l.*, and the reduction in the annual charge 1,750,000*l.* The accumulated surplus of the whole period was 19,535,988*l.*, or, deducting the loan raised at the time of the Irish famine, 11,535,988*l.* The ordinary revenue without the Income Tax stood in 1853-4 a trifle higher than in 1842, and the rate of expenditure also was substantially the same in the two years. The cost of the Supply services had been increased by about the same amount as that by which the charge for the debt had been diminished. Symptoms of a disposition to depart from Sir Robert Peel's policy with regard to the Income Tax, however, had been shown in the years 1848 and 1851, and Parliament had begun to look upon it as a tax which might be used as a permanent source of revenue, might be renewed annually, and might be varied in its rate. Feeling, however, that it could not well be used in this manner without some alteration in its framework, the House of Commons had begun to review it with the purpose of meeting the demands of those who were calling for its reform. If that reform could have been made upon principles satisfactory to the majority, the Income Tax would have become the makeweight of our financial system, and would probably have been freely used to effect remissions of taxation on the one hand and additions to expenditure on the other. This was what we appeared to be coming to, when Mr. Gladstone carried the great measures of 1853, and restored for the time the policy of Sir Robert Peel. Seeing the danger of attempting either to remodel or to perpetuate the Income Tax, he made a bold, but by no means a too bold, effort to stamp the impost with the character of a temporary and provisional source of revenue, designed, as Sir Robert Peel had designed it, to carry the finances through the period of an experiment.

The Russian war, in its direct and still more in its indirect consequences, put an end to the policy of 1853. It was that war which, as I have already observed, not only rendered large expenditure necessary, but infected the whole nation, and not this nation only but all Europe also, with ideas of extravagance. The importance of maintaining an annual surplus of income over expenditure, and of making some provision for the reduction of our debt, has been lost sight of. Some persons have been for reducing taxes, others for increasing expenditure, without any apparent respect to the consequent effect upon our balance-sheet, or upon the amount of our unredeemed debt. It would be unfair to reproach any particular minister or any particular party for this line of conduct. All have been more or less responsible, and each may retort upon the other the arguments which any one may use. This, however, is perfectly clear,—that if we are to put an end to this state of things we must leave off wrangling as to who is most to blame, and must apply ourselves in earnest to find a remedy. Public spirit must take precedence of party spirit;

and a general view of the policy most conducive to the interests of England must not be eclipsed by our attachment to particular theories and particular measures. It is with a sincere conviction that the financial condition of the country is such as to render it our duty to lay aside all private and personal prejudices, and to cooperate heartily in setting right that which is amiss, that I close this chapter.

APPENDICES.

APPENDIX A.

Table of Budgets.

HE following Table is made out by taking the estimates of revenue and expenditure from the Budget Speeches of each year, and the results from the Finance Accounts, which do not however show the actual expenditure on each head of service, but only the Exchequer issues on account of it up to the close of the year.

The column headed " Basis of Estimate" shows the amount anticipated by the Chancellor of the Exchequer before making any alteration in taxation. When this column is left blank it is because no alteration was made in that year.

Budget of 1842-3.

(March 11, 1842.)

REVENUE.

Head of Revenue.	Basis of Estimate.	Estimate.	Result.	Remarks.
	£	£	£	
Customs	22,500,000	21,560,000	20,754,185	Income Tax imposed at 7d. in the pound.
Excise	13,459,000	13,700,000	12,500,627	Export duty laid on Coals.
Stamps	7,100,000	7,190,000	6,977,358	
Taxes	4,400,000	4,400,000	4,265,537	Spirit duties and Stamp duties in Ireland increased.
Post Office	500,000	500,000	610,000	
Crown Lands	150,000	150,000	117,500	Expected gain 4,300,000l.
Miscellaneous	250,000	250,000	552,559	Customs' duties to the estimated extent of 1,200,000l. remitted.
Income Tax	...	3,700,000	2,456,287	
China Payment	...	...	511,407	
Total	48,350,000	51,450,000	48,745,460	
Surplus	...	631,000	...	
Deficiency	2,469,000	...	2,421,776	

EXPENDITURE.

Head of Service.	Estimate.	Result.	Remarks.
	£	£	
Debt	29,427,000	29,434,891	
Cons. Fund Charges	2,368,000	2,408,377	
Army	6,617,000	6,308,602	
Navy	6,739,000	6,680,163	
Ordnance	2,084,000	1,893,425	
Miscellaneous	2,800,000	3,182,432	
Canada, Clothing of Volunteers	108,000	150,062	
Chinese Expedition	675,000	1,079,487	
Unclaimed Dividends	...	29,796	
Total	50,819,000	51,167,236	

Budget of 1843-4.
(May 8, 1843.)

REVENUE.

Head of Revenue.	Basis of Estimate.	Estimate.	Result.	Remarks.
		£	£	
Customs	...	19,000,000	21,426,632	No alteration of taxation this year.
Excise	...	13,000,000	12,962,011	
Stamps	...	7,000,000	7,011,937	
Taxes	...	4,200,000	4,192,473	
Post Office . . .	...	600,000	628,000	
Crown Lands . .	...	130,000	147,500	
Miscellaneous . .	...	250,000	305,881	
China Money . .	...	870,000	803,802	
Income Tax . .	...	5,100,000	5,356,888	
Total . . .	...	50,150,000	52,835,125	
Surplus . .	...	762,355	2,095,428	
Deficiency .	...	...	...	

EXPENDITURE.

Head of Service.	Estimate.	Result.	Remarks.
	£	£	
Debt	29,178,734	29,132,784	The money applied to the payment of the opium compensation, and the settlement of the debt to the East India Company had not been estimated for. Excluding this item, the expenditure was about 700,000l. below the amount of the estimate. But the great apparent reduction in the Army expenditure arose partly from certain repayments having been made by the East India Company, and partly from the reduction of the balances which it had been necessary to keep in the Commissariat chests abroad during the China war.
Cons. Fund Charges	2,357,000	2,352,264	
Army	6,619,788	6,118,656	
Navy	6,382,990	6,286,056	
Ordnance . . .	1,849,142	1,941,926	
Miscellaneous . . } Insurrect. in Canada }	3,000,000	{ 2,812,294 { 25,300	
Opium Compensation & Debt to E. I. Co. for China war }	...	2,070,416	
Total . . .	49,387,645	50,739,697	

Budget of 1844-5.

(April 29, 1844.)

REVENUE.

Head of Revenue.	Basis of Estimate.	Estimate.	Result.	Remarks.
	£	£	£	
Customs . .	21,500,000	21,260,000	22,312,365	Reductions made on
Excise . .	13,000,000	12,950,000	13,431,883	EXCISE. £
Stamps . .	7,000,000	6,900,000	7,267,342	Flint Glass 35,000
Assessed Taxes	4,200,000	4,200,000	4,217,749	Vinegar 12,000
Income Tax	5,100,000	5,100,000	5,104,448	CUSTOMS.
Post Office .	600,000	600,000	699,000	Currants 90,000
Crown Lands	130,000	130,000	125,000	Coffee 50,000
Miscellaneous	250,000	250,000	482,755	Wool 100,000
China Payment	...	...	777,073	STAMPS.
				Marine Insurances . 100,000
Total . .	51,790,000	51,390,000	54,417,615	About . . £400,000
Surplus .	3,146,830	2,746,830	6,342,436	
Deficiency	...	...	...	

EXPENDITURE.

Head of Service.	Estimate.	Result.	Remarks.
	£	£	
Debt.	27,697,000	27,672,918	Charge for the debt apparently reduced by 1,435,000*l.* on account of the alteration of the time of paying dividends. Real reduction only 313,000*l.* for one half-year.
Cons. Fund Charges	2,400,000		
Dissentient fundhldrs.	250,000	2,737,945	
South Sea Company	239,000		
Army	6,616,868	6,415,394	Consolidated Fund charges include 104,275*l.* for dissentient fundholders, and 222,211*l.* for South Sea Company.
Navy	6,250,128	6,218,219	
Ordnance . . .	1,840,064	1,973,511	
Miscellaneous . .	3,000,000	3,026,266	
Opium Compensation	...	30,926	
E. I. Company for China war . . }	400,000	...	This sum was not required within the year.
Total . . .	48,643,170	48,075,179	

Budget of 1845-6.

(Feb. 14, 1845.)

REVENUE.

Head of Revenue.	Basis of Estimate.	Estimate.	Result.	Remarks.
	£	£	£	
Customs . .	22,000,000	19,582,000	19,768,393	Income Tax renewed at 7d. in the pound.
Excise . .	13,500,000	12,580,000	13,296,620	Reduction of Sugar £ duties 1,300,000
Stamps . .	7,100,000	7,100,000	7,660,340	
Assessed Taxes	4,200,000	4,200,000	4,224,039	Repeal of Export duties 118,000
Post Office .	700,000	700,000	791,000	
Crown Lands	150,000	150,000	130,000	Repeal and remission of 430 duties . . 320,000
Income Tax	2,600,000	5,200,000	5,084,741	Repeal of duty on Cotton Wool . . . 680,000
Miscellaneous	250,000	250,000	303,333	
China Payment	600,000	600,000	750,859	Total Customs £2,418,000
Total . .	51,100,000	50,362,000	52,009,324	Repeal of Auction duty. 250,000
Surplus .	1,410,000	672,000	2,380,600	Do. of Glass duty 640,000
Deficiency	...	...	...	Total Excise . . £890,000
				Total . . £3,308,000

EXPENDITURE.

Head of Service.	Estimate.*	Result.	Remarks.
	£	£	
Debt	28,395,000	28,213,523	About 1,000,000l. added to the Navy Estimates, in order to enable us to create a respectable Steam Navy, and to maintain ten sail of the line.
Cons. Fund Charges	2,400,000	2,394,138	
Army	6,678,000	6,715,409	
Navy	6,936,000	6,968,917	
Ordnance . . .	2,142,000	2,236,507	* These figures are Sir R. Peel's; but the detail does not bear out the total.
Miscellaneous . .	3,200,000	2,871,673	
Unclaimed Dividends	...	228,557	
Total . . .	49,690,000	49,628,724	

Budget of 1846-7.

(May 29, 1846.)

REVENUE.

Head of Revenue.	Basis of Estimate.	Estimate.	Result.	Remarks.
	£	£	£	
Customs	19,768,000	19,500,000	21,086,265	Customs' Duties to the amount of 1,041,000*l.* were remitted this year.
Excise	...	13,400,000	13,958,391	
Stamps	...	7,450,000	7,638,765	
Taxes	...	4,230,000	4,257,159	
Income Tax . .	...	5,100,000	5,464,580	
Post Office . . .	...	850,000	856,000	
Crown Lands . .	...	120,000	112,000	
Miscellaneous .	...	300,000	432,957	
China Payment .	...	700,000	667,644	
Total . . .	...	51,650,000	54,473,762	
Surplus . .	...	777,000	2,765,191	
Deficiency .	...	...	...	

EXPENDITURE.

Head of Service.	Estimate.	Result.	Remarks.
	£	£	
Debt	28,100,000	28,055,202	
Cons. Fund Charges	2,550,000	2,807,043	
Army	6,697,000	6,534,699	
Navy	7,521,000	7,708,293	
Ordnance . . .	2,543,000	2,645,646	
Miscellaneous . .	3,435,000	3,957,687	Including 550,000*l.* on account of Irish distress.
Total . . .	50,873,000	51,708,571	

Budget of 1847-8.

(Feb. 22, 1847.)

REVENUE.

Head of Revenue.	Basis of Estimate.	Estimate.	Result.	Remarks.
		£	£	
Customs	...	20,000,000	19,940,296	The falling-off on Malt and Spirits this year was no less than 1,400,000l., yet the whole revenue was only 432,000l. below the estimate.
Excise	...	13,700,000	13,276,879	
Stamps	...	7,500,000	7,319,053	
Taxes	...	4,270,000	4,347,571	
Income Tax	...	5,300,000	5,459,368	
Post Office	...	845,000	932,000	
Crown Lands	...	120,000	61,000	
Miscellaneous	...	330,000	291,569	
China Payment	...	450,000	455,021	
Total	...	52,515,000	52,082,757	
Surplus	...	332,000	...	
Deficiency	...	...	3,092,285	

EXPENDITURE.

Head of Service.	Estimate.	Result.	Remarks.
	£	£	
Debt	28,045,000	} 28,427,232	
Addl. Int. on Ex. Bills	142,000		
Interest on Loan	280,000		
Cons. Fund Charges	2,700,000	2,724,971	
Army	6,840,074	7,357,689	
Navy	7,561,876	} 8,157,287	
Navy Excess (1845-6)	185,000		
Ordnance	2,679,127	2,726,698	
Miscellaneous	3,750,000	3,614,329	
Unclaimed Dividends	...	91,835	
Total	52,183,077	...	
Irish Distress	...	975,000	
Kaffir War	...	1,100,000	
	52,183,077	55,175,042	

Budget of 1848-9.

(Feb. 18, and Aug. 25, 1848.)

REVENUE.

Head of Revenue.	Basis of Estimate.	Estimate.	Result.	Remarks.
	£	£	£	
Customs	19,750,000	19,710,000	21,170,860	Duty on Copper ore taken off, 41,000*l.*
Excise	13,000,000	} 20,540,000 {	13,932,277	Increase of Income Tax to one shilling in the pound proposed, but abandoned. Loan of 2,000,000*l.* in Exchequer Bills authorised.
Stamps	7,200,000		6,565,365	
Taxes	4,340,000	4,340,000	4,318,903	
Income Tax	5,200,000	5,200,000	5,317,245	
Post Office	900,000	900,000	812,000	
Crown Lands	60,000	60,000	100,000	
Miscellaneous	300,000	300,000	232,040	
China Money	...	80,000	84,284	
Appropriations in aid	...	500,000	484,758	
Total	51,250,000	52,130,000	53,017,733	
Addit. Income Tax	3,500,000	..	...	
Surplus	113,000	...	...	
Deficiency	...	2,031,256	269,378	

EXPENDITURE.

Head of Service.	Estimate.	Result.	Remarks.
	£	£	
Debt	28,530,600	28,489,860	In consequence of the Reports of the Committees which sat upon the Military, Naval, and upon the Miscellaneous Estimates, the estimates originally framed, and which amounted to 21,970,000*l.* for those heads of Expenditure were reduced to 21,141,735*l.* as shown in the table. Sir C. Wood took the expenditure for the Kafir War into the account for this year, but as it was paid out of the balances in the Exchequer before the termination of the financial year 1847-8, it belongs properly to that year, and is there entered.
Cons. Fund Charges	2,750,000	2,811,557	
Army	7,012,795	6,743,634	
Navy	7,518,610	} 7,962,397	
Naval Excess, 1846-7	245,411		
Ordnance	2,801,760	3,001,128	
Miscellaneous	3,783,570	3,888,615	
Pensioners	25,000	...	
Kafir War	1,100,000	...	
Irish Distress	262,545	389,920	
Emigrants to Canada	130,965	...	
Total	54,161,256	53,287,111	

Budget of 1849-50.
(June 22, 1849.)

REVENUE.

Head of Revenue.	Basis of Estimate.	Estimate.	Result.	Remarks.
		£	£	
Customs . . .	...	20,450,000	20,442,759	
Excise	...	13,710,000	14,043,064	
Stamps	...	6,750,000	6,843,546	
Taxes	...	4,300,000	4,332,980	
Income Tax . .	...	5,275,000	5,466,249	
Post Office . .	...	800,000	823,000	
Crown Lands . .	...	180,000	160,000	
Miscellaneous . .	...	222,000	267,023	
Old Stores . . .	...	485,000	437,453	
Surplus Fees . .	...	90,000	100,845	
Total . . .	...	52,262,000	52,916,919	
Surplus . .	...	104,304	2,538,502	
Deficiency .	...	...	...	

EXPENDITURE.

Head of Service.	Estimate.	Result.	Remarks.
	£	£	
Debt	28,243,527	28,194,507	In these estimates the gross amount of the sums required for the Army, Navy, and Ordnance is voted for the first time; appropriations in aid being carried to the account of revenue.
Cons. Fund Charges	2,831,556	2,740,761	
Army	6,787,083	6,490,475	
Navy	7,021,724	6,711,724	
Ordnance . . .	2,654,270	2,485,387	The vote for the Navy includes the cost of the Packet Service (748,296*l.*) and that of the Arctic Expedition (12,688*l.*)
Miscellaneous . .	3,924,731	3,755,563	
Repaym. of an Escheat	52,173	...	
Excess Navy, 1847-8	323,787	...	
,, Ordnance, 1846	97,984	...	These Excesses are included in the payments made for Army, Navy, and Ordnance.
,, Army, 1847-8	119,950	...	
,, Ordnance ,,	35,386	...	
,, Commiss^t. ,,	65,525	...	
Total . . .	52,157,696	50,378,417	

Budget of 1850-1.

(March 15, 1850.)

REVENUE.

Head of Revenue.	Basis of Estimate.	Estimate.	Result.	Remarks.	
	£	£	£		£
Customs	20,000,000	20,000,000	20,572,324	Alteration of Stamp Duties	300,000
Excise	14,045,000	13,590,000	14,453,795		
Stamps	6,860,000	6,560,000	6,567,858	Abolition of Excise on Bricks	455,000
Taxes	4,320,000	4,320,000	4,350,731		
Income Tax	5,410,000	5,410,000	5,403,379		
Post Office	820,000	820,000	861,000	Total reductions	755,000
Crown Lands	160,000	160,000	160,000		
Miscellaneous	260,000	260,000	268,387		
Old Stores	410,000	410,000	419,580		
Total	52,285,000	51,530,000	53,057,053		
Surplus	1,521,418	766,418	3,174,731		
Deficiency	...	...	...		

EXPENDITURE.

Head of Service.	Estimate.	Result.	Remarks.
	£	£	
Debt	28,105,000	28,090,911	The sum of 248,550*l.* paid out of the Consolidated Fund in discharge of the debt to the Equivalent Company, is not included in this account.
Cons. Fund Charges	2,620,000	2,588,643	
Army	6,629,347	6,571,883	
Navy	6,613,659	6,401,076	
Ordnance	2,434,417	2,400,078	
Miscellaneous	4,000,000	3,822,980	
Margin for Contings.	150,000	...	
Unclaimed Dividends	...	6,751	
Total	50,763,582	49,882,322	

Budget of 1851-2.

(Feb. 17 & April 4, 1851.)

REVENUE.

Head of Revenue.	Basis of Estimate.	Estimate.	Result.	Remarks.	
	£	£	£		£
Customs	20,400,000	20,000,000	20,673,954	Window Tax repealed	1,856,000
Excise	14,000,000	14,000,000	14,543,895	House Tax imposed	720,000
Stamps	6,310,000	6,310,000	6,346,311		
Taxes	4,348,000	3,780,000	3,691,226		
Income Tax	5,380,000	5,380,000	5,283,800	Loss	1,136,000
Post Office	830,000	830,000	1,056,000	Timber and Coffee Duties reduced : loss	400,000
Crown Lands	160,000	160,000	190,000		
Miscellaneous	262,000	262,000	287,845		
Old Stores	450,000	450,000	395,287	But deduct moiety of Window Tax receivable this year	1,536,000
Total	52,140,000	51,172,000	52,468,319		568,000
Surplus	1,892,829	925,000	2,176,996		
Deficiency	...	...	...	Net Loss	968,000

EXPENDITURE.

Head of Service.	Estimate.	Result.	Remarks.
	£	£	
Debt	28,092,000	27,978,526	
Cons. Fund Charges	2,600,000	2,614,416	
Army	6,593,945	6,828,662	
Navy	6,537,055	6,010,000	
Ordnance	2,424,171	2,338,442	
Miscellaneous	4,000,000	4,114,266	
Kafir War	...	300,000	
Unclaimed Dividends	...	107,009	
Total	50,247,171	50,291,323	

Budget of 1852-3.

(April 30, 1852.)

REVENUE.

Head of Revenue.	Basis of Estimate.	Estimate.	Result.	Remarks.
	£	£	£	Income Tax continued for one year. Revenue from Crown Lands increased by transfer of some charges to the head of Miscellaneous Expenditure.
Customs . . .	20,572,000	...	20,396,828	
Excise	14,604,000	...	14,890,382	
Stamps	6,339,000	...	6,920,373	
Taxes	3,090,000	...	3,194,271	
Income Tax . .	2,600,000	5,187,000	5,593,043	
Post Office . . .	938,000	...	1,045,000	
Crown Lands . .	235,000	...	252,000	
Miscellaneous . .	260,000	...	487,175	
Old Stores . . .	400,000	...	464,146	
Total . . .	49,038,000	51,625,000	53,243,218	
Surplus . .	...	461,000	2,460,742	
Deficiency .	2,125,000	...	...	

EXPENDITURE.

Head of Service.	Estimate.	Result.	Remarks.
	£	£	Miscellaneous estimates increased by transfer of charges from the Crown Lands' revenue.
Debt	27,950,000	27,918,027	
Cons. Fund Charges	2,600,000	2,533,826	
Army	6,491,000	6,768,488	
Militia	350,000		
Navy	6,493,000	6,511,540	
Ordnance . . .	2,437,000	2,488,389	
Miscellaneous . .	4,182,000	4,132,207	
Kafir War . . .	660,000	430,000	
Total . . .	51,163,000	50,782,476	

Budget of 1853-4.

(April 18, 1853.)

REVENUE.

Head of Revenue.	Basis of Estimate.	Estimate.	Result.	Remarks.
	£	£	£	
Customs . . .	20,680,000	20,022,000	20,703,048	New duties imposed, net gain, 1,344,000*l*. Old duties reduced or repealed, net loss 1,656,000*l*.
Excise	14,640,000	14,391,000	15,263,549	
Stamps	6,700,000	7,000,000	6,956,819	
Taxes . . .	3,250,000	3,250,000	3,241,701	
Income Tax . .	5,550,000	5,845,000	6,117,303	
Post Office . .	900,000	900,000	1,104,000	
Crown Lands . .	*390,000	390,000	395,888	* The estimate for the Crown Lands was swelled by a sum of 135,000*l*. on account of repayments in respect of Metropolitan Improvements.
Miscellaneous . .	320,000	320,000	511,450	
Old Stores . . .	460,000	460,000	481,146	
Total . . .	52,890,000	52,578,000	54,774,905	
Surplus . .	807,000	495,000	3,524,785	
Deficiency .	...	...	...	

EXPENDITURE.

Head of Service.	Estimate.	Result.	Remarks.
	£	£	
Debt	27,804,000	27,738,927	The estimate for the Army as here given includes the vote for the Commissariat; and the estimate for the Navy includes that for the Packet Service, though Mr. Gladstone stated them separately.
Cons. Fund Charges	2,503,000	2,500,529	
Army	6,582,000	6,415,000	
Militia	530,000		
Navy	7,035,000	6,942,769	
Ordnance . . .	3,053,000	2,900,000	
Miscellaneous . .	4,476,000	4,471,559	
Kafir War . . .	200,000	230,000	
Unclaimed Dividends	...	51,336	
Total . . .	52,183,000	...	
Estimated saving on conversion of Stock .	100,000	...	
Total . . .	52,083,000	51,250,120	

Budget of 1854-5.
(March 6 & May 8, 1854.)

REVENUE.

Head of Revenue.	Basis of Estimate.	Estimate.	Result.	Remarks.
	£	£	£	
Customs	20,175,000	20,875,000	20,496,659	Income Tax raised to 14*d*. in the £. Duty on Scotch and Irish spirits raised. Malt duty raised from 2*s*. 8½*d*. to 4*s*. per bushel. Sugar duties raised.
Excise	14,595,000	17,495,000	16,179,169	
Stamps	7,090,000	7,090,000	6,965,514	
Taxes	3,015,000	3,015,000	3,036,136	
Income Tax	6,275,000	12,832,000	10,515,369	
Post Office	1,200,000	1,200,000	1,299,156	Amount of unfunded debt created this year:—
Crown Lands	259,000	259,000	272,572	£.
Miscellaneous	320,000	320,000	316,904	Exchequer bills 1,750,000
Old Stores	420,000	420,000	414,674	,, bonds 5,375,513
				£7,125,513
Total	53,349,000	63,506,000*	59,496,154	* This sum shows the estimated ultimate produce of the new taxes, but the whole amount expected within the year was 59,496,000*l.*, the deficiency of 1,543,000*l.* being provided for by the issue of Exchequer bonds.
Surplus	...	...	...	
Deficiency	2,840,000	3,543,000*	6,196,808	

EXPENDITURE.

Head of Service.	Estimate, March 6.	Estimate, May 8.	Result.	Remarks.
	£	£	£	
Debt	27,546,000	27,546,000	27,864,533	
Cons. Fund Charges	2,460,000	2,460,000	1,839,290	
Army & Commiss.	7,502,000	7,802,000	} 8,380,882	
Militia	530,000	1,030,000		
Navy & Packets	8,280,000	12,830,000	14,490,105	
Ordnance	3,846,000	4,486,000	5,450,720	
Miscellaneous	4,775,000	4,775,000	5,867,432	
Extraordinary Military Services	1,250,000	2,100,000	1,800,000	
Total	56,189,000	63,039,000	65,692,962	

Budget of 1855-6.

(April 20 & Aug 2, 1855.)

REVENUE.

Head of Revenue.	Basis of Estimate.	Estimate.	Result.	Remarks.
	£	£	£	
Customs	20,500,000	22,450,000	21,788,771	Sugar, Tea, and Cof
Excise	17,071,000	17,921,000	16,636,670	fee duties increased. Irish
Stamps	6,815,000	6,815,000	6,894,307	and Scotch Spirit dutie raised. Income Tax fixe
Taxes	2,920,000	2,920,000	2,958,626	at 1s. 4d. in the pound.
Income Tax	13,535,000	14,535,000	14,814,757	
Post Office	1,438,000	1,438,000	1,171,696	Loan of 16,000,000l.
Crown Lands	260,000	260,000	281,516	
Miscellaneous	800,000	800,000	1,158,148	
Total	63,339,000	67,139,000	65,704,491	
Surplus	...	...	...	
Deficiency	16,560,519	18,895,000	22,723,854	

EXPENDITURE.

Head of Service.	Estimate, April 20.	Estimate, August 2.	Result.	Remarks.
	£	£	£	
Debt	27,974,000	27,974,000	28,112,824	These sums are no included in the expen diture.
Cons. Fund Charges	1,750,000	1,750,000	1,723,420	
Army	16,214,477	18,789,532	17,395,059	* In addition to thi
Navy	16,653,042	19,379,013	19,654,585	amount, the Chancello
Ordnance	7,808,000	8,644,292	10,411,544	of the Exchequer pro
Miscellaneous	6,500,000	6,500,000	6,930,913	vided for 2,000,000l further expenditure
Vote of Credit	3,000,000	3,000,000	4,200,000	viz. 1,000,000l. to pa off Ways and Mean
Total	79,899,519	86,034,000*	88,428,345	Bills, issued in 1854-5 and 1,000,000l. in pai of loan to Sardinia.

Budget of 1856-7.

(May 19, 1856.)

REVENUE.

Head of Revenue.	Basis of Estimate.	Estimate.	Result.	Remarks.
	£	£	£	
Customs	22,524,000	23,850,000	23,321,843	This being the first year in which the gross revenue has been estimated, I have given under the head of "Basis of Estimate" the sums which would have been estimated as net revenue upon the former system. No alterations were made in taxation this year.
Excise	16,348,000	17,170,000	18,165,000	
Stamps	7,000,000	7,185,000	7,372,209	
Taxes	2,950,000	3,110,000	3,116,046	
Income Tax	16,000,000	16,355,000	16,089,933	
Post Office	1,070,000	2,810,000	2,886,000	
Crown Lands	260,000	260,000	284,857	
Miscellaneous	1,000,000	1,000,000	1,098,174	
Total	67,152,000	71,740,000	72,334,062	
Surplus	...	...	...	
Deficiency	13,961,000	9,373,000	3,254,605	

EXPENDITURE.

Head of Service.	Estimate.	Result.	Remarks.
	£	£	
Debt	28,660,000	28,681,177	The original estimates for the Army and Navy were as follow:—
Cons. Fund Charges	1,750,000	1,773,726	
Army	20,747,000	20,811,242	£
Navy	16,568,000	13,459,013	Army 34,998,000
Miscellaneous	6,800,000	6,626,734	Navy 19,876,000
Collection of Revenue	4,588,000	4,236,775	The reduction in consequence of the peace was 17,559,000*l*.
Vote of Credit	2,000,000	...	
Total	81,113,000	75,588,667	
Loan to Sardinia	1,000,000	1,000,000	

Budget of 1857-8.

(Feb. 13, and July 17, 1857.)

REVENUE.

Head of Revenue.	Basis of Estimate.	Estimate.	Result.	Remarks.
		£	£	
Customs	...	22,850,000	23,109,105	The original estimate was
Excise	...	17,000,000	17,825,000	for a surplus of 891,000*l.*
Stamps	...	7,450,000	7,415,719	after paying off 2,250,000
Taxes	...	3,150,000	3,152,033	of debt; the result shows
Income Tax	...	11,450,000	11,586,114	a deficiency of 247,346
Post Office	...	3,000,000	2,920,000	without reckoning the
Crown Lands	...	265,000	276,654	debt. If the debt is reckoned, the deficiency
Miscellaneous	...	1,200,000	1,596,887	2,497,346*l.*
Total	...	66,365,000	67,881,513	
Surplus	...	891,000	...	
Deficiency	...	...	247,346	

EXPENDITURE.

Head of Service.	Estimate.	Result.	Remarks.
	£	£	
Debt	28,550,000	28,627,103	The Expenditure includes a
Cons. Fund Charges	1,770,000	2,919,198	sum of 1,125,206*l.* paid out
Army	11,625,000	12,915,157	of the Consolidated Fund
Navy	8,109,000	10,590,000	for the purpose of redeeming the Sound dues.
Packet Service	965,000		
Miscellaneous	7,250,000	7,227,719	From statement made the
Collection of Revenue	4,690,000	4,358,988	17th of July, the total estimated expenditure appears
Persian War	265,000	900,000	67,684,000*l.*; deduct from
China War	...	590,693	this 2,250,000*l.* (Debt.)
	63,224,000	68,128,859	Estimate of ordinary expenditure = 65,434,000*l.*,
Repayment of Debt	2,250,000	2,250,000	leaving estimated surplus of 931,000*l.*
Total	65,474,000	70,378,859	

Budget of 1858-9.

(April 19, 1858.)

REVENUE.

Head of Revenue.	Basis of Estimate.	Estimate.	Result.	Remarks.
	£	£	£	
Customs . . .	23,400,000	23,400,000	24,117,943	Irish Spirit duties raised to 8s. per gallon. Stamp duty on bankers' cheques.
Excise	18,100,000	18,600,000	17,902,000	
Stamps	7,550,000	7,850,000	8,005,769	
Taxes	3,200,000	3,200,000	3,162,000	
Income Tax . .	6,100,000	6,100,000	6,683,587	
Post Office . . .	3,200,000	3,200,000	3,200,000	
Crown Lands . .	270,000	270,000	280,040	
Miscellaneous . .	1,300,000	1,300,000	2,125,944	
Total . . .	63,120,000	63,920,000	65,477,284	
Surplus . .	...	310,000	813,402	
Deficiency .	3,990,000	...	...	

EXPENDITURE.

Head of Service.	Estimate.	Result.	Remarks.
	£	£	
Debt	28,400,000	28,527,484	The expenditure would have been greater by 3,500,000l. if the Sinking Fund had not been put an end to, and the Exchequer Bonds reissued.
Cons. Fund Charges	1,900,000	1,940,655	
Army	11,750,000	12,512,291	
Navy & Packet Service	9,860,000	9,215,487	
Miscellaneous . .	7,000,000	7,169,473	
Revenue Collection	4,700,000	4,515,969	
Expenses of China War (Naval) .	...	391,943	
Expenses of Russian War . .	...	390,580	
Total . . .	63,610,000	64,663,882	
War Sinking Fund	1,500,000	...	
Exchequer Bonds .	2,000,000	...	
	67,110,000	...	

Budget of 1859-60.

(July 18, 1859.)

REVENUE.

Head of Revenue.	Basis of Estimate.	Estimate.	Result.	Remarks.
	£	£	£	
Customs	23,850,000	23,850,000	24,460,901	Income Tax raised from 5d. to 9d. in the pound; but the whole of the additional 4d. levied in the first half-year.
Excise	18,530,000	19,310,000	20,361,000	
Stamps	8,100,000	8,100,000	8,043,598	
Taxes	3,200,000	3,200,000	3,232,000	
Income Tax	5,600,000	9,940,000	9,596,106	
Post Office	3,250,000	3,250,000	3,310,000	Malt credit abridged by six weeks, estimated produce 780,000*l*.
Crown Lands	280,000	280,000	284,479	
Miscellaneous	1,530,000	1,530,000	1,801,584	256,000*l*. repaid by the Spanish Government is included in the Miscellaneous Revenue.
Total	64,340,000	69,460,000	71,089,669	
Surplus	...	253,000	1,587,380	
Deficiency	4,867,000	...	...	

EXPENDITURE.

Head of Service.	Estimate.	Result.	Remarks.
	£	£	
Debt	28,600,000	28,638,726	Charge for the debt increased by the fact that a certain part of the Long Annuities fell in upon the 5th of Jan. 1860, and that a quarter's payment had to be made upon that day, whereas the regular time for the half-yearly payments was April 5.
Cons. Fund Charges	1,960,000	1,964,394	
Army and Militia	13,300,000	14,057,186	
Navy & Packet Service	12,782,000	11,823,859	
Miscellaneous	7,825,000	7,721,519	
Revenue Collection	4,740,000	4,438,548	
China War	...	858,057	
Total	69,207,000	69,502,289	

Budget of 1860-1.

(Feb. 10 & July 16, 1860.)

REVENUE.

Head of Revenue.	Basis of Estimate.	Estimate.	Result.	Remarks.
	£	£	£	The figures given in the second column show the amount of the revenue estimated on the 16th of July, after the bill for repealing the Paper duty had been thrown out, and the duty on Spirits had been increased. According to the original estimate in February, the income would have been 70,478,000*l*., the expenditure 70,014,000*l*., and the surplus 464,000*l*. The amount of duties intended to have been remitted was on
Customs	22,700,000	23,430,000	23,305,777	
Excise	19,170,000	21,361,000	19,435,000	
Stamps	8,000,000	8,295,000	8,348,412	
Taxes	3,250,000	3,110,000	3,127,000	
Income Tax	2,400,000	10,872,000	10,923,816	
Post Office	3,400,000	3,400,000	3,400,000	
Crown Lands	280,000	280,000	290,568	
Miscellaneous	1,500,000	1,500,000	1,453,101	
				£
				Customs 2,776,000
				Excise 1,155,000
Total	60,700,000	72,248,000	70,283,674	Total relief . £3,931,000
				Net loss to revenue . £2,108,000
Surplus	...	...	...	Income Tax fixed at 10*d*. in the pound.
Deficit	9,400,000	1,286,000	2,558,385	Malt and Hop credits further shortened. Spirit duties raised to 10*s*. per gallon.

EXPENDITURE.

Head of Service.	Estimate.	Result.	Remarks.
	£	£	
Debt	26,200,000	26,231,018	The expenditure includes a sum of 50,000*l*. for fortifications, charged upon the Consolidated Fund, but not included in the Budget estimate.
Cons. Fund Charges	2,000,000	2,296,430	
Army and Militia	15,300,000	14,970,000	
Navy & Packet Service	13,900,000	14,401,446	
Vote of Credit	500,000	3,043,896	
Miscellaneous	7,500,000	7,411,820	
Revenue Collection	4,700,000	4,487,448	
Total	70,100,000	72,842,059	
Supp^y. Vote of Credit	3,300,000		
Revenue Estimates	220,000		
	73,620,000		
Expected Savings in Revenue Deprtmnt.	86,000		
	73,534,000		

Budget of 1861-2.

(April 15, 1861.)

REVENUE.

Head of Revenue.	Basis of Estimate.	Estimate.	Result.	Remarks.
	£	£	£	
Customs	23,585,000	23,570,000	23,674,000	Paper Duty repealed from Oct. 1, 1861. Estimated loss 665,000*l*. Income Tax reduced to 9*d*. Estimated loss 850,030*l*. If the expenditure on fortifications be deducted the deficiency is 1,442,006*l*.
Excise	19,463,000	18,788,000	18,332,000	
Stamps	8,460,000	8,460,000	8,590,945	
Taxes	3,150,000	3,150,000	3,160,000	
Income Tax . .	11,200,000	10,350,000	10,365,000	
Post Office . . .	3,520,000	3,520,000	3,510,000	
Crown Lands . .	295,000	295,000	295,000	
Miscellaneous . .	1,400,000	1,400,000	1,481,534	
China indemnity .	750,000	750,000	266,000	
Total . . .	71,823,000	70,283,000	69,674,479	
Surplus . .	1,920,000	408,000	...	
Deficiency .	...	...	2,412,006	

EXPENDITURE.

Head of Service.	Estimate.	Result.	Remarks.
	£	£	
Debt	26,180,000	26,142,606	
Cons. Fund Charges	1,930,000	1,945,572	
Army	15,256,000	15,570,869	
Navy	12,029,000	12,598,042	
Vote of Credit . .	1,000,000	1,230,000	
Miscellaneous . .	7,737,000	7,984,463	
Revenue Departments	4,780,000	4,699,581	
Packet Service . .	995,000	891,920	
Expenses of Russian War . . . . }	...	53,431	
Fortifications . .	...	970,000	This item was not included in the Budget estimate, being provided for by loan.
	69,902,000	...	
Deduct for Savings .	25,000	...	
Total . . .	69,875,000	72,086,485	

APPENDIX B.

See page 141.

HAVE found much difficulty in obtaining the materials necessary for a fair comparison of the Taxation of 1840 and 1860 with that of 1850. The information which we possess as to local taxation is very imperfect, though we are now, I hope, in way of getting it much more satisfactorily than heretofore. I have to thank Mr. Bowring and Mr. Bucknall of the Board of Trade for the assistance they have kindly rendered me in procuring such information as is here made use of.

I. *General Taxation not falling directly on Property :—*

	1840 £	1850 £	1860 £
Taxes on articles of Food, and Tobacco	29,862,522	31,820,798	39,136,758
Manufactured Articles	3,519,446	2,452,658	1,561,490
Raw Materials	2,975,974	764,000	319,309
Duties affecting Trades and Professions	2,908,759	4,464,906	6,400,745
Conveyances	696,279	648,487	582,068
Newspapers and Advertisements	382,142	511,418	139,402
Assessed Taxes (except Window Duty and House Tax)	1,566,761	1,491,308	1,312,697
Total of general Taxation not falling directly on Property	41,911,883	42,153,575	49,452,469

Appendix B.

II. *General Taxation falling directly on Property* :—

	1840	1850	1860
Land Tax, House Tax, Window Tax, Probate, Legacy, Succession, and Insurance Duties, &c. Stamps on Deeds and other instruments affecting Property, and Schedules A and C of the Income Tax.	£ 7,703,513	£ 12,451,776	£ 15,143,714

It will be observed that the great increase in the produce of indirect taxation arises under the head of duties on articles in the nature of food, and on tobacco. The increase is due, not to additions to taxation, but to the large increase of consumption of taxable articles. The only articles included under this head upon which the duties have been raised since 1840 are these two,—

  Spirits.
  Chicory.

The articles upon which the duties remain unchanged are,—

  Tobacco.
  Malt.
  Pepper.

The principal articles upon which the duties have been reduced are,—

  Tea.
  Sugar and Molasses.
  Coffee.
  Cocoa.
  Corn.
  Wine.
  Vinegar (foreign).
  Hops (now repealed).
  Sago.
  Fruit (preserved and dried).

The principal articles which have been entirely set free from duty are,—

  Fruit (fresh).

Meat.
Salt provisions.
Animals (living).
Butter.
Cheese.
Eggs.
Rice (except dust).
Spices (except pepper).
Vinegar (British).

Under the head of Duties affecting Trades and Professions are included Licence Duties, certain Stamp Duties, and the Income Tax, Schedules B, D, and E.

Under the head of Taxation falling directly on property are included,—

Land Tax.
House Tax.
Schedules A and C of the Income Tax.
Stamps on Deeds.
Probates.
Legacy and Succession Duties.
Fire and Marine Insurances.

III. *Local Taxation.*

The items of the following return show the amounts derived from the principal sources of our Local Taxation, so far as reliable information can be obtained. Although the amounts do not all apply to the same year, I am assured that they are in the main nearly the same as the aggregate amount of any recent year.

In addition to these items, however, there are many others of which it is at present impossible to estimate the amount with any confidence; such as Sewers' Rates; Lighting and Watching Rates; Improvement Rates; Metropolitan Rates, Tolls, and Dues; Scotch Burgh Rates and County Assessments.

The returns required under the Local Taxation Returns Act (1860) are, however, fast approaching completion; and these will put an end to all uncertainty.

Appendix B.

RATES.

	£
Poor Rates, England and Wales, 1859 to Lady-day 1860	7,715,948
„ Scotland, Whit Sunday 1859 to 1860	671,516
„ Ireland, Lady-day, 1860	503,813
County Receipts, England and Wales, to Michaelmas, 1860	1,222,765
Highways, Parish, England and Wales, to 25th of March, 1859	2,174,962
Turnpikes, to 31st Dec. 1858, Eng. and Wales	1,047,308
„ Scotland, to Whit Sunday, 1859	238,048
Church Rates, 1853-4, England and Wales	482,500
Grand Jury (Ireland) Presentments, 1861	1,034,926
Scotland, Burgh Rates, 1854 (*Sums paid for prosecutions*)	400,000
„ County Police	24,000
Metropolitan (City) Rates and Duties	200,000
Total	£15,715,786

Adding the sums here given to the amount of general taxation, under head II, we arrive at a total of nearly 31,000,000*l.* as the amount of the taxation falling directly on property in 1860, as compared with 25,451,000*l.* in 1850.

I must, however, repeat that I am not fully satisfied with the data on which this calculation is founded, nor do I feel sure that my calculations are made on precisely the same principle as those of Sir C. Wood.

www.ingramcontent.com/pod-product-compliance
Lightning Source LLC
Chambersburg PA
CBHW050848300426
44111CB00010B/1174